D1175518

ROOTS & BRANCHES

A FAMILY SAGA LIKE NO OTHER

MICHAEL M. MEGUID MD

Copyright ©2020 by Michael M Meguid

All rights reserved.

No part of this publication may be reproduced, stored in a retrievable system, or transmitted, in any form or by any means without the prior written permission of the publisher, nor be otherwise circulated in any form of binding or cover other than in which it is published and without a similar condition being imposed on the subsequent purchaser/reader.

ISBN 978-0-9992988-5-5

M3 Scientific Media
Marco Island, Florida 34145, USA
www.michaelmeguid.com

Cover image: Krizvector - Freepik.com

ALSO BY MICHAEL M. MEGUID

MASTERING THE KNIFE

Seeking Identity & Finding Belonging

Mastering the Knife is a coming of age story based on biographic events of a young Egyptian medical student in London in the 1960s hounded by failure, self-doubt and cultural identity. In learning to heal others, he ultimately finds himself.

MAKING THE CUT

Overcoming a childhood of abandonment and neglect, Dr. Meguid became a world-renowned surgeon. But before that, he had to learn how to become a man. Now, that story is revealed.

makingthecutpodcast.com

DEDICATED TO

Bonnie, my morning sunshine,
Robert, my evening moon,
Sam, a bright man,
Lucy, the shadow of my soul,
Natalie, my meadow flower,
Cameron, the velvet fist . . .
not to forget those that may follow.
And
to Victoria, who couldn't have known her man for he didn't
know himself.

*Men go forth to wonder at the height of mountains,
the huge waves of the sea, the broad flow of the rivers,
the extent of the ocean, and the courses of the stars,
and omit to wonder at themselves.*
—St. Augustine, Confessions.

CONTENTS

AUTHOR'S NOTE

The occurrences in this book are subject to time and perspective but are inspired by my memory of factual events. Some characters and scenes are composites, and certain experiences were reordered. The names and identifying characteristics of some individuals have been changed to protect their privacy; as unique individuals, however, they may discover themselves in these pages. In other cases, I used names in accordance with historical facts and records.

The narratives are my recollection of events during my youth in Egypt, Germany and England. I've endeavored to be as authentic as possible, relying on my personal archives, including a journal, letters, photo albums, report cards, and stories from familial verbal history. Quotes from letters originate from correspondence. This account does not attempt to tell the whole story. Others may recall things differently or have their own versions of what transpired.

PROLOGUE

1957-1960

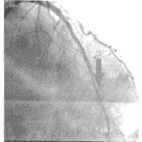

Obstructed Main Coronary Artery-before & after stent

Rage, rage against the dying light.
—Dylan Thomas

Continental flight 8758 arrives into Newark from Syracuse—four hours late. It's 6:40 p.m. Most passengers have missed their connections. My wife Debbie and I are booked through to Amsterdam, where we will start our river cruise to Vienna, where I will attend a four-day clinical congress of the European Society of Parenteral and Enteral Nutrition. As Editor-in-Chief of *Nutrition, The International Journal of Applied and Basic Nutritional Sciences*, I had spent several months with my managing editor planning a work meeting with the Editorial Board, whose international members are congregating from around the globe. Because of the delay we are slated to depart from JFK to Frankfurt at 9:35 p.m., with an onward connection to Amsterdam the next morning. We have 175 minutes to get from Newark to JFK during Friday-night rush hour.

Our commuter flight pulls into Continental gate C-99. There is no passenger ramp; the plane parks on the scalding hot apron close to the gate, one of the farthest from the main terminal. I'm first down the steps, Debbie hanging on to my jacket, because she has mild Alzheimer's and is terrified of losing me. Tempers are hotter than the sweltering August air as passengers chaotically jostle about the gate-check cart. I push through the milling throng of people, crying kids, heaped car seats, and the disorganized and helpless ground crew to grab our two carry-ons, each weighing 20 pounds. We burst free from the scrum into the cool terminal, hurtle up escalators through the indifferent crowds clogging Concourse C and run, dragging our bags, toward the main entrance. I am laden down with my backpack stuffed with books, camera, and laptop. Breathless, perspiring, I charge through people movers, roll apologetically over feet in the walk lane, and sprint past a non-working sidewalk. I am 65 years old, accustomed to the academic surgeon's life: high-octane, doppio-fueled, stress addicted.

Assaulted by the noise of incomprehensible gate announcements, by now I am really sweating. My legs feel heavy as they try to propel me forward. With Debbie just behind me, we reach the beginning of Concourse C in 17 minutes. We have 158 minutes to take-off and our vacation.

Feeling dazed and breathless, I press on, rushing toward the street exit. I bound down two escalators, two steps at a time. My roll-on bounces erratically off the narrow sidewalls, just missing the legs of fellow riders. I fight for air with each breath, my heart thumping in my chest. Debbie is nowhere in sight. She is tired and must be riding the escalator down, because I do not see her as I wait at the bottom. Mentally I urge her on: *Come on, hustle, hustle, or we'll miss our connection.*

Meanwhile, I curse my luggage and catch my breath. My heart beats in my mouth, which feels like cardboard—parched. Sweat trickles down my back. Debbie eventually comes into view. Relieved to see me, the uncertainty and anxiety vanish from her face. We resume our roll toward the automatic door, which opens like magic, a barrier between the cool-dry terminal air and the sweltering 91° F with 65% humidity of the New Jersey sidewalk: 148 minutes before our departure.

I see a row of yellow taxis like a serpent, shimmering in the distant heat, and I set off in a laser-straight line to the topmost taxi. My lungs burn with each inhaled breath. As I step off the curb, a shrill whistle stops me. A gesticulating cop jabs the air in the direction of a street crossing 50 yards in the other direction. *Damn it, I can barely breathe, and now this added detour...* Without breaking stride, we change direction, dragging our luggage, which feels progressively heavier and wobbles behind us as we charge across the four-lane-wide crosswalk.

Keep going, I urge myself, *you have to keep going,* even as I gasp with each breath. When we reach the other side, a taxi blocks the crossing. I try to enter. The driver yells, "No, go to dispatcher," pointing up the rank to the snake's head.

Inhaling with great effort, I run parallel to twenty-plus idling yellow blurs. The dispatcher is in an intense argument with five Indian passengers, surrounded by a heap of oversized bags, the first taxi driver by his side. I bypass them, bearing down on the second taxi. Again, I am waved off, directed to the dispatcher, as I barge through the haggling crowd.

"JFK..." I barely muster through my desiccated mouth, my chest heaving. My wife catches up. He thrusts a yellow ticket into my hand. Turning, I head again for the second cab. The driver's face showed his astonishment at the speed of unfolding events. As if moving through molasses, he gradually extracts himself from his seat, opens the passenger door, and my wife collapses into the taxi. He slowly lifts the two carry-ons into the trunk, and I swing my heavy backpack into it.

"JFK please, as fast as you can…" He slams shut the trunk, points to the traffic and shrugs. It is 7:10 p.m. and boiling hot—the cab is not air-conditioned. We now have only 139 minutes left. Will we make it? He pulls out into the flowing traffic of the airport and is immediately snarled in the stall and crawl of the JFK Expressway.

"I've only got sixty minutes. Use the local roads," I shout from the back.

"It'll go faster on the Belt Parkway, and on the Verrazano," he says into the mirror, stepping on the gas, changing lanes. The taxi lurches forward. He is obviously a seasoned driver, and from his accent probably from Afghanistan. He does not use the local roads. It is 7:21 p.m. We now have used up eleven of the sixty minutes. Even if we get to JFK within my allotted time, we'll have to get to the counter, book two seats together, clear security, walk to a distant gate—all in only 79 minutes before the Airbus pushes back from the gate.

He crawls faster in the outside lane. It is 7:30 p.m. when Mr. Mohsin Abdulla, as the taxi nametag identifies him, exits the expressway and merges into the Belt Parkway. We cross onto Staten Island, driving marginally faster.

With all the running, the fruit salad, bagel, and large coffee I had seven hours earlier at the Syracuse Airport are now coming to revisit me—especially the black coffee.

I become aware of the sudden onset of a vague feeling of indigestion at the end of my sternum, the breastbone, above my stomach, like substernal chest pain. I chew three Ultra 1000 TUMS and get some relief. Suddenly, I start to diaphoresis—profusely sweating from my head, face, neck, chest, arms—and the cold sweat floods me. My shirt is soaking and the stiff, hot wind through the windows has no drying effect. It cools me, but I continue to perspire uncontrollably.

I feel lightheaded and slide down the seat. I rest my head in my wife's lap, my legs dangling from the seat half-on, half-off. The substernal chest pain waxes and wanes in severity, though I can still bear it. I grab my chest through my shirt. I become lightheaded and still more lightheaded. I'm about to faint, or am I going to throw-up? I do neither.

"My husband has a backache," she says to the driver frowning and staring at us in the rearview mirror. "How much longer to JFK?" she adds.

Abruptly, I get a sharp, exquisitely excruciating burst of pain in my chest. It is in my mid-sternum, searing hot and spreading radially in all directions, like a starburst. I grunt uncontrollably, then again but louder, trying to tolerate it. *Breathe. Breathe…don't hold your breath. Pant as if it is labor,* I tell myself. And as I do, I become lightheaded and my head begins to swim.

God? Please. Make this indigestion.

I chew three more TUMS with some relief, I think. Or am I imagining it? The pain diminishes some, replaced by a dull chest agony. I close my eyes, trying to rest and remain calm.

God? Is this indigestion? I know I'm stressed out and doing too many things. Let this be indigestion, and I promise I'll cut back on my commitments when I return from Vienna, I say to Him.

Utter fatigue overwhelms me. The heat in the backseat is a furnace. With my eyes closed, I sense our crawl through the slow-moving traffic, hear the rush of the cars in the opposite direction.

The searing chest pain abates some and moves to my stomach again. *It's a deal, Lord. You've given me severe indigestion with acid reflux…heartburn. Oh, thank you God! Thank you for this dispensation—a warning; I absolutely promise to slow down and, take things easy…*

Nothing in medical school, in books, or in the movies describes this type of pain as a heart attack. My momentary suspicion was obviously wrong. I am just tired, thanks to this mad dash from gate C-99, the stress of the time crunch, and the draining heat and humidity.

A sudden onset of still greater lightheadedness and the searing chest pain returns. It travels to my left shoulder, then radiates to my left neck, my left ear lobe. The cold sweat resumes. I grab my chest and writhe uncomfortably in the back-seat and lose track of time. Did I pass out? Fall asleep?

When I open my eyes, it is dusk and I see my wife's face above me. She looks alarmed and confused. "Are you OK?" she whispers as I groan and squirm about with pain, my face contorted, and I try not to hold my breath. I nod uncon-vincingly.

God? You just warned me this would be indigestion and nothing else. What happened to our deal? Lord, are you listening? Do you hear me? I will slow down my life and take it easy from now on. I'll get out of the fast lane, I promise, I promise, I promise.

"Where are we now?" I ask the driver, my voice strained.

"Belt Parkway on Staten Island heading to the Verrazano Bridge," he says, turning his head to catch a glance of the back seat. "Are you all right, sir?"

"Yes, just very tired. I have some indigestion, that's all. Just get us to JFK, as fast as you can."

The pain gets worse. It's going down both arms. I feel faint; I feel very, very tired. I just want to close my eyes. It can't be indi-gestion. Think clearly . . . think objectively . . . It can only be a heart attack.

If someone came to me with these symptoms, there is no question what my diagnosis would be, so why fool myself? Yet how can it be? I have no previous history of chest pain. It's a ridiculous diagnosis! I have a touch of controlled high blood pressure, and before starting on a statin, my cholesterol was in the low 200s. Now it's about 187, and as of three weeks ago my good cholesterol is above the upper limit of normal and my bad cholesterol is within normal limits. There is no measure for stress. It just doesn't add up. I'm not a candidate for a heart attack.

God? Are you there? What's going on? I did really promise things would change on my return. But right now, I just want your help! I must go on to Vienna. It's my meeting… all my editors from Latin America, Asia, Europe and their assistants are attending this critical yearly gathering. I've been preparing for months, so I have to turn up. Really, Lord, I'll slow down. God, are you listening? Do we have a deal?

The chest tightness and pain recur abruptly but worse. It persists, going down to my left elbow. My shortness of breath gets worse. I am now convinced: it can only be a heart attack.

Why Lord, why? Why, when I have so much still to do? Lord, if this is a test, I promise I will listen carefully to your cues. I promise! I'll quit my surgical professorship and only focus on being editor of the journal. I can't give that up—surely you understand that? Please Lord, help me out now. Please.

The pain ebbs somewhat. At 7:43 p.m. I call my son Rob, a surgical chief resident at Johns Hopkins Hospital in Baltimore. He answers right away. I tell him my predicament and self-diagnosis. He replies with professional coolness. "Dad, take an aspirin right away. Do you have some?"

I look up and see my wife's silhouette in the approaching dusk. She sobs. She prays. She grabs my hand.

"All my meds are in my backpack in the trunk."

"Pull over and get one," he commands. We hang up. I dismiss the idea: I'm already on daily baby aspirin, a statin, and taking Omega-3 fish oil, and we are stuck in bumper-to-bumper traffic with lanes of cars hemming us in on both sides.

The driver gets wind of our strained conversation. I tell him, "Listen, I don't feel well. Cancel JFK. Go directly to New York-Presbyterian Emergency Room."

"OK. Do you want to go to an ER that's nearer? In New Jersey?"

"No, just head towards 68th Street," I groan. He gets off the

Verrazano Bridge and speeds in the lighter traffic towards the Brooklyn/Queens Expressway, heading for the 59th Street Bridge to Manhattan, and onto the FDR Drive. It is equally clogged, and we shuffle along in the heat like it's a death march. It's almost 8 p.m., and I've abandoned the idea of a vacation. If my diagnosis is wrong, we'll travel tomorrow.

I lie on the back seat with my wife still praying and weeping, begging me not to die. It suddenly occurs to me that this is a very real possibility. I regret that my children know so little of their dad. I'm not even sure myself of who I am and who I have become.

I feel very faint and close my eyes. The last thing I'm aware of before I black out is the relentless chest pain, my labored breathing, and Debbie's quiet sobbing, "Don't leave me."

As I close my eyes, and the traffic noise fades, I have an epiphany. I see two white hills in front of me, plain black lines representing some achievements I still have to accomplish. It gives me the sense that my time has not yet come, but that I need urgent medical help to survive. I feel a strange feeling of hope and encouragement that says, "Hang in there; do not yield, persevere."

At 7:49 p.m., Rob calls again to ask how I'm feeling. My reply convinces him it is the real thing.

"Rob," I groan, "call the head of the ER at New York-Pres-byterian and alert him to my arrival so I can get rapid attention. I feel I'm losing ground." He agrees and hangs up.

We are stuck in very slow-moving rush hour traffic. I sit up, and in the last light before dusk I see a police cruiser crawling at a snail's pass in the next lane. I holler and wave to them through the open window, the taxi driver honks his horn to get their attention, and my wife yells to them, pleading for their help. I make the sign of a crushed fist on my chest as she shouts, "He's having a heart attack. Help us please. Lead the way and we will follow to Presbyterian." They look at us, and then as if it is a joke start laughing. It is clear they have no intention to assist. I slump back onto the back seat of the taxi.

At 8 p.m. my son calls again. "I spoke to their chief and they're waiting for you. When do you think you'll be there?" I can't tell him. With the pain abating and my breathing slightly easier, I tell the taxi driver. He is encouraged and replies, "I'll take the next exit, and we'll go on city streets." The pain gets much worse, spreading again to my neck and jaw and into my left arm—I am winded. Is this the end? *Please Lord, I don't want to die yet. It's too soon. I haven't left my mark in life yet.* I open my eyes, and see my wife crying and saying a prayer. "I'll be all right, don't worry," I tell her.

God? Are you still there? Deb needs me. She cared for me self- lessly after my divorce and after my last back operation. She helped me get on my feet; I can't abandon her now, with her condition. I have to take care of her... please God.

I feel increasingly tired and fatigued as I lie on the back seat and the taxi crawls forward. The pain has become dull and flits between my chest and left shoulder. I open my eyes again and Deb is still sobbing quietly, praying, and repeating, "Please don't die."

"How are we doing?" I ask the driver, trying to sit up and steady myself. I don't have the strength and fall back, clutching my cell phone in one hand and my chest with the other. The quality of the neck pain is now the worst I have ever experienced —one I can't begin to describe.

At 8:11 p.m. my son calls back. "Yes, it's still there. It's getting worse. We're on surface streets heading north." The pain grows more intense, my head swims. Is this the end? What about my epiphany? Life is so fickle. One moment we are living, with the wondrous spectrum of human emotions, the next we are dead, pure organic material—soulless.

At 8:16 p.m. Rob call again. "Yes, son. I'm hanging on."

At 8:23 p.m. the taxi pulls up in front of the ER, its neon lights glowing like a beacon.

I call Rob. "Arrived." I hang up, open the back door, and stagger out into the dark like a drunk, short of breath, pain increasing, my legs bucking. I'm rapidly approached by a guard who grabs me and steadies me. He looks like he has seen a ghost as he assists me a few yards into the ER.

"I'm a surgeon and I am having a heart attack," I tell him. The ER is familiar territory: blazing lights, stretchers, crowds of sick people hanging around. I wobble through the gauntlet of aides, nurses, patients, relatives, and uniformed personnel hanging about the corridor as I head for a stretcher. *I've got to make it to the stretcher or I'll faint.* The guard guides me in the direction of the Triage Nurse Office and I bust through the door, which he does not enter. A surprised elderly nurse sitting at a teller's window stands up as I stagger toward the stretcher on the far wall and fling myself on it crying out, "I'm a surgeon and I am having a heart attack."

In my 35 years of active duty as a surgeon at a variety of emergency rooms about Boston's Harvard teaching hospitals during my residency, and then at Boston City Hospital covering trauma in my first job as general surgeon, I have worked with the most battle-hardened, competent, and highly regarded nurses. Never have I experienced what I lived through next.

An angry battle-axe, slighted by my intrusion, yells, "Who the hell are you? I don't care if you're a surgeon or not, bursting into my office like that. You are the rudest person I've ever seen. I have to triage you first. You come right over here and sit down on this chair before I can get your vitals and paper work!"

"Lady, I am sorry. I am having crushing chest pain . . . I'm going to faint," I groan. I toss her my wallet, which lands on the desk next to her. In its window is a New York State Physician Identification card, with my name, address and the crucial information needed to pass a police check in the event of an emergency. "I'm dying of an MI," I yell at her. She adamantly points to the chair next to her desk, turns her back on me, and without looking in my direction, starts sorting out the papers in her inbox, ignoring me and the ID lying next to her: an egomaniac power play while I'm dying.

I make a supreme effort to rouse myself off the stretcher and struggle the three yards across to her chair. A nurse in scrubs enters through another door. She becomes my savior, gives a drop-dead look to the sulking triage nurse, and nudges me back onto the stretcher. She lifts my shirt and says calmly, "I need a 12 lead EKG," slaps the silver leads on my chest, and runs a strip as I lie in a twilight of pain and supreme aggravation.

She rips off the EKG paper capturing the ongoing MI and disappears for a moment. Within seconds she returns and helps me out of the triage office to an ER bay, where a full complement of nurses, technicians, residents, cardiac fellows, and physicians wait. They pounce on me and start their magic. It looks like chaos, but the hustle and bustle are the same intense process as the well-rehearsed precision on an aircraft carrier flight deck.

I am placed on a stretcher and they go into full swing to stabilize me. A highly choreographed, effective team of skilled and dedicated individuals perform their assigned jobs. They extract information about the vital functions of the patient so as to accurately assess their medical status. Several intravenous catheters are inserted in both my arms, intravenous fluids are started, and medications as dictated by the team leader begin to flow. Oxygen prongs are placed up my nose. They measure my oxygen saturation level, monitor my heart activity, and ask me direct questions, known in the trade as "taking a history." The questions are very familiar to me. I answer and describe a precise time-sequence of the symptoms. They make sure I am not allergic to medications; I give them a record of my prescriptions, while others undress me and place an ID band on my wrist: I am a patient.

My wife enters the bay with my backpack and sits in a corner looking overwhelmed and dazed. A nurse reassures her and helps her fill out more paperwork.

"We are going to give you a mixture of anticoagulants and

aspirin, so we have to do a rectal exam and test your stool for active bleeding in your gut," someone tells me. With that, my pants are whipped off and a gloved finger is inserted. It is negative. I swallow a cocktail of medications with a sip of water. The cardiac monitor beeps away rhythmically, and the chatter and commands decrease as they get control of the urgency of my situation.

Several young doctors introduce themselves and mention their specialty as they wade in and out of the three-to-four-person deep team working on me. The names are too much for me to remember, and I regret that they do not hand out business cards. Mentally I check off the right services: a dynamic Italian cardiac fellow with a Modigliani face and a singsong voice; a bright-eyed medical resident probably from Pakistan, her medical student pale and nervous at her elbow; and a smart-looking ER resident from the Bronx. A nurse yells out, "Dr. Moussa is on his way in." He's the interventional radiologist.

I hear the magic words, "Let's go," and place my last call to Rob to let him know that I love him and we are on our way to the cardiac catheter suite. It's 9 p.m., seventy-seven minutes since the onset of my negotiation with God, thirty-seven minutes since I entered the ER, and thirty-two minutes since I received the life-enhancing cardiac cocktail. *Thank you, God. You sent Moses to work miracles on my heart. Oh! Thank you, Lord! I think I might make it.*

The stretcher bearing me, a portable cardiac monitor, an oxygen tank, and a green bag with my clothes is rolled rapidly down the corridors as the Modigliani cardiac fellow and another Italian colleague run. I begin to feel lightheaded again and close my eyes as we whiz around several corners. We enter a cooler, semi-dark room with glowing monitors. I am transferred onto an X-ray table by friendly hands.

A new set of faces introduce themselves—veteran-type technicians, looking down at my face over the masks and glowing monitors that separate us. Again, the identification ritual, the medication and Latex allergy questions. My hospital gown is lifted and my pubic hair is shaved and lavishly washed with cold antiseptic. Some of the solution trickles down between my scrotum and thigh, and I wonder if this will become a source of future irritation as it settles between my buttocks. My arms are tucked by my sides; I am swaddled by sheets as preparatory steps continue in the semi-darkness.

I feel a bit sheepish when I tell the nurse, just before local anesthesia is to be injected into my right groin, "Nurse, I have to pee, badly," without adding that I've not had the chance since leaving Syracuse. She is remarkably calm in her response and automatically washes down my penis and tapes a condom-catheter to its shaft. "OK. Go ahead."

"Sorry, there's no way I can pee lying down, and my bladder is bursting," I say factually, a tone of apology in my voice, without adding that my inhibitory instincts are so strong and ingrained that it will take an act of Satan for me to pee into a condom. I have hardly finished this thought when she rips off the tape holding the condom-catheter in place, removing any remnant of a foreskin that may have escaped circumcision 65 years ago. She shoves a Foley catheter up my urethra into my bladder. The catheter is at least several sizes too big and gouges a most excruciating burning track. I cry out with pain, wondering if she is a man-hater. The pain subsides as my bladder drains. "Seven hundred ccs," she says. She tapes the catheter to my thigh and covers the area.

"Hello. I'm Dr. Moussa," I hear. I open my eyes for a brief glimpse of his between the surgical cap and mask in the now-darkened room. "How bad is the pain?" he asks.

"Ten," I reply, while local anesthesia is injected into my right groin and I feel him palpating for my femoral vessel. He makes the cut a few seconds before the local anesthesia overwhelms the area.

"Has everyone got lead on?" he questions his team. From the mixture of the responses there must be four to five people assisting him. I feel the urgent probing and pushing in my groin, visualizing their activities. I unexpectedly feel my heart being pushed around by their vascular catheter, which elicits no pain, only the sensation of a pencil being pushed through a balloon. I become short of breath. Is it real, or am I just apprehensive and anxious? I feel the X-ray contrast as a warm flush, and hear my cardiac monitor. There is a low murmuring and minimum discussion as the X-ray monitors are activated and de-activated. Dr. Moussa works rapidly, proceeding in silence. My cardiac pain persists. I am apprehensive and also curious. What does he see and what is he doing?

"Dr. Moussa, can you give me a running commentary on what you're doing?"

There is long silence. I'm about to repeat the question, when he says, "I can't concentrate when you're asking me questions." Turning to the nurse he says. "Give him one milligram of Versed."

I get his message: be a patient, not a doctor. "OK, I'll shut up," I say.

After a while he says, "How is the pain? Any better?"

"No. Worse. It's radiating into my left shoulder." Another long silence follows while they work, peppered only by his asking for a specific type of stent to be loaded onto catheters that are inserted into my groin and pushed up into my heart vessels, to unblock my coronary artery.

"The pain is getting worse," I report. He orders another milligram of Versed.

Again, he asks, "How is the pain? Any better?"

"No better," I reply, wondering if he senses my further apprehension.

I'm feeling worse. *God? Are you still there? Can this still go wrong? Can my heart go into ventricular fibrillation and stop?* I suddenly realize that being in the cardiac suite led me to a false sense of security. I'm still in danger and could die. I could be dead in seconds. Then what? A post-mortem?

The Versed works and I drift off. In my dreamy haze, I relive my very first post-mortem when I was a medical student some forty years ago. Some idiot arranged for the teaching post-mortem to be just before lunch break in the cafeteria. Twelve of us filed into the room and stood two deep behind a banister separating us from a body lying on a slab. The chest cage was opened, the face covered by the pulled-down scalp revealing the brain, and the midline abdominal incision exposed the guts. I felt queasy. It was not the sight, but the sweet smell permeating the room. I stood in the second row behind a girl named Judy, and buried my face in her lacquered beehive hair-do, breathing only enough to prevent myself from fainting.

The pathology professor held up an enlarged heart in one gloved hand; in the other, he waved forceps with a tiny clot. "This rather corpulent bobby," referring to the policeman's corpse lying behind him, "dropped dead last night in Trafalgar Square. This man of great authority and holding a venerated social position was smitten by this tiny clot that blocked his coronary artery," he emphasized as he waved the forceps with the yellow-reddish blob about our faces. "He suffered from coronary artery disease, probably due to our Western diet of high sugar, meat, and fat. The Masai, mainly meat eaters, do not suffer from CAD because they spend a lifetime chasing their cattle. They do not have sedentary lives; the constant exercise doubles the size of their coronary arteries. They die of other afflictions." I heard his voice in my Versed-induced dream, when Dr. Moussa addressed me.

"Dr. Meguid, you had a burst plaque in the middle of your left descending coronary artery. Your middle right coronary had a 99% critical narrowing. I have restored blood flow through each, placing a medicated stent to keep it open. Because of the likely duration of your blocked coronary vessels, you have an area of infarcted dead cardiac wall and a surrounding area of stunned, damaged heart muscle, so that your ejection fraction is only 40% instead of 60%. With each contraction of your left ventricle, just a tad more than one-third of your blood is pushed out. I have inserted a balloon assist device into your abdominal aorta. When your heart contracts the balloon will inflate, pushing more blood down through your coronary arteries. Depending on your recovery, we'll decide when to remove the balloon, but probably in 24 to 48 hours. In the meantime, you'll continue to be on blood thinners, full dose aspirin, and Plavix."

"Thank you," I mumble as he leaves. It is 9:35 p.m. and flight LH 405 to Frankfurt is pushing away from the gate with two empty business class seats.

Debbie appears beside my bed in the ICU. She hugs me, relieved to see me alive. I share her sentiment. I know she will gradually lose her faculties, including her speech, and I want to care for her. "God, is that one of the mountains you had in mind?" I whisper. Since I now feel better than I have for a long time, I irreverently joke that we could fly tonight.

By morning, my children sit in my room with me. Rob and his wife drove overnight from Baltimore while my daughter flew in from Rochester, New York. I see relief clearly expressed on their faces. I find comfort in their presence and know it comes with the obligation I had negotiated for the extension of my life. I will tell them the story of their ancestral past, starting with the remarkable story of their grandparents.

God, is that the other mountain you had in mind?

I had one more question for God. *How much time are you giving me to assault and surmount my second hill?*

I receive no sign or indication—it is obviously His call.

"Honey, please pass me my laptop." I open it and begin.

PART I

1905-1949

The farther backward you can look,
the farther forward you can see.
—Sir Winston Churchill

1

EGYPTIAN STRIPES
BENI HAREM, UPPER EGYPT

Buffalo driven Sakia with Fallah

Who am I, and why?
The Aeneid

Four hundred km south of Cairo, in the province of Assuit in a narrowing green Nile valley, lies the village of Beni Harem, my ancestral home. The sunbaked village is nestled in a clearing close to a forest of date palms, and obscured by tall fields of sugar cane. For centuries, before the first Aswan Dam controlled the yearly torrents of rainwater from the central African highlands that lay to the south, the annual floods deposited rich alluvial mud.

Donkeys and the occasional bicycle were the primary forms of travel along the heavily trodden mud paths beside the canals that cut through alfalfa and cotton fields. These strips of cultivatable land were bounded by desert.

Each day was ushered in with the roosters' rousing cries and the muezzin's call to *fajr*—dawn prayer, the first of five punctuating the day's rhythms. Donkey-riding peasants headed to their fields and barefoot children in cool cotton *galabeyas* hustled to school along the narrow alleyways, books in hand, starting early to avoid the oppressive mid-day heat.

Sheikh Amin, a tall, slender man with the sturdy Sa'idi genes of an Upper Egyptian peasant, greeted them at the door. A bookish man in his twenties, he was the teacher and principal of the one room schoolhouse. I would eventually call Sheikh Amin *Giddi,* grandfather. His younger brother was the *omda*, the influential village chief.

On the first day of July 1905, Sheikh Amin had barely started classes when he received word that Khadiga, his sixteen-year-old wife—his first cousin by tradition—had delivered their first child. He rushed toward their mud-brick house in his *galabeya,* holding tight to the white cotton turban wrapped about his skullcap, and his grey *binish*, an overcoat, flapping behind him.

Women in Arab dresses and *hijabs* with infants in arms stood outside their houses and shouted *"Alf mabrouk"* as he hurried through the narrow alleys. He rushed past the coffee house where a few elderly, early risers sat in the shade playing backgammon, drinking glasses of hot, sweet tea, and smoking their *shisha*. Sheikh Amin's students followed, shouting excitedly and expecting treats on this happy occasion.

On entering their whitewashed adobe home, the midwife presented him with a swaddled newborn. Khadiga had blessed

Sheikh Amin with a son. First-born sons were especially esteemed: in this agrarian society, he would be socially responsible to take care of his aging parents. As he grew physically stronger, he would relieve them from working the land, providing more sources of food and more wealth. The first-born son would continue the family line, gradually occupy a dominant position within the family, and eventually hold primary power and the predominant role of leadership, moral authority, social privilege, and control of the majority of the family property. Khadiga had indeed done well. She bore a son whose loyalty to her was blood-connected and unquestionable. Her son would always take care of her—his mother.

Jubilant women telegraphed the news of another *Ibn-el balad* —native son—to their menfolk in the fields by a series of high-pitched tongue trills. The sounds reverberated among the cluster of huts, echoing through the narrow alleys, past well sweeps and courtyards where languorous black-horned buffalos powered the *sakias*—waterwheels.

Sheikh Amin handed his son to Khadiga, thanking the Almighty for a safe delivery. Their hut was similar to the others throughout the tightly knit community. The outer wall of Amin's adobe home was whitewashed, the paint attesting to his *Hajj*, a pilgrimage to Mecca, and the secular, respectful title of Sheikh. They lived with their animals in close quarters to provide nightly warmth and a ready supply of fresh milk and cream and a source for yogurt. Khadiga lay on a straw mattress in a corner of their windowless, one-room home in the early sun that pierced the beaded-curtain door that kept out the ubiquitous flies. The midwife milked a goat to nourish Khadiga, who started to nurse her son.

The following day, Sheikh Amin mounted his donkey—no saddle, merely a blanket thrown across its back—and rode east, his dangling legs moving rhythmically with each trot. In Assuit, the regional capital, he registered the birth of his son, Abdel Aziz Amin Abdel Meguid. Abdel Aziz—the servant of the Almighty

—the given name of the man I would lovingly call Baba, and eventually Daddy.

Four-year-old Abdel Aziz chased his brother, two-year-old Abdel Shaffei, as he ran barefoot into the dirt yard, into the buffalo's circular path beneath the swinging crossbeam and the groaning *sakia*: a danger zone not intended for play. Khadiga, with her third infant son Abdel Sabour in her arms, followed, driven by a mother's apprehension to get them out of harm's way. She did not see the crossbeam of the waterwheel. It struck her mid-back. There was a snap. She collapsed, screaming with pain. With her shrieks, the boys' cries of panic and fear, and the wailing baby, the womenfolk rushed to her side. They dragged Khadiga out of the danger zone and summoned Sheikh Amin. When my father related this story to me, he always hesitated saying "snap." I could see the pain on his face as he stared into the distance.

When mothers died in childbirth, and life expectancy at that time was forty, what was the point of calling for the doctor in Assuit? If called, would he come? What could he do for a woman paralyzed from the waist down? The villagers consoled Sheikh Amin, saying it was *maktoob*—fate—as written in the Qur'an (6:17): "If God afflicts you with evil, none can remove it but He; and if He blesses you with good fortune, know that He has power over all things."

Along with his teaching job, Sheikh Amin cared for Khadiga as best he could with the help of the womenfolk while she lay immobilized on a constantly soiled straw mattress. The responsibility for caring for his younger siblings fell on Abdel Aziz. He watched helplessly as, over a few weeks, his mother's health gradually declined and she died. My father was factual as he recounted these events to me when, as a curious boy in England, I asked him about his youth.

After the mandatory one-year mourning period, Sheikh Amin remarried. Nazifa had once been his brightest student, my father boasted. The following year, his stepmother expelled him from the family in Beni Harem. His innocent crime was that Sabri, a half-brother, was born to Nazifa and displaced him from the pinnacle of sibling hierarchy. My father knew that Sabri was endowed with the authority of the first-born male to Nazifa. "She was an evil woman," he said, even as he understood that Sabri's loyalty to Nazifa was unquestionable.

With tears in his eyes, my grandfather, Sheikh Amin, seated his six-year-old son in a third-class carriage of a Cairo-bound train. He was to live with an elderly aunt with the expectation that he be schooled. Seeing an opportunity to make some money, Auntie sold Abdel Aziz into bondage to a *makwagi*—a launderer. My father labored in the shop long hours for his meals and slept on a mat under the counter. After a few months, and unbeknownst to Sheikh Amin, he ran away and joined others as a boarder at the madrasa of Al Azhar Mosque, which for centuries was the institution of learning and the seat of religious authority in the Islamic and Arab world. "I was determined to make my own way in life," he told me.

Abdel Aziz at Al Azhar, and with younger brothers in Cairo

He learned the Qur'an by rote, rapidly excelling in its rhetoric recitation according to the rules of pronunciation and caesura—the pauses near the middle of a line between words—

making him a pupil of note and praise. Convinced that education was the path to betterment, at thirteen he moved back to the teeming Cairo suburb, with his now-infirm Auntie, for he had to have an address to attend school. He earned extra money for his keep by recitations of the Qur'an at neighborhood functions. On completing high school at sixteen, he returned to Al Azhar to study Arabic and Islamic culture.

At nineteen, Abdel Aziz was a confident, self-assured, ambitious young man who graduated to become a respected but meagerly salaried employee of the Ministry of Education, teaching the Arabic language to first graders in a government-run school. As the eldest, a self-made man, a government employee, and now the most learned, he earned the respect of Nazifa, whom he kept at arm's length. His father had broken tradition by leaving Beni Harem. Together with Nazifa and their growing brood, Sheikh Amin had sought the prosperity of city life by joining the massive migration from impoverished Nile villages to Cairo. Their meeting was the first time in several years that Abdel Aziz saw his scrawny younger siblings, for whose education he took responsibility. His voice was also heard when it came to the topic of appropriate grooms for his half sisters.

Government salaries were puny and the prospect of promotion was slim. My young father lacked professional connections and influence. Fearing the capricious decisions of bribed bureaucrats that permeated Cairo's civil service and the academic world, he contemplated his options. Recognizing that his continued educational success furthered the status of the entire family and the marriage prospects of his sisters, Abdel Aziz joined the Department of Education at Cairo University.

2

BABA GOES TO ENGLAND

EXETER 1930

Baba in the street of Exeter

England is the paradise of individuality, eccentricity, heresy, anomalies, hobbies and humors.

—George Santayana

I n 1928, Abdel Aziz applied for a scholarship from the British Council to enroll in a teacher training program at Saint Luke's College in Exeter, Devon, England. His application was successful, but a visa would only be issued if his physical examination was normal. The dread of failing haunted him. He had slept with the farm animals in Beni Harem as an infant, and had frequent sore throats during his childhood, and he had heard this might progress to rheumatic fever. Uncertain of his health, he substituted a friend's normal chest X-ray. Before his appointment with the ophthalmologist, and in keeping with the times, he bribed the receptionist to let him into the office to memorize the eye chart. With a clean bill of health, he received his visa. By the time he arrived in Britain in 1930, his self-assurance had been weakened and replaced by insecurity. With each upward move he would have to prove himself again.

Once accepted, overseas students and others from the British Dominions and Empire had to attend intensive courses in English and pass a proficiency test before joining the teacher training program. During this time, Abdel Aziz lived in a dorm with other Egyptians who were also studying in Exeter. One afternoon, two fellow students persuaded him to join them at a picnic where they  met several young German au pairs, among them Margarete Martha Steinbach, who called herself Gretchen.

In Arab culture, men did not mingle freely with unmarried women without a chaperone. The closest my father came to admiring women was sitting on his parents' balcony in Sayeda Zeinab after graduating from Al Azhar. He told me that he had torn a discreet hole at the centerfold of a daily newspaper and scanned the girls from surrounding flats as they walked out to hang the family wash, beat the carpets, or lower a basket to hawkers below. Had one of them appealed to him, he would have told his father, who would tell Nazifa to contact the girl's family and arrange a meeting between their families. Encountering young au pairs in England must have been exciting and nerve-racking.

———

In the years before WWII, life in Germany was changing rapidly. The National Socialist Party was a mass movement embraced by demoralized Germans. Initially it was not the totalitarianism of Hitler and his diabolic followers. The early movement redressed national disorders of food shortages, low wages and high prices, and built the autobahn, hospitals, houses, and schools—instilling pride in German nationalism. In contradiction to sanctions imposed by the Versailles Treaty, the government sent troops into the demilitarized zone of the Rhineland with impunity and stopped the gold payment of very large reparations to the Allies. In sum, the National Socialist Party restored national pride, self-esteem, dignity, and a sense of superiority that bordered on arrogance, given that there was weak international pushback. With it came the Nazi ideology in which the putative Nordic or Aryan races, predominant among Germans and other northern European peoples, were deemed highest in the racial hierarchy.

A cornerstone of Aryan ideology was a call for young women to produce blond, blue-eyed babies. The Fatherland, anticipating a need for more male soldiers, developed *Lebensborn,* "procreation farms." Hitler's movement also closed the progressive *Frauen-Schule,* women's schools, preventing women from obtaining their high school certificate with eligibility for university application, causing unrest among the progressive women's movement. In Gretchen's case, the high school principal had counseled her and other like-minded women to go to England to serve as nannies or housekeepers while seeking opportunities to pursue higher education.

At home in Wedel, on the western outskirts of Hamburg, Gretchen announced her intentions of going to England to advance her education. Her Prussian authoritarian father ridiculed and strenuously opposed the idea, perhaps because he was a veteran of WWI, when England was the enemy. Her mother was more sympathetic; she understood her daughter's independent character and her desire to grow.

As a teen, Gretchen followed the conventional path of a blue-collar family daughter, attending the local school, staying home, studying, and taking a Lutheran Confirmation at fourteen. By sixteen, the appeal of going further afield led her to petition to attend the progressive Frauen-Schule in distant Hamburg. For the next three years, she caught the early morning train, leaving before breakfast and returning in the late evening after extracurricular activities—sports, choir, and school plays—thereby avoiding her autocratic father.

Gretchen met Heini, who was in a senior class, and probably joined him in the Hitler Youth League of German Workers in order to spend weekends and summers hiking and sailing. As their relationship developed, he became a frequent visitor in their Wedel home. Heini became Gretchen's sweetheart and eventually her lover.

Heini was tall and fair, with blue eyes. An ardent supporter of the prevailing political ideology, his aim was to become a lawyer. He was the man everyone expected Gretchen would marry, and it would be a comfortably predictable union. Heini opposed the idea of his future wife going to England. He recognized her passion for higher educational opportunities, yet feared such an endeavor could weaken their bonds.

Although Gretchen claimed that the desire to advance herself through further education drew her to follow several of her class friends across the Channel in 1935, that wasn't the only reason. Apart from aspiring to be the first in the family to attend university, she wanted to escape her father, who negated her ambitions and inhibited her desire to explore her womanhood. At twenty, without her father's blessings and to Heini's disappointment, she asserted her independence and left for Exeter to work as an au pair to an English family with two young children.

At the picnic, Gretchen met Abdel Aziz. She beguiled him with her open charm. She was outspoken, espousing progressive European views—so different from the few demurring Egyptian women he had met. She was attractive, with shoulder-length auburn hair parted in the middle, a wide forehead, and manicured eyebrows that framed her inquisitive light blue eyes. A hint of freckles fell across her prominent cheekbones. The young Egyptian was smitten.

However, she had a secret. In Hamburg, prior to her departure, Heini proposed their engagement with the intent to marry his sweetheart on her return. This informal understanding gave cause for an unofficial celebration, which her mother arranged on a Sunday afternoon, with coffee, cake, and whipped cream. Her father's objection to her trip was somewhat assuaged. She tentatively accepted Heini's proposal.

After the picnic, Gretchen and Abdel Aziz met more frequently, at first with her newly acquired circle of German girlfriends, including her close friend Trudel. Her English family invited Abdel Aziz for tea, and then he accompanied Gretchen on outings with the two youngsters. Eventually, they met alone. He progressively declared his growing feelings for her in letters.

```
Exeter 1936
My beloved Gretel,

I find great happiness in writing to
you. I feel like writing every day
because I feel strangeness without you.
```

```
I never had such a feeling before. It is
really strange. It has been always my
motto "Reason before affection," but at
times, I am weak. I forget myself and go
on thinking of you, of our future, of
our common life. My love, and affections
for you.

Yours,
Meguid
```

She wrote back that she found him handsome and charming and was intrigued by his alien culture. She noted his playfulness, intelligence, extreme ambition, and kindness, along with his sensitivity to her needs and dreams of an education. He seemed a worldly man with profound human insight. One could not blame her if she thought he was far more interesting than the man she was expected to marry.

The following summer Abdel Aziz completed his bachelor's degree in English and pedagogy at Saint Luke's College and immediately enrolled in London's School of Oriental and African Studies, primarily to study Arabic. He also signed up for a graduate course at University College London with the eminent educational psychologist Sir Cyril Burt. When he moved to London, Gretchen followed, living near him for the remaining few months of her legal one-year visa. Abdel Aziz encouraged her to prepare for her college education by continuing English lessons and starting courses in typing and shorthand. That summer, when her guest visa expired, she returned to

Wedel with the promise to write frequently and return to him shortly.

Surely, she must have felt some nagging ambivalence of loving an Egyptian—a non-Aryan. How would such a union work when their cultural outlook was diametrically opposite? Arab society was based on communal relationships and rooted in honor, shame, and disgrace. Western society was entrenched in the individual. They argued about this divide, seeking harmony. There was also the issue of Heini in Hamburg.

She prolonged her absence from London that autumn, staying away until Christmas. Abdel Aziz presumed she was with her parents in Wedel, but suspected and worried she might be with Heini in Hamburg, too, who would no doubt try to talk her out of her newfound ideas. In a flurry of letters, Abdel Aziz expressed astonishment and unease at her long silence.

London 1937
My dear Gretchen,

It is surprising to me that I have not heard from you. The family I am staying with has noticed my anxiety and frequent inquiry for your letters every time the postman passes. Do you not have my address? Or are there some more impor-tant affairs which take all your time?

I'm longing, my dear, to have some news from you. You must write and it must be a long letter.

Goodbye my angel,
Meguid

When he got no response, his letters took on tones of anger

and jealousy. What could she be doing in Germany? He relentlessly sought to persuade her to return to London, to continue her dream of obtaining a degree in psychology. Between the lines were tantalizing intimations of their living together, with suggestions of wanting a more lasting relationship. He had difficulty reading her occasional non-committal responses; her handwriting was akin to chicken scratch.

In December, a different letter arrived from her. She recounted that she had met Heini at Altona's main railroad station when he returned for his military furlough. He disembarked from his train late one afternoon and they went to the station restaurant. She feigned not being hungry, unsure about his ability to pay for the dinner. He ordered a lavish meal of *Kartofelsalat* and *Wurst*—potato salad and sausage, with beer. When it was served, he devoured it without offering to share a bite, and without any conversation. As they sat in silence, she could only think of her father tucking into his meal while her mother ate in the ensuing silence. "I decided then and there," she wrote, "that I could never marry him."

She broke off their seven-year relationship, agreeing not to tell her parents because Heini did not know how to face them and deal with what her father would say. She wrote to Abdel Aziz with the news of her plans to return and in his last letter to her before she came, Abdel Aziz swore he would kiss every inch of her body on her arrival. He met her at the train station in December 1936. In April 1937, on the occasion of Gretchen's upcoming twenty-third birthday, Abdel Aziz presented her with a portable Olivetti typewriter.

Heini soon sent a letter that would have unforseen consequences.

Hamburg, April 25, 1937
My dearest Gretchen!

Even today, I am very sorry and

sincerely regret that things happened
the way they did, that you want to move
away, and that you will be lost from all
of us. You had obviously made the decision regarding our relationship much
earlier. . . because of your decision.
For me, too, everything has changed.

You have been a secure support and
compass for me for a long time. And you
know very well that in spite of all the
conditions while you were here [*sic*
autumn 1936], we were attracted to each
other quite a bit. What will your
parents say, should I meet them again at
some point? I know that I am unable to
change anything; only you are in the
position to do that. And if I reflect
further about Cairo, with its 8% of
foreigners and mix of cultures, quite a
few worries come to mind.

. . . think about how it will be when
you're older? Will you be able to endure
the absence from here, will the longing
not be too strong for everything that
you are giving up today? Will the people
over there be able to fill your entire
life? Particularly when one grows older,
one reflects more and more about the
things and problems that have never
arisen in your youth. Presently the
longing for your homeland, and thus for
your relatives and friends, does not
know any limits . . . Being homesick and

```
longing for something familiar may cause
a lot of sorrow for people; it may even
cause unrest and depression. I only want
the best for you. If I cannot be your
lover, consider me as your big broth-
er . . . write often. Will you read my
letters while alone? I remain your
friend and I will never forget you,

Heini
```

With this letter, had Heini wormed into her mind the uncertainty of her future happiness in Cairo, living far from family, friends, and her incessant longing for her homeland? Nevertheless, once Gretchen was back in London, she and Abdel Aziz set up house together.

Abdel Aziz recognized his own romantic dream of marrying a western woman to declare his progressiveness, although he remained unsure of the wisdom of a cross-cultural relationship —a love cocktail of hubris and naiveté. A few months later, while they were briefly apart, he wrote about his discussion with an Egyptian art student about his conflict.

```
London November 1937
Gretchen,

I met some Egyptians yesterday who had
come just recently from Egypt and we
discussed the strong need of the nation
for reformation and improvement. I also
discussed with one of them my intention
to marry a European. "No," he said. "You
will never feel happy with her. She
wants you all for herself. She would
stand in your way whenever you behave in
```

the context of your culture. And
besides, she will have her own ways and
her friends and her own visits, etc."
But I went on explaining to him the type
of girl I am going to marry, how she
will be my supporter and inspiration,
and how she will stand by me in good
times and bad. "This type of girl is
very rare," he said. "Yes, I agree with
you," I replied, "and I am lucky to find
this rare girl."

I am sorry my dear to tell you this,
because I feel I must not hide anything
from you. On the other-hand, I shall be
miserable all my life if I ever lose
you. You are mine. You are everything to
me. You are the dearest creature to me.
Say something to console me!

Meguid

Apparently, she must have, for they continued their life
together and she completed her typing and shorthand courses at
the Pittman's School.

3

THE CURSE OF THE PROMISE

LONDON 1938

Abdel Aziz, Gretchen, and Heini

Abdel Aziz submitted his doctoral thesis to University College by the late summer of 1938. After he was awarded his doctorate, he officially became Professor of Arabic and Pedagogy at Cairo University and received tenure. With the threats of war and the completion of his studies, he and Gretchen hastily married on September 20, 1938, without the presence of family from Egypt or Germany. No honeymoon followed. Given the political atmosphere in Europe they anticipated the potential onset of a major conflict that might affect his return to his family in Cairo.

Gretchen had converted to Islam, adopting the Muslim name Nadia, forgoing the usual lengthy, formal religious education and spiritual transformation desirable for living in a Muslim culture. This shortcut would turn out to be a costly mistake with far-reaching effects, for it denied her the deeper insights that would have eased her integration into and acceptance of her adopted Egyptian community. Critically, it deprived her of a sympathetic appreciation of Islam's intimate role in Egypt's daily life, a consequence that left her an emotional outsider, reluctant to embrace the ambient culture.

By marrying and accompanying Abdel Aziz to Cairo, Gretchen deferred her own educational dream. She never failed to remind him of his solemn promise that they would return to England to embark on *her studies*. In the absence of a practical timeline, the promise became a curse—a sword hanging over Abdel Aziz and the Meguid progeny. The promise would influence the career decisions that he would make.

On their way to Cairo, they planned to stop in Germany for him to meet his new in-laws. Gretchen traveled ahead to Wedel to explain her new status as wife to an Arab. He stopped first in Heidelberg, to attend an intense German language course. Unbeknownst to Abdel Aziz, Heidelberg was teeming with roaming Brown Shirts, harassing Jews and anyone who didn't look Aryan.

When I was eleven, my father told me of his experience in Heidelberg to teach me the moral of the tale. "These unemployed Germans were pumped up by Hitler's hate-mongering rhetoric about the undesirables. Gypsies, intellectuals, homosexuals, and Jews were blamed for Germany's economic depression. They would beat, terrorize, and arrest anyone who did not look like them. One minute I was walking to class through the bustling city streets clutching my briefcase, and the next, I hear the Brown Shirts shout, *'Einer von Denen!'* One of them." Because he looked different, a throng of capricious young men had accosted him. They harangued him, pushing him about; his briefcase was yanked away, and they arrested him.

Sitting at a bus stop in the early morning sun next to the

Nile awaiting a bus, he carried on with his story. Although there were crowds milling about us in Cairo, his words transported us into the past and to that other world. "They took me to a police station, stripped me, and made me stand on a long table in a cold cellar where the only light was a single bulb hanging from the ceiling. They paraded me about, shoving me in all directions and taunting me, banging the table with their clenched fists, screaming, *'Jude, Jude, Jude...'* They were convinced I was Jewish. My dark complexion, my curly hair, my circumcision."

He told me he had been terrified, fearful of their unpredictable hysteria. The humiliation did not stop until a black-uniformed SS officer in knee-high boots marched into the room and blew his whistle. The room fell silent. My father felt his heart in his throat, he said, as he stood shivering in the cold. "I wondered—deportation to a camp?"

Saluting with an outstretched arm, the officer declared that my father was a guest student from Egypt, a Muslim married to a good Aryan, Christian, German woman.

"In an instant," he related, clutching my arm, "the ominous atmosphere changed. The mortal threats became exuberant praises of my physique. The Brown Shirts expressed joviality, displayed friendliness to the Arab race, and feigned camaraderie, saying it was all a joke. Once dressed, I was escorted onto the streets of Heidelberg." His gaze tracked a Felucca sailing down the Nile. A long silence followed.

Abdel Aziz with his new, German in-laws

"Son, 'one of them' is someone who is different from our social norms, someone we don't respect or love, someone we can live without." Our bus approached. "Keep this in mind." He quoted Napoleon, saying, "Those who come to cheer me today will come to see me hang tomorrow."

Back in Wedel, when Gretchen's parents met Abdel Aziz, they were impressed by his deferential attitude and his perseverance in trying at conversing with them in German, despite his limited ability. His new mother-in-law adored him. His father-in-law, now a committed National Socialist, reserved judgment. He wondered if his new son-in-law would be interested in joining him as a hand when he next went sailing on the Elbe.

Opa and Oma Steinbach in their boat "Möve" sailing on the Elbe river

4

SUDAN
1939-1943

Graduation of Abdel Aziz's first teacher training class.

Natural abilities are like natural plants,
that need pruning by study.
—Francis Bacon

T he Meguid clan in Sayeda Zeinab welcomed their eldest son. They embraced his foreign wife, bestowing the couple with belated wedding gifts and serving them lavish meals. In the custom of Egyptian hospitality and generosity, around food and drink one could sit, relax, and converse with family and friends, although Gretchen's language barrier, and her lack of familiarity with local customs deeply influenced by Islamic tradition, made things awkward. She wanted to eat and then clear up, but they sat around and chatted in a mixture of Arabic and English. While his German wife enhanced Abdel Aziz's already elevated educational standing, her pragmatic Teutonic habits of tidiness and hygiene did not always allow her to accept or understand the nuances of the honors given to her by her new Egyptian family, as well as his Arab university colleagues. Such disparity in behavior concerning what was expected and what was displayed was the source of tension between the newlyweds. For example, she would discard the surplus of a meal rather than give it to the blind beggar on the corner.

That first strained introduction into Arab communal family life, however, only lasted eight months. After agitating the Department of Education to establish a formal educational program—one he could organize and supervise, an ambitious and grand scheme for the time—Abdel Aziz was assigned to the Egyptian University in Bakht El Roda in Ed Dueim, some 2,433 km from Cairo to the south, in Sudan. Politically, Sudan was then part of the Anglo-Egyptian Territory, governed by the British. There were no direct roads or flights to Ed Dueim.

Gretchen wrote a colorful letter to her parents about their move, twenty-four days before the start of World War II in Europe.

Ed Dueim, August 8, 1939
Dear loved ones in Hamburg

Our trip from Cairo to Dueim was one of
the most beautiful journeys I have ever
experienced. We took the train from
Cairo as far as Shalala in Upper Egypt.
There we had to take a Nile steamer to
Wadi Halfa at the border with Sudan and

the site of the Nile's first major
cataract. We became acquainted with a
"new" Nile so very different to the Nile
as we knew it in Cairo. Here the fast-
moving river cuts through huge boulders
of bare rocks, which form islands and
steep riverbanks encroached by the
Sahara Desert.

We transferred from the train to a Nile
steamer and traveled on the Nile to the
cataract at Wadi Halfa, passing Abu
Simbel—an ancient Egyptian temple hewed
into the rock facing west and guarded by
four mammoth Pharaonic figures.
We disembarked and took a bus on a
winding road gradually rising above the
waterfall of Wadi Halfa, which is
already in Sudan. From there we took the
train from Wadi Halfa to Khartoum by

train—a 34-hour trip through desert. In
Khartoum we transferred onto another
Nile steamer. We travelled for seven
days through Africa to where the White
Nile meets the Blue Nile. At their
confluence lies Sudan's second largest
city, Ed Dueim—in the heart of Africa,
where Bakht El Roda University lies. The
trip took ten days.

We were prepared to share our life with
the natives, but much to our surprise,
we found a minor paradise. We were
assigned a small house set amidst a huge
English garden with well-kept lawn and
flowerbeds. Our new home was hidden from
the outside world with a variety of
flowering bushes and trees. It reminded
me of England. The White Nile flowed
past the bottom of our garden. It is a
wide river with fast moving currents
towards the north. Standing on the edge
of my new garden and seeing the White
Nile, I was reminded of my childhood
home—Wedel and standing by the river
Elbe.

In the morning, we milk our cow, Elsa.
We feed our visitors—feral cats, two
gazelles, and my leopard cub.
The Egyptian daily, *Al Ahram*, reaches us
almost a week behind the time. Sometimes
we get the *Times* of London and other
English papers. These dailies limp into
Ed Dueim seven days late. Alas, no

German papers for me now. On the wireless, the Reuter news is in telegram
form. These are the only communication
with the outside world.

The British community's swimming pool is
set amongst trees and behind hedges for
privacy where we meet our English
friends every afternoon for tea after we
play tennis. We then have drinks, which
I am not accustomed to.

Gretchen

Her letter would certainly have reached her parents ten to
fourteen days later. Each letter to Germany—to an Axis power
—passed via the British military censors. They opened each
missive, read its contents, and if it contained innocuous news it
was taped shut using censorship tape and mailed. Gretchen was
either unaware of or chose to ignore this. She spoke English with
a lilt, her foreign accent and German sentence construction
clearly revealed her national origin, raising suspicions of her
loyalty.

The majority of the University staff were British. My father
was the only Egyptian and headed the Arabic Department. His
task was to train primary school teachers, to reform and stan-
dardize the Arabic syllabus across the Sudanese school system, and
to write textbooks reinforcing the teaching of Modern Standard
Arabic. After a couple of years, in 1940, he proudly graduated his
first class of teachers. Transforming the Arabic curriculum in
Sudan was a monumental achievement. By virtue of this assignment, he developed a life-long flair for writing textbooks to
promote his native language, earning him respect and admiration
on his return to Egypt, and eventually throughout the Arab world.

Abdel Rahman & Abdel Raheem

During their five-year stay in Ed Dueim, from 1939 until early 1943, my mother typed more than 150 letters to her parents describing their luxurious lifestyle. Her nostalgic pangs for her homeland were mollified when she discovered that storks, which traditionally nested on northern German chimneys in spring, wintered in Sudan. In her early letters, she described their spacious villa with her senior cook Suleiman, who constantly nibbled at their European food, and the two houseboys, Abdel Rahman and Abdel Raheem, who she trained in German housekeeping ways.

Gretchen wrote of their lush British garden cared for by three gardeners, and the many exotic birds along the banks of the White Nile. She raved about her enchanting, gracious, colonial British lifestyle, as she socialized with the gentrified British society wives.

She played tennis and attended leisurely luncheons served by white-gloved Sudanese butlers. Some afternoons, she participated in organized outings into the bush. In lavishly furnished tents, tall, black Sudanese waiters wearing white robes and turbans poured Ceylon tea from silver pots into Wedgwood cups. The women were served finger sandwiches, scones, strawberry jam, and clotted cream on bone china plates—all imported from Britain.

On special occasions they attended an afternoon reception at the Colonial Administrator's Palace. Gretchen wore traditional black outfits which contrasted with the British dress code of colored flowery dresses. In the evenings, she attended formal dinners wearing evening gowns, with Abdel Aziz in black tie. Though they were outsiders, an Egyptian and a German, their

British education elevated them into privileged colonial society
—the posh life.

As newlyweds, they received belated wedding gifts, including
copper coasters engraved with their names and marriage year,
and a six-piece fish cutlery set of silver with ivory handles. My
mother kept these souvenirs throughout her life. In her letters,
she pleaded with her parents and little brother, seven years
younger, to visit Sudan because of its exciting novelty. It is ques-
tionable whether such pleading was sincere or if it reflected her
lack of understanding of the tense situation in Europe.

When the shooting in Europe began, Abdel Aziz was visiting
schools some distance from Ed Dueim, prolonging his absence.
Gretchen felt alone and marooned in Ed Dueim, and the first
blush of their love was wearing off. She found herself with many
lonely hours that dragged on through the day. She wasn't a
serious reader and she didn't play cards, board games, or a
musical instrument. With her Germanic social background, she
had little in common with the other wives who were British. The
Sudanese women didn't even merit a mention in her voluminous
correspondence, presumably because there was no mixing of the
races. The tone of her letters began to reveal increasing loneliness
and homesickness and her attitude grew more critical. In
October 1939, she wrote:

Dear loved ones in Hamburg,

Dueim is a town of some standing and
rank (the second largest in Sudan after
the capital, Khartoum). To me it is just
another mud village. The words ugly,
bare, monotonous are appropriate if I
was to try to give you a description of
Dueim city. With the sun brooding over
it all day long, the place becomes more
desolate and uninviting.

Gretchen

Dueim. Gretchen's Photograph

Her letters underscored her superior European-Germanic
interpretation of Sudanese culture, which she described as
simple, just short of primitive. In Ed Dueim, even though she
had two radios, allowing her to follow events of the war via the
BBC and Radio Berlin, she felt out of touch, mainly with her
family. Mail and newspapers were delivered weekly, arriving on
the Sunday boat coming down the White Nile from Khartoum.
In February 1940, despite British censorship, she praised
Deustschland by writing:

> . . . in the deepest little corner of my
> heart, it is a 'heart's desire' to soon
> be able to be with you! The dear, good
> Vaterland—one will never forget it.

It may have been the poetic reaching of a lonely, homesick woman, but to British military censors, mention of the Vaterland was synonymous with the National Socialist Party, the warmongering Hitler, the ruthless SS, and racial cleansing. It must have raised red flags. Her name was no doubt placed on a watch list of foreigners with potential sympathy toward the enemy, undependable when it came to potential hostile activity. All this occurred without her husband knowing.

Gretchen became increasingly melancholy. Her moods were, no doubt, exacerbated by her physical and emotional isolation; Abdel Aziz was a workaholic, gone all day and pre-occupied with his projects during the evening and at weekends. Given the war, she didn't receive mail from her family. What was the status of her brother, who would now be of conscription age? And maybe she also wondered about Heini. Perhaps she was having marriage regrets about leaving Germany.

Her British friends distanced themselves from her; perhaps early in the war she had touted or alluded to Axis victories and other Nazi triumphs, or bored them with subtle, perchance references to the superiority of the Nordic races, themes that had prevailed when she lived in Germany. In talking about this among her British women friends, she sought a confidant, some consolation rather than merely to make herself important, but the war and the British army wives made the times, place, and audience wrong for seeking comfort.

To ease her discomfort Abdel Aziz began taking her on his long trips to faraway Sudanese village schools. When they went south to Juba for three weeks, she described her experience in a letter to her family:

Ed Dueim, Sudan, December 8, 1939
Dear loved ones,

Such a tour is well prepared ahead of
time. We took two cots and mattresses,
mosquito net, two armchairs, a table, a
bathing tub, washbasin, all kinds of
cooking supplies with provisions, buckets, and water containers. In addition
to our everyday clothes, I packed a long
evening gown and Meguid's jacket and
black-tie outfit.

Apart from our wonderfully comfortable
car, we had a truck for all of the
luggage and two servants. The loaded
truck with the servants and a local
policeman proceeded ahead to establish
camp at our destination. We usually
traveled across country, during the day,
attempting to reach our camp before
dark, since it was too dangerous to
drive by night.

After the dusty trip over rocks and
stones, the prepared warm bath by one of
the servants was welcome. It shed the
dust and dirt and rejuvenated me.
We dressed, and after a served dinner, a
few important local dignitaries would
appear. We served coffee that was drunk
from small cups, sitting in a "familiar
circle." As a sign of appreciation, the
coffee was slurped very loudly. The
louder one drank, the greater the sign

of gratitude. Then Meguid and I would
drop into our cots exhausted.

The next day, we received half a dozen
chickens and a lamb as a gift. These
were butchered and served roasted over
an open pit the next night.

Abdel Aziz did not take his European wife to the work
setting. She stayed in the tent and occupied herself writing to
her friends and family in Europe, unaware of the war situation.
She had further correspondence with her family during progressive stages of the war, through the International Red Cross.
Gretchen focused on sending food packages via Switzerland, or
sending money via her Steinbach cousins who had immigrated
to Pennsylvania before the war, asking them to help her parents
in any way they could. Her yearning to "return to my *Heimat*
[homeland], to be with you," was a recurring theme, perhaps
echoing the sentiments in Heini's insidious letter.

In the midst of war, the British censors in Sudan intercepted
her mail to and from Germany. They concluded that her letters
were those of a person with Axis sympathies. It is no wonder
that the buzz among the British community became that she
might be a German alien at best, or a spy at worst. The British

authorities demanded her internment with other Nazi-leaning nationals.

Hearing this, Abdel Aziz impressed upon the Mahdi, the spiritual Sudanese leader, that his wife Nadia was Muslim, and an Egyptian national, and he was the head of the Arabic Department at Baht el Roda. His crucial work would cease if they interned her. The Mahdi interceded with the British authorities on his behalf, and the matter of internment did not come up again. In return, the Mahdi asked Abdel Aziz to take a seven-year-old street-smart Sudanese orphan boy, Ibrahim, under his wing to tutor and nurture him.

Amazed by Ibrahim's intelligence and affability, Abdel Aziz immediately liked him. Was he subconsciously slaking his desire for a son? After a few weeks, he discussed with his wife the possibility of adopting Ibrahim. Gretchen was not in favor of the idea. Perhaps the conception of their first-born occurred to placate Abdel Aziz's desire for a son, or to dispel any speculations about Gretchen's identity and loyalty. With a new baby at home, his restless wife would certainly be kept busy and, at least for the time being, she'd focus on other issues and not her homesickness.

Expecting an addition to the family, Abdel Aziz applied for a transfer to a lecture position in the Education Department in Cairo. A daughter, Gulnar, was born in 1941 in the prestigious Civilian Hospital in Om Dur Man, near Khartoum. The announcement of my father's appointment appeared in the "Notice" section of Cairo's prominent daily *Al Ahram*. Abdel Aziz only learned of his appointment when Sheikh Amin wired the good news to his son, that his job would begin in January 1943, and the family of three returned to Cairo.

5

AL HAMDULIL ALLAH—A SON

CAIRO, 1944

Marwan at seven months—always a happy child

*A father is a man who expects his son
to be as good a man as he meant to be.*
—Frank A. Clark

According to my mother, I was ten days late when I was born on the second Friday of April, 1944. In the male-centric Muslim society of the Arab world, including Cairo, Egypt, there was no higher asset, no greater social benefit, than the birth of a male offspring. My Baba shouted from the balcony of our flat in Giza to the passing pedestrians below, "I have a son! A son, a son." Raising his hands to the heavens, he proclaimed in a loud voice, "Praise be to Allah—*Al Hamdulil Allah.*" He had established the beginning of an academic dynasty.

The overjoyed feeling was not shared by my mother and sister. My mother found the pregnancy inconvenient, for it derailed her plans to return to England to complete her education—the promise my father had made to her in London in 1938 before marriage, almost as inducement. And Gulnar, my older sister, was incensed at being physically and emotionally usurped. She was no longer the center of her parents' or her many Egyptian aunt's devotion. She began to be a rival for attention, setting up a life-long fateful conflict, for in her eyes no one was going to devalue or displace her.

On the day of my birth Mother's water broke around seven in the morning on a cloudless day with the half-moon lingering above the desert's edge and the apricot trees in full bloom. Sister Edith Röske, a young German nurse and close friend, accompanied Mother to Papaioannou Hospital. I glided into the world after a short labor, at about eleven. Sister Röske assisted an Egyptian midwife delivering me at a Greek hospital in the shadow of the great Pyramid of Cheops on the edge of the Giza Plateau, overlooking the green Nile valley. I was immediately circumcised by a Muslim cleric.

The tranquility of my arrival belied cataclysmic events abroad and at home. In the previous summer's battles in the desert west of Alexandria, the Allies had halted the advancing Axis troops at El Alamein, forcing their retreat to Tunisia along the North African coast. The German approach to Cairo had encouraged those Egyptians who were struggling against sixty years of British colonial rule and hoped a German presence in Cairo would usher in Egyptian independence.

Domestically, there was mass migration from the rural Nile valley to Cairo's teeming, proliferating slums. Cairo's population increased rapidly, and the infrastructure strained under the burden of the influx. Cholera outbreaks were frequent.

In neighboring Palestine, the continuous flow of refugees from central Europe and Poland who seized Arab lands, encouraged by the Zionist movement, caused unrest in Egypt and in the surrounding Arab countries, foreshadowing the creation of Israel in 1948 and the first Arab-Israeli war. Against this turbulent backdrop, my childhood in Cairo would unfold.

When we saw each other for our first face-to-face meeting sixteen years later, Sister Röske told me that the vitality of my first bellow reflected the vigor of a healthy baby. And as I would have expected, the midwife dangled me, cut the cord, and spanked my slippery bottom. My cries mingled with the muezzin's mid-morning call to prayer—*dhuhr*—which wafted through the open delivery room window from neighborhood minarets.

Sister Röske said I looked about in wonderment, seeking the warmth of my mother's breast. Mother, however, was hesitant and reluctant to hold me. As Sister Röske swaddled me, she noted my strikingly long, slender fingers and predicted that I might become a pianist, a violinist, or even a surgeon one day. Sister placed me in a bassinet within my mother's view, hoping she would take to this new vulnerable stranger who had unintentionally disrupted her plans.

A messenger hurried along the dusty road leading from Papaioannou Hospital toward the shady, two-story villa where my parents occupied the top flat. It was set back from the main street on the fringes of an expanding Cairo in the middle-class district of Dokki, Giza—a ten-minute walk from the university, the zoo, and the botanical gardens. Baba was at home on this Friday Sabbath. He was the youngest professor in the Department of Arabic and Pedagogy at Cairo University. As I would come to accept during his life, he was working, as usual busy on a manuscript, on one of his many upcoming new Arabic textbooks. The servant kept an eye on Gulnar while he anxiously awaited the outcome of the birth. He hoped that his second child would be a son—an heir—to bolster his standing as a man.

The messenger burst into the house, rushed into Baba's book-lined study and shouted, "A son, Master—*Ya effendi*. You have a son, *alf mabrouk*, a thousand congratulations!"

Baba's joy and pride, he told me more than once, was such that he emptied his pocket of all its change to reward the messenger. "Mind you, I had only a few coins," he would add each time he related this story to me with a wry smile. "I rested my pen on the manuscript and rose from my desk with immodesty. News of a son filled me with such elation it popped my shirt buttons. I stepped out onto our balcony to proclaim my joy."

Baba first set eyes on me during visiting hours later that evening. I wonder if he thought of the zebra, with its two types of stripes: Gulnar expressed his dark, enigmatic Arab ones, and to his surprise, I, his son, had the lighter ones, fair skin, and a shock of blond hair.

6

THE EGYPTIAN CLAN

1944

Sheikh Amin and Sit Nazifa

To the family–that dear octopus from whose tentacles we never quite escape, nor, in our innermost hearts ever quite wish to.
—Dodie Smith

On the day of my birth, Baba was the bearer of good news for Sheikh Amin and the Meguid clan, a very different experience from Gulnar's birth. At the time of Gulnar's birth, he had been inspecting a school's Arabic curriculum in Ed Dueim, Sudan. Due to his "duty complex," he was not with Gretchen at the Civilian Hospital in Khartoum after the delivery. Instead, he had sent her a handwritten letter reflecting his hope and fear of disappointment.

```
Ed Dueim, Sudan,
November 15, 1941

My dearest,
I am assuming you are already in the
hospital, and already mother of a sweet
baby. Yes, I can see him; a lovely
little thing laying in his cot . . . It
is also wondering what is going on round
him it; a different world from the one
it has been used to. I've been referring
to the baby by it, because I do not want
to be disappointed by saying "he."

Meguid
```

The "it" had been Gulnar—a beautiful, brown-skinned, Sa'idi-looking girl with almond eyes and straight black hair, absent of any visible Teutonic genes. If he was disappointed that he didn't have a son, he did not show it.

Now, two years later, on his way to deliver the news of my birth to Sheikh Amin, Abdel Aziz left the overcrowded tram at Sayed's square in the heart of the ancient city of *Al Qahira*—Cairo. He picked his way through the noisy, winding streets in the early afternoon heat as Friday crowds thronged the area. Music blared from sidewalk cafés and customers enjoyed their *shisha*—single- or multi-stemmed pipes for vaping, or smoking flavored tobacco or opium. Baba surged past donkey carts and sputtering old cars honking their way through an oncoming sea of hawkers, artisans, and galabeyaed workers who navigated on and off the street and pavement. Cafes, restaurants, and shops spilled out onto the roadway's edge. Avoiding mangy stray dogs, he strode past walkways littered with trash and pools of sewage from broken pipes. Continuing, he turned into narrow alleyways, passing irreversibly decaying buildings, finally arriving at 7 Haret Omar Street. He climbed up the stairs through a flurry of feral cats to our clan's third-floor flat in a block of old houses.

The aging Sheikh Amin, revered head of the Cairo clan, was now slender, silver-haired, and kind, with a dark, sun-wrinkled face bisected by a grey walrus mustache. He was dressed in a clean, high-quality gabardine *galabeya*—an open, V-neck, collarless robe with billowing sleeves—his head wrapped in a traditional white cotton *kafiyeh*. He wore no glasses over his rheumy eyes.

Sit Nazifa, rotund in her black *abaya*, had a prominent dimple in her chin. She had once been a slender, beautiful young woman, with the feared tongue of a snake and an equally malicious personality. Her lineage was pure Sa'ida, and she spoke in the *Sa'idi* dialect with my aunts and uncles. Despite once having been Giddi's promising student in Beni Harem, she was not facile at reading or writing. Having evicted Abdel Aziz when he was six and not expecting him to survive, she now feared him. Baba, however, focused his attention entirely on his father, Sheikh Amin, never dealing directly with her concerning family matters. He essentially ignored and disregarded her.

Baba's parents heaped praise on my father when they heard his good news. Their second grandchild was a boy. Baba accompanied Giddi to Friday's afternoon service in the historic mosque, Our Lady of Sayeda Zeinab, to give thanks to Allah for my safe arrival. The strong bond between father and son was respected by Sheikh Amin's other sons and none attempted to insert themselves into their relationship.

Baba's younger siblings, many in school and living at home, bestowed congratulations as they gathered for the late Friday lunch. After Sheikh Amin pronounced the customary benediction, *Bismillah, ar-Rahman, ar-Rahim*—In the name of Allah, the Compassionate, the Merciful—the meal began promptly.

The feast, prepared by my step-grandmother with help from my aunts, was unusually lavish to mark the special occasion. The table was laden with platters of stuffed vine leaves, kabobs, deep-fried aubergine, spiced lentils, okra in tomato sauce browned in garlic and onions, saffron rice with raisins, and fried pigeons, a delicacy. Another special dish: the delicious and uniquely Egyptian *Mulukheia* soup—the food of kings—made of the green leaves of the mellow plant. It had taken all morning to prepare. There was also blackened freshwater Moses fish from the Nile, and mango and guava juice. As a show of affluence, they also drank Pepsi Cola. Seasonal fruits topped off the savory offerings: tangerines, mangos, grapes, guava, a variety of dates, and small, sweet bananas. Completing the meal was sugary mint tea or Turkish coffee. The spread far exceeded even the luxurious splendor of the yearly feast after Ramadan.

The sharing of family news, gossip, and rumors mingled with the cries of hawkers exaggerating their craft and declaring the virtue of their wares. Noise rose from the streets below, along with Qur'anic recitations from Cairo Radio drifting through the open windows, blended with the strains of Egyptian music from sidewalk cafes. Fans whirled to alleviate the stiffening early spring heat wave. Rumors of an influx of World War II Jewish migrants usurping land and displacing indigenous Palestinians, and murmurs and fears of the cholera epidemic, were set aside. My father basked in the glory of showered praise. Thanks to my arrival, Abdel Aziz's status had risen.

In his exuberance, my father neglected his duty to register my birth. Weeks later, when my mother asked to see the certificate, he remembered he had forgotten, and trotted off to the local police station.

"April—sir?" asked the sergeant, pen in hand, sitting in front of a huge ledger. "If it's April you must pay a fine because you failed to register within three weeks of the happy event."

"April? Did I say April? Ah, no. I am so happy to have a son that I misspoke. You know what it's like to have a son. I meant he was born a week or so ago. In what month are we now?" And so the month of my birth became May, the penalty averted; a modest tip, *baksheesh*, was discreetly slipped into the sergeant's outstretched hand.

Baba hastened home with a copy of my birth certificate, speedily signed and sealed, to show my mother. My name reflected traditional Arab culture and disregarded any German heritage or genealogy: Amin Marwan Abdel Aziz Abdel Meguid. The first name honored my Egyptian grandfather. The second was my given name. The third reflected my father's name, followed by Abdel Meguid, the family name.

Was my mother disappointed that her son did not have at least one German name? Had she objected? Did she understand the implication that in giving me a series of Egyptian names my father expected his son to live, work, and thrive in his culture? In her voluminous correspondence to her German friends and family, she never spoke of this, even when she wrote about me.

7

THE INEXORABLE GERMAN PULL

Gretchen & Abdel Aziz

I loved her against reason, against promise, against peace, against hope, against happiness, against all discouragement that could be.
—Charles Dickens

E gyptian children call their mothers Mama. Mine wanted me to call her by the German Mutti, but she remained Mama for a long time. In letters to her parents reaching Germany via the Red Cross while the war was raging, Mama said that I was a "string bean," born at a mere five pounds, but 23 inches long. She bragged that I looked more German than Egyptian, describing me as a "*Kleiner* (miniature) Steinbach." I had fair skin with blue eyes, and a squarish head like her father, Wilhelm. She boasted, ". . . he sees everything, nothing escapes him, he hears everything, he smells everything; loves every animal . . . in short he loves life and the world."

Some years later, when I was sixteen, I met Sister Röske at Hamburg's Eppendorf University Hospital on one of my visits to my grandparents in Wedel. I was eager to share the news that perhaps I intended to apply to medical school. I wanted to see her, having heard much about her stay in Cairo, and her prediction of my becoming a surgeon. Curious, I asked her how she knew my mother.

She had met my mother in Cairo on their return from Sudan. They were both young German women who came from Hamburg and became fast friends. She was a nurse in the Red Cross and had been sent to Cairo to teach young Egyptian nurses. The war stranded her in Egypt.

During their many chats, Mother confided about being homesick, missing her friends, and dreaming of returning to Europe to complete her education. "It wasn't just a dream," Sister Röske told me. "You see, your father had promised her this before their marriage." She continued, saying that my mother supported his commitments to his work, but could not understand the endless investment of time and effort into his family. She did not understand that in an Arab society, loyalty to kin was part of the weave of the culture into which she had readily married. She described the family as being too dependent on him, unable to help themselves—by her German standards, useless! Sister Röske added, "She believed they stood in her way. Your father's endless sense of duty deferred her dream: first, by returning to Egypt, then living in Sudan, then the war, and the birth of your sister. Toward the end of the war, when the prospects of returning had increased, she found herself pregnant once more."

We sat in the cafeteria—I, an eager teenager, she projecting middle-age security and established authority in her nurse's uniform and Red Cross embossed cap. It was approaching lunchtime and patrons were filing in. Sister Röske leaned forward on her elbows and continued in a solemn tone. "Your father promised to return to England. Your mother was an impatient woman, irritated by these delays. She wanted to leave what she described as 'primitive Egypt' and return to what she believed was the civilized Europe she had left behind."

She paused, looked about, and seemed to choose her words carefully. "Your birth further derailed her plans, deepened the longing for her Vaterland, and impeded her unrelenting dream of a university degree." Lowering her voice almost to a whisper, she leaned even closer. "Your mother referred to her pregnancy as 'inconvenient,' and in a moment of anger even explored the idea of a backstreet abortion." Sister Röske sat back, as if shocked at her own disclosure. I too was shocked. The force of the message that I wasn't wanted was as strong as my immediate urge to vomit. I didn't, but the revelation explained my mother's constant distancing—no kisses, no hugs, or encouragements.

8

THE SCORPION'S STING

Marwan, age four, with Gulnar

Said the scorpion to the frog:
Give me a ride across the Nile—it's wide and swift.
Frog: No, you will sting and kill me.
Scorpion: If I did, I'd also drown. I can't swim.
Frog: Very well, hop onto my back.
Halfway across the Nile the scorpion stung him.
Paralyzed the frog began to sink.
Frog: Why?
Scorpion: I can't help myself. It is in my nature.

Egyptian Adaptation of Aesop's Fable

Named after the red Persian pomegranate flower, Gulnar was born in November 1941 under the astrological sign of Scorpio. She was exotically attractive, with smoky eyes, jet black hair, and a dark complexion, favoring Baba's genes rather than her mother's fairer Nordic ones. Like the scorpion, she was unpredictable.

She was Baba's special little girl. When she was little and no brother existed, he'd improvise songs for her—songs of praise, of her beauty and wondrousness. Mama would arrange Gulnar's braids into a crowning wreath, or hanging down with red ribbons, while telling her how beautiful she was. For three years she was the princess, the beauty, the sweetest infant girl in the family—the center of attention, garnering all the praise and compliments from Baba, grandparents, aunts and uncles—she had no rivals. Mama described her development from a baby into a young girl in almost every letter sent to her parents, throughout the war and into the post-war years, until Gulnar and her German grandparents finally met.

I don't know if my parents had prepared her for my arrival. Either way, the tectonic shift of attention from Gulnar to the highly prized male was hard for her. In an instant not of her making, she was suddenly displaced by a baby—a cute boy who, as my parents casually confessed, overshadowed her in value and primacy. She watched as parents, aunts, and uncles expressed appreciation, joy, praise, or gratitude for Abdel Aziz's son. But he was the intruder into her world. As the phrase *Al Hamdulil Allah* —a son, profound in Egyptian society—began to sink in, she understood that she, a female and subsequently a woman, was considered less valuable. Furthermore, this son held the potential of power over her destiny.

Her aunts encouraged her to foster a big-sister attitude of caring, deference, and unending praise for the boy. Instead, she developed a brother complex: extreme envy and jealousy, which grew to hatred, with the sting of a scorpion.

Gulnar must have found herself in a sudden state of disequilibrium as Baba raised her brother above her. Her Baba had betrayed her. She probably felt forsaken, deceived by her first love, the one she had called Dadadadah. He had held her hand as his precious princess until suddenly, and without warning, his demeanor changed to benign neglect. Baba had sung to her, called her "my special girl," held her, made a fuss over her, spoiled her—all in contrast to her impatient, irritable, compulsive mother who pushed to potty train her and who regimented her days.

Early photographs of her taken in the absence of a sibling portrayed a happy and radiant girl; subsequent photos in which her little nemesis was present clearly showed her unhappy demeanor as captured by the family Leica. The smile, the laughter she had shown the world became the sober glare of one who connives. Any joviality she may have displayed toward me was a façade for what became a very secretive personality—the scheming Gulnar I have known all my life. Then as now, I felt uneasy when her eyes fixed on me, for I was unable to guess what she was thinking. I became the vulnerable object of her devious gaze and developed a big-sister apprehension. To this day I carry the scars of revenge so deeply that I live with its heightened awareness and sensitivity.

Mama told me that due to the war, the cholera endemic, and the lack of pasteurized milk, she breastfed me. I would like to think now that enveloped in her arms, I experienced her warmth, her comfort, her lingering scent, the moistness of her nipple. Mama told me repeatedly that during such special interludes, the scorpion would stealthily creep up from behind like a cat on its prey. She would look up to see Gulnar cautiously approaching with a deceptively benign smile. Before Mama could gently sweep her aside, Gulnar would swiftly pinch me on my arms or on my bare thighs, making me cry out. The scorpion had successfully struck!

Gulnar would skip away as if nothing had happened.

Though each repetitive intrusion unfolded in a similar way, Mama did little to anticipate or prevent these attacks. My apprehension progressively grew on seeing Gulnar's approach. I would struggle and cry to forewarn Mama of my impending pain. She merely fussed with her breast, leaving me with a feeling of being let down by her.

Gulnar's resentment of me developed into a physical illness. Her unresolved anguish manifested itself psychosomatically in chronic urticaria, an allergic trigger of distressing skin rashes over her entire body. She had red, raised, itchy welts, which she scratched incessantly until they bled, preventing her from sleeping, but bringing Mama's attention. The outbreak lasted more than six weeks, until finally Baba took her, shortly before my second birthday, to the seaside in Alexandria. They returned a month later, her urticaria cured, her love for her father restored. Yet I was still there.

The little Devil—Afreet

During her absence, Mama sat me on a white enamel pot, leaving me alone in the tiled entrance hall to potty train, periodically checking to see if there was a result. She said I mimed the nursery rhymes not understanding their words, my legs propelling me forward about the foyer. The pot scooted with ease over the smooth floor from one end of the room to the other. How long this went on, is, of course my conjecture. It ended when I wore a hole through the pot's enamel base, coinciding with my use of the toilet and my sister's return.

Gulnar's assaults on me resumed with greater malice. This was not ordinary sibling rivalry; it was sibling annihilation. My next recollection is of sitting in a high chair trapped in place by a tray in front of me. I was a sitting duck. Mama was on the other side of the swinging kitchen door preparing my usual lunch— beans in tomato sauce, rice, and a little minced lamb. Gulnar approached me wielding a broom handle held at shoulder level like a bat, ready to swing it full force into my face. I squirmed in my seat, yelling, "Mama, Mama, Mama!" I threw my spoon with a primal shriek of distress. Gulnar ducked and the spoon missed. In the off-balance instant, Mama swung through the door and disarmed her.

Occasionally we agreed to play together. When Sister Edith Röske returned to Germany after the war, she sent us two sheets of paper dolls, a boy and a girl with separately printed clothing. Mama glued them on thin cardboard after cutting them out. Gulnar and I played "Mommy and Daddy." It was fun to dress and undress "Hansi" and "Ursula" and see their different body outlines. I always wanted the doll Gulnar had, and she would not let me have my way. Gulnar said that the daddy went to work to earn money. I would ride off around the flat on my scooter with Hansi, making engine noises and bargaining with pretend friends to bring money back to Gulnar. In the meantime, Gulnar and Ursula played with the children at our imaginary house. This worked quite well for a couple of days, until I protested. I wanted to be the mommy, to change Hansi and Ursula's clothes. Gulnar could be the daddy.

"You can't be," Gulnar would say, "you're a boy."

Not getting my way, I would furiously stomp my foot, forcefully pushing and shoving her to get what I wanted—I was the privileged son. The argument went back and forth until my parents intervened. Mama was impatient with me, siding with Gulnar and telling her under her voice to divert my attention. Baba, my best friend, was always there for me. He would solve our arguments patiently, impartially, until the play resumed.

When our maid came of a marriageable age, she returned to Beni Harem and the *omda* promptly sent us a new one—Bakhita. Mama was not pleased with Bakhita, telling Baba she was barely twelve years old—a mere child, more of a liability than an asset. Mama described her to a close friend in Germany:

> We spent one day delousing her of para-
> sites, and she seemed to feel much
> better in her own skin because she
> started to sing, not so much work.

Giddi reassured Mama that she would work out. It was Bakhita's first time away from the village. Like many Arabic words, her name had a double meaning depending on the context: "fortunate" in classical Arabic or "stupid" in the colloquial tongue. The condescending tone of Mama's voice when she called her had the latter inflection. I felt sorry for Bakhita to be so repeatedly humiliated. Having no experience, she was assigned the chores of scullery maid, and on rare occasion, babysitter. Bakhita, who had to take off her shoes by the door, was only a couple of heads taller than Gulnar, and was petite, shy, and soft-spoken. Her coconut-brown skin was highlighted by the white knee-length dress and framed by the white head-scarf Mama made her wear, in keeping with other servants of her European acquaintances.

Our play progressed from dolls to doctor, which we indulged in with curiosity in our parents' absence. Gulnar determined that I be the doctor, telling me to listen to Bakhita's heart with our toy stethoscope and ordering Bakhita to lie down on one of our long low tables, and to bare her chest. Gulnar directed me to use our toy iron to flatten Bakhita's young breast mounds. Fascinated, I ironed with enthusiasm and focused engagement, making car noises as I pushed the iron back and forth as Gulnar watched. She threw the bolt across the door of the entrance hall. I attempted to flatten Bakhita's erect nipples, excited by her closed eyes and trance-like state. The more I ran my flat iron over them, the more they swelled and the louder she whimpered.

Gulnar heard my parents returning, unlocked the door and vanished. Bakhita lay in a daze, her breasts exposed, her eyes closed to impending danger, as my parents walked through the front door. I stood there, flat iron in hand.

Mama scolded me severely. "You are a bad boy. A bad, bad boy. You shouldn't take her clothes off and be doing such things." Bakhita was shamed, told to get dressed and go into the kitchen. Baba merely glanced at me as he headed to his study. Did he disapprove, also?

My four-year-old self felt intense shame from the harsh reprimand, and I was confused as well. I had thought it was only a fun game; I did not understand its sexual implications. I didn't know it was bad. At that moment, I wanted hugs and kisses in all the ways a mother could give me that are right, good, and pure. I stood in shame while, from around the corner, Gulnar smirked.

FAMILY LIFE

At Cairo's botanical garden

Everything you say,
your child absorbs, catalogues,
and remembers.

Mama had a sewing room flooded by sunlight through its large side-facing window. Her portable Singer lived there, along with her Olivetti, which sat firmly on a table with a heavy blanket underneath it to dull the pounding clatter that reverberated through the tiled floor. She daily retreated to her sanctuary, shutting its opaque glass door. We would see her shadowy figure sitting by the machine as we played in the living room under the servant's casual watch. She would bang out one dispatch after another, some three hundred and fifty of them to her parents, holding herself apart from the "primitive life in Egypt," as her letters referred to it, dwelling in the ideal world of her remembered Germany.

I always wanted to go into her room simply to see what she was doing, and to be near her. Occasionally she left the door open, and the aroma of coffee floated out to me. Sneaking in one morning, I was curious about the black-lettered sheet rolled in the typewriter and wondered what it said. Pushing all the keys with my open palm, I was amazed at the oblique swinging arms until they stuck together in midair—alarming. Moving around the table, I touched the opaque airmail paper, the onionskin, and the carbon paper in their open boxes. Her carbon-copied missives were pinned to their replies, and occasionally to an envelope lying in a pile at the end of the table. She shooed me out impatiently the instant she returned, closing the door firmly behind me. That room wasn't a place for a youngster—as if I could read her fantasy world.

Baba had a study with a balcony facing the front of the house, where he wrote, received students, and burrowed into his academic work; he occasionally found time in his busy day to read Arabic stories to me. In keeping with the times, he left domestic issues to his wife. Baba usually left in the morning around nine or ten, always with a laden briefcase. He headed to the university or to meetings with his writing group at well-known literary cafés. They read and edited each other's manu-scripts, discussed literary ideas, and spun out plans for new book series, frugally nursing one Turkish coffee each while asking the waiter for many glasses of water throughout the morning. When I was sick, or Mama wanted peace and quiet, Gulnar accompa-nied Baba to his literary meetings. He never missed a chance to show her off to his friends. As Gulnar wrote years later, she found refuge under the coffee tables, surrounded and impressed by the freshly pressed, bright clothes of struggling young writers, among them Taha Hussein, Tewfik El Hakim, whose short stories were widely popular, and Naguib Mahfouz, who would go on to win a Nobel Prize in Literature.

When Baba returned from his office in the early afternoon, Mama offered him a hot meal and news from letters she had received, or the latest gossip. Preoccupied with his work, he made small talk, and in the heat of the afternoon he retired for his siesta in a bed that had been set in the corner of his study. We wanted to play with him, but he would close his study door, shutting us out.

Up on the roof

Gulnar and I played in the living room with our toys. Since I always wanted whatever she had, a wild chase through the house often followed, with her loud protestations and tears that finally forced Mama to leave her type-writer. In the afternoon the noise of our games or arguments frequently brought Baba out of his study where he was having his siestas, irritated at being disturbed. He would grab the presumed noisemaker, usually me, and clutching me under his arm, drag me into his bed, imploring me to nap while he drifted back to sleep. I carefully freed myself of his grasp and crawled toward the door giggling loudly, only to have him pounce on me and haul me back to bed. I played this game repeatedly until I eventually fell asleep in his clutches. When I awoke during the early evening, I'd see him writing at his desk lit by his single lamp.

As was his habit, he wrote late into the night, interrupted only by a light evening meal, numerous cups of black tea, or the ritual of putting us to bed. We rode one on each shoulder while he pretended to be a camel rocking from side to side, sighing loudly under our heavy load as he carried us through the large flat. We giggled, tumbling into our beds.

When it was Mama's turn, she sang to me the same German nursery rhyme, words I did not understand. No matter who tucked us in, I slept soundly. I was a trusting child.

The landlord kept his chickens on the flat-tiled roof of our house. After breakfast, Gulnar and I, accompanied by Bakhita, occasionally went up to the roof. I would chase the chickens, but never caught one, despite my determination. From there I could see the white ibises noisily nesting in the neighboring eucalyptus trees. When they ignored my hoots, I would throw a shoe at them and a few birds flew away. I did this often enough that during that part of my childhood I usually wore two different-colored shoes. It also taught me that I could influence the things around me.

In the Botanical Garden

Several mornings a week, Mama took us with Bakhita to the Cairo Zoo, where we met other children with German mothers. The women chatted, looking out for us while we ran from cage to cage. The pacing tigers fascinated me. I enjoyed being with the other children who were all about my age. We spoke in Arabic while playing. Unlike Gulnar, they posed no challenge to me.

My position in the family and the constant praise from my uncles and aunts gave me confidence, and I became the leader, devising mischievous games to outsmart the others.

Due to the ongoing Egyptian cholera endemic of September 1947 in the eastern Nile delta just north of Cairo, Mama did not trust Bakhita to buy our produce and went to the local market herself. After she brought them home the vegetables were soaked in the purple-colored water of potassium permanganate, considered the best cholera disinfectant at the time. Standing on a stool in front of the kitchen sink, I would sing and splash about in the soaking vegetables, fascinated by the color and its effects on the raw vegetables. I overheard Mama tell Baba we should not eat vegetables at Giddi's Friday lunches, and I heard Baba tell Mama that cholera had spread because farmers took their dead from the east to their western family burial plots under mounds of vegetables on their carts. As I stood each morning on the balcony and saw the donkey carts laden with carrots or sugar cane pass our house, I wondered if dead people lay underneath the mounds of produce.

Sometimes, Gulnar, Bakhita, and I visited the lush garden at Papaioannou Hospital. To get to the garden we had to walk through the morgue, a cold dim chamber with a sweet, acrid scent I would come to recognize years later, in medical school, when I dissected a corpse. I closed my eyes, holding tightly to Bakhita's hand. Dead people frightened me. In the garden, we played under the watchful eyes of either the Catholic sisters or Sister Röske. Occasionally other children joined us—Egyptian-German kids of our age. When I was the only boy, I'd be the leader, bossing them around. They accepted from a boy the ideas of what the play would be—as I improvised our games.

When it was time to go home, I grasp Bakhita's hand again, hurrying through the morgue, eyes tightly shut, holding my breath until we stood on the pavement, where I would gasp with relief. Almost three years older than me and less fearful, Gulnar led the way through the morgue in both directions. I secretly admired her courage, thinking that if I were like her, she would be my friend. No matter how hard I tried, she was always taller, stronger, and older than I was, but I never gave up trying to compete with her. I desperately wanted to be accepted, to be praised by her. Her refusal was a powerful weapon that she repeatedly used against me. This was hurtful since I wanted her to trust and recognize me, instead of ignoring me.

One day Bakhita stopped us on the curb, telling us to be silent. Others stood there too, hats in hand. In a whisper, she explained that a funeral cortege was passing. The horse-drawn vehicle held a coffin visible through its etched-glass sides. The hearse had four black corner posts with black-feathered plumes menacingly pointing into the sky. I looked away and started to whimper. Holding my hand, Bakhita insisted I look and told me I need not be frightened of the dead. Gulnar forced my head in the direction of the coffin. The hearse slowly inched past. A single old driver sat hunched at the front, holding the reins. The dark horse, all skin and bones, had a black plume on its head and wore blinders. I had nightmares about the black hearse that night. Bakhita may have been trying to cure me of my fear, but surely Gulnar, who insisted I keep my eyes open, was hoping to frighten me.

One night in May 1948, Baba took us onto our balcony and pointed eastward to show us the red glow of raging fires in the Mokattam hills far across the Nile valley. The munitions dump in the hills was ablaze. It was the beginning of the first Arab-Israeli war, as I eventually worked it out. By that time, Gulnar and I occasionally walked alone to Papaioannou Hospital's garden. On our way home once, she saw a plane overhead and took my hand and we scurried under a tree. "They won't see us here, or drop a bomb on us," she said. At that moment, I was glad that she was a good sister. She was six then, and I was four and too young to understand fully the connections between these two disparate events in the ongoing war. Gulnar would cry whenever the air raid sirens wailed, piercing our ears. Usually our male servant picked us both up and, with Mama leading the way, we joined the other tenants in a rush to the basement. We stayed there until we heard the all clear sirens.

Our lives continued, despite the war. Each summer from the mid-1940s onward, we, including our servant, joined University of Cairo's camp, which was on a stretch of remote coast along the shores of the Mediterranean, past the delta village of Balteem. We rode in the university bus some four to eight hours —190 km to 255 km depending on the route that was open in the absence of highways. The baggage included a fully supplied kitchen, one large canvas tent per family and our luggage. This was loaded on a lorry that preceded the bus. By the time we arrived the tents had been set up. We stayed the entire month of August to escape Cairo's oppressive heat and humidity. Every family had their own army tent cooled by the constant sea breeze. These huge tents were well-spaced along the remote beach, set side by side, and a judicious distance above the high tide mark.

University Camp in Balteem. Marwan age 3

Waves crashed onto the wide yellow sand beach and rushed toward us; a mixture of sea, foam, and crabs. A kitchen tent manned by university cooks was set at the far end of the row, beside a mess tent with a flagpole. The community of sixty—professors, their families, and students—would congregate each morning, observing the raising of the green Egyptian flag and exchanging newsworthy items. Some distance behind the family tents was a communal long-drop, a pit latrine, with a privacy screen of woven palm leaves. About 50 yards beyond that, sand dunes towered, off which rose the sea breeze, whistling a precise C major, into a cloudless blue sky. On the other side of the dunes were acres of vineyards and fig trees. There were no newspapers, radios, or electricity, only sun, sea, sand, and solitude. Mama spent most of her time congregating with the other German wives, rather than the Egyptian ones.

Baba, Gulnar and I spoke Arabic amongst ourselves. Mama persisted in socializing with foreign women and not Egyptian ones, including my loving aunts Amal, Souad, Fardous, Sanaa, and Mustakima, as if they were not good enough. By her conduct she indicated that they were not her equal. I felt embarrassed for her and minimized my time being with her and her foreign friends. Her superiority complex towards Egyptians and her attitude toward Bakhita and my relatives angered me. As a young boy I was unable to crystalize or verbalize my discomfort toward her behavior. No wonder the bits and pieces of gossip that I picked up from my aunts about Mama were not favorable.

On the sand dunes behind the camp

At night, families gathered about the campfire under the Milky Way and listened to the *hakawati*—the storyteller in the ancient Arab tradition of oral history—recite epic poems or spin a fable. The sole intrusion was the stealthy Nubian camel patrol passing at dusk and dawn, materializing from one horizon and disappearing along the empty seashore in the opposite direction, the smells of the camels stronger than the sea air.

Baba played with Gulnar and me, hauling wet sand in our Mickey Mouse buckets. When I was three, he first coaxed me into the cold Mediterranean. I clung onto him, screaming as we jumped into the air to ride over the rolling waves. Baba laughed with infectious joy. It was there that I first noticed his thin left leg. It had less hair, although he was quite a hairy man. He later told me that when he lived in Beni Harem, he became unaccountably sick with a high fever lasting several weeks. The illness weakened the muscles of his left leg, and he wondered if he had had polio. Baba would certainly not have checked "polio" on an occupational health form, fearing that the disclosure would affect his work status or his advancement. He considered admitting to any physical limitation a weakness.

Gulnar & I with Baba in the sea

In the hot summer of 1947, we were returning from our annual Balteem vacation. The faculty rode in a bus that rumbled through the numerous Nile Delta villages toward Cairo along a single-lane, black-ribbon road by irrigation canals, shaded by eucalyptus trees. Several lorry convoys carrying the tents and supplies followed. The fleet slowed when we passed a cluster of mud houses, where life spilled over onto the road.

In one village, when the peasants saw the foreign women sitting at the open windows, they ran along the bus and threw stones, smashing some windows. The women on the bus screamed and ducked and the bus veered to a stop. My father grabbed Gulnar and me from the front seat and pushed us into the middle of the bus. In their fury, peasants beat the chassis with sticks, yelling, "No Jews here."

The Egyptian university crew rushed from the lorries and shoved back the villagers, screaming that the passengers were Egyptian professors from Cairo University returning from Balteem. The mob refused to accept this and continued to attack the bus. When the village elders arrived, a semblance of calm descended. The helpers continued to push the crowd back, allowing the bus to move forward again. Still, peasants threw themselves onto the road ahead, determined to extract the foreign women.

My father stepped into the open bus door. He raised his hands in a gesture of peace, ducking the stones flying in his direction. He started to recite verses from the Qur'an, which quieted the throng grouped about

Baba relaxing. Note his left leg, which is smaller post-polio.

the bus. He cried, "*Allah ho Akbar*—God is great," and exclaimed, "Our wives are Egyptians—Muslims." He continued to recite verses of tolerance and peace, in the words of the prophet.

Frightened, I started to cry. Gulnar sat on an aisle seat next to Mama, whose face was ashen. Anxiously, Mama shushed me. My terror grew when Baba stepped off the bus into the crowd to meet the village elders, calming those who surrounded him. I was so afraid; were they going to take him away? Would he come back to us? Would they attack and kill him? Following an apparent understanding between the elders and Baba, the rabble reluctantly dispersed, Baba returned, and the bus resumed its journey. He sat in a middle row behind Mama and us, away from the windows. In silence, above the whine of the engine, the passengers contemplated the fate they had narrowly avoided. Proud of Baba's courage, I climbed onto his lap, surprised to discover his knees were shaking.

10

THE RELUCTANT EGYPTIAN

We do not see things the way they are,
We see things the way we are.
The Talmud

Every Friday, the Meguid clan congregated for lunch at my grandparents' flat, usually after communal prayer at the old Sayeda Zeinab Mosque. Before we left our flat in Dokki, Giza, I would hear my parents arguing behind Baba's closed study door. They spoke in a mixture of English and German, with a few sharp Arabic words occasionally emitted by Baba. Mama refused to come with us.

By age four I was most fluent in Arabic, and I understood some phrases in English and German. Their raised voices spiked my anxiety. Why were they having a row in such accusatory and bitter tones? Had I done something wrong? Gulnar would start crying and bang on their door, pleading with them to stop. I overheard Mama tell Baba that she did not like the noisy family gathering, their heavy, greasy food, their stinking toilets, their grey towels, and their lack of English, which was ironic since she made no effort to learn sufficient Arabic to converse with them. The arguments were a regular weekly staple: Baba wanting his wife to accompany him, she adamantly refusing. I always felt bad and wished she would come and be part of our family.

After we left, Mama retreated to her sewing room with a cup of Nescafé. A letter she wrote her parents described her unhappiness:

Cairo,
Dear Mutti und Vatie,

I can't grow any roots or feel a sense of belonging, despite husband and children. I basically feel that I'm stuck here by coincidence during my travels, and always wait for the day of my departure. Today is the most important Arabic festival: the Arabic Christmas. Meguid went very early in the morning with children and servant to his parents to celebrate. I thought this was a wonderful chance to be able to write to you without interruption. Even if I wanted to, I cannot manage to be in a

```
festive mood! Their celebrating consists
in eating too much, mostly anything with
meat. It is customary that families
slaughter a lamb and the entire clan
congregates. Gulnar and Marwan prefer
the in-laws to being with me! Once they
are there, they munch all day . . .
Nothing is not allowed, only toys as we
know them won't be found there and if I
tell Gulnar about dolls, picture books,
forests and fields, about rain and snow,
then she gets all lost in her thoughts
and thinks Germany would be the most
beautiful country, which I then confirm.
```

```
Gretchen
```

The family must have quietly resented her absence, signaling their response to her disdainful, superior attitude. She did not know why he had to visit his parents each Friday—*the one day*, she emphasized, that he was free to be at home with her and the children; the one day they could visit her friends as a couple. His family was a drain. They were too demanding, too dependent—a competitor for his attention.

I began to understand the gist of these arguments during my third and fourth years of life. Mama furiously scolded, "Did you not promise to return to Europe after fulfilling your professional commitment in Egypt? It is now time for my education."

After a brief silence, he would storm out of the room, slamming the door behind him. I was near tears and Gulnar watched in wordless bewilderment.

On Fridays we'd leave our flat around ten in the morning, heading on foot toward Cairo's eastern suburb. Gulnar, feeling older, refused Baba's hand and walked ahead. Not wanting to lose her among the sidewalk throngs, Baba tried to keep up with her, dragging me behind, with Bakhita forming the rear of the phalanx.

Baba gripped my wrist firmly, almost dragging me along, as if his anger were toward me. We walked east across *Kubri Inglisi* —English Bridge—that spanned the narrow western branch of the Nile. The affluent island of Zamalek accommodated the exclusive Gezira Sporting and Jockey Club in its upper two-thirds, with a marathon racehorse track and eighteen-hole golf course, the UN headquarters, most foreign embassies, and the upper-middle-class residential area. As we traversed the lower third of the island, Baba's mood gradually improved. His grip softened and moved from my wrist to my hand.

He had walked the same route on the day of my birth. We then crossed the southern tip of Zamalek, weaving our way through the noisy Friday crowds across *Kubri El Nil*—the Nile Bridge—guarded by two majestic bronze lions, which spanned the main, eastern branch of the Nile leading into Midan Tahrir. It was a long trek. Baba's grasp moved once more to my wrist as I began to grow weary and cranky, until we finally reached the central tram station. There we boarded an already crowded tram at the beginning of its route, sitting in first class. In her white tunic with headscarf, conspicuous to the surrounding crowds, Bakhita crammed into the rear, riding second class, the compartment where passengers overflowed the tram's open sides or avoided paying their fares by hanging onto the running board.

Gulnar always took the window seat. I sat on Baba's lap and looked out through the open window at the milling crowds, the honking cars, donkey carts laden with fresh vegetables, a herd of camels driven to market. I noted the smells of rotten garbage and the black clouds of exhaust from old cars; heard the strains of music and the Qur'an; along with the unending presence of buzzing flies: the hubbub of a vibrant city.

Watching life in the passing streets, I often reached up to Baba's face, the squarish head, high forehead, and prominent chin. I touched his well-shaved skin, smooth with few wrinkles, feeling the tension in his face and frown lines between his bushy eyebrows. Baba had full lips, and his smile revealed his dimples. Sitting on his knee, fingering his face, I perceived his earlobes were detached—free from his face, like mine—a recessive gene I would later learn. I liked to tweak the few coarse hairs that grew around his ear lobes—a way of getting his immediate attention. I knew he did not like it, though he would laugh and kiss the top of my head. It was a game we played. He had black curly hair parted on the left. I remember when Mama first parted mine, she softly said, almost to herself, "Just like your father." His nose was straight and his skin had the lingering fragrance of pearl soap—a bouquet of spring flowers.

As the eldest son, Baba was culturally obligated to care for his parents and to ensure his unmarried sisters were educated, with secure, well-paying jobs. To meet his aging parents' needs he had to acquire a family mausoleum in the City of the Dead, at that time on the distant outskirts of Cairo. Mama did not understand these responsibilities, which were the cause of her constant unhappiness in Egypt. She demanded Baba work over-seas, preferably in England, to quench her ceaseless yearning *"für meine Heimat."* The promise he had made her about returning to Europe hung over our family like a guillotine and was a recur-ring theme in their arguments.

Once we reached Sayeda Zeinab, Baba would muscle us off the crowded tram into the throngs that swept us along the dusty, littered streets, to the apartment block with my grandparents' small flat. When we entered, I was enveloped in my grandmoth-er's cloud of garlic from her breath and her sweat.

She hugged me effusively, smothering me with wet kisses on my cheeks, my forehead, my eyes, warding off the "evil eye," protecting me from envy. Engulfed in her bosom I smelled henna, caraway, and fresh coriander. *"Nawartuni"*—you light up my day—she said repeatedly as part of her ritual greeting phrases. She told me how handsome I was, how important I was, and what a great man I would become. She pinned gold amulets to my shirt to protect me. I loved hearing her *Sa'idi* dialectic phrases and wanted to believe every word she uttered. Aside from the occasional Arabic phrase, she spoke mainly in *Sa'idi*, blessing me, asking God to take care of me. When she sensed I did not understand, she repeated herself with a little laugh. I picked up whole sentences. I would pun with her words, getting her to smile in triumph and show her missing front teeth. My chest would swell with the attention and compliments I received, not bestowed on my sister. The sense of belonging was divine. In my grandparents' home I was the preeminent child, the first son of their eldest son.

My grandmother Sit Nazifa—meaning pure—with her older daughters, Tante Mustakima and Tante Souad, spent all morning cooking, making the dishes we loved. The small flat filled with a thousand aromas. The oiled tablecloth was barely visible underneath the products of their toil, among them my favorite, *fattaa*—a rice and toasted bread dish soaked in garlic-infused chicken broth. I was always hungry and squirmed with

Mustakima, Souad & Sit Nazifa

anticipation until the men returned from the mosque and we could eat.

Giddi presided over the clan, sitting with dignity at the head of the table, watching his brood in his thoughtful, kind way, barely able to get a word in edgewise in his soft voice. He wore his usual *galabeya* and white turban. I sat to his right, and Baba to the left of his father. Sheikh Amin was not an *imam*—a religious leader—although the family looked up to him, as he was prudent and knowledgeable about most things that affected his family. Baba, because of his university education, his title of professor, and his position as eldest son, also commanded great respect and authority.

My five uncles, their wives, and the unmarried aunts squeezed a plate on the edge of the crowded table. The dining room brimmed with noise—sometimes cheerful, sometimes acrimonious—with family discussions, promises, confessions of problems, multiple gratuitous solutions, rehashed misunderstandings and slights, and everyone trying to drown out the other in raised Arabic voices. They ate and gesticulated with hands full of food to make a point. Sit Nazifa, the proud matriarch, barely five feet tall, in her traditional black *abaya* and headscarf, assumed the mantle of cheerleader. She energetically circled the table behind our chairs, conversing in shouts, carrying on multiple conversations with her children, entreating us to eat, placing more food on our plates: "Sweet mangos brought by your aunt," she'd say or, "Have another banana from Uncle Azmi's tree." Gulnar, sitting between aunts, was happy with the spoiling attention from the womenfolk who doted on her. Baba was relaxed and content and the room overflowed with love and laughter. Phrases punctuated the air, emitted by people with full mouths eating with gusto across the food-laden table. Words like *Ma'alesh*—the compassionate, forgiving "never mind"; the reassuringly vague *Insha Allah*—God willing; and the comforting, encouraging *Shid de halak*—do your best. Despite this chaos in a family of eleven siblings, they were always respectful to my grandparents and deferential to Baba. I loved being at my grandparents' home. The environment was warm and caring, and there was an air of love and compassion. This was my family. No one missed Mama, including me.

When lunch was over, my uncles usually dispersed. Giddi went to his bedroom. He lay down, accompanied by Baba, to discuss serious family affairs, including the purchase of a mausoleum in the City of the Dead on the distant outskirts of Cairo, and a potential husband for Tante Souad—possibly Giddi's nephew, Mohammed, the *omda*'s son, fostering family solidarity. I joined them, sitting on his brown, coarse, camel hair bed cover. The women busied themselves clearing the table, working in the kitchen, and playing with Gulnar.

I was about four and a half when I saw Gulnar alone, deep in conversation with Sit Nazifa. Curious, I walked into the small parlor. Gulnar sat on the sofa, leaning against the cushions, her knees drawn up, exposing her white panties. Sit Nazifa put her hands on Gulnar's knees, spreading her thighs, and mimicked a cutting motion with her index finger. I saw the horror on Gulnar's face as she pulled away. Sit Nazifa tried to reassure her, saying it would not hurt, that it would be over quickly. Knowing it had to do with Gulnar's privates, I called out for Baba. He came quickly and collected our things to go home, my aunts consoling a crying Gulnar. In the chaos, Sit Nazifa seemed puzzled at the reaction.

On our return home, a distraught Gulnar related to Mama what had happened and Mama vented her fury at Baba. "That old, illiterate peasant will not interfere with my daughter. Gulnar will not go to the lunches anymore." The arguments continued, but Mama, the reluctant Egyptian, never again went to the family home for any reason. She made no effort to integrate into the clan, nor did she avail herself of its social advantages. Without her acceptance of the only family I knew, I lived with a growing sense of incompleteness and conflict.

11

OFF RAMP TO EUROPE

I loved my Vaterland dearly. Then I went to Sudan and Egypt.
After leaving these forsaken lands,
every particle of dust in Germany seems sacred to me.
—Gretchen, in a letter to her parents

My mother's yearning for "the most beautiful country" persisted. She wrote to her parents in late 1946 that her husband had bought land near the Pyramids with the intent of building a villa, a new house for them—a status symbol in accord with Baba's increased income and in keeping with Egyptian society. Yet Mother saw it as the laying down of roots in concrete, a sense of permanency similar to the nearby Pyramids, an anchor preventing her flight from Egypt. Mother wrote to her family, "I'm not interested in that at all. First of all, I want to come to you!"

It was not that she was isolated or did not have a social life. On the contrary; she regularly met with a gathering of European women and expats married to Egyptians. They came over every Thursday afternoon for an English tea, which she went to great lengths to prepare. She started in the morning by visiting Vasilakis, the Greek grocer. She bought imported Danish Lurpak butter, Dutch blue cheese, sliced Wonder bread, freshly ground Kenyan coffee, loose tea leaves from Ceylon, fresh milk, Nestlé's sweetened condensed milk, tomatoes, and small cucumbers, paying exorbitant prices, when around the corner on Hassan Sabery Street there was a local green grocer with fresh vegetables from the delta.

Back home, she mixed the blue cheese with butter to make finger sandwiches. Bakhita, relegated to scullery maid, washed the vegetables. Mama cut the edges off the white bread once she had finished making the sandwiches, wrapped them in moist cheesecloth, and refrigerated them. She baked a sliced apple or pear tart with fruit imported from Lebanon, topped off with frangipane. The baking smells made me salivate. Gulnar and I watched, forbidden to touch or taste her creations. Sometimes she went with Baba to the exclusive Café Groppi, near Tahrir Square, to buy elaborately decorated sweet gateaux. I always had my eyes on the chestnut cream meringues covered in confectioners' sugar, though there were seldom any leftovers.

The women arrived in the afternoon when the day's heat was abating. They spoke a mixture of German, English, and occasionally some colloquial Arabic. They compared affronts of their domestics, gossip, and complaints. The group ate the delicacies while drinking freshly ground black coffee. Auntie Jo was among the regular guests. She was English, born of Belgian refugees who fled to England during WWI. She married an Egyptian engineering student in London. Widowed two years after their arrival in Cairo, she survived by forming a close relationship with her brother-in-law; she integrated into her Egyptian family and learned Arabic for the sake of her two-year-old son. He accompanied her, and I was expected to play with him. She was one of Mama's close friends and a lifelong confidant.

While I played with Auntie Jo's son, who was one year younger, Mother periodically called me. Thinking I was going to get a sweet morsel, I was instead asked if I needed to pee. Mortified in front of her friends, I always said no. She would look into my eyes and say, "Oh! It's about to overflow. Quickly go and pee." I would rush off to the bathroom, at the same time knowing she was tricking me. I fell for the bluff each time, despite worrying what Auntie Jo's son was doing with my toys in my absence.

Sometimes the women overstayed their welcome, encroaching into Gulnar's and my evening mealtime. We would interrupt their *kaffeeklatsch*, trying to end the party. One day, when it came time to leave, Auntie Jo's son would not relinquish my only Dinky toy car. I objected. "It's *mine*. It's my *only* car, my only toy. I *want* it," I cried, tears welling up in my eyes as I stretched out my hands to retrieve it. He held it behind his back and started to rise from the floor where we had played.

"Oh, let him have it," Mama said dismissively, "He is father-less." Resentfully, I gave up my toy and Auntie Jo and her son left. I felt betrayed. Not only had Mama embarrassed me with her bluff, but she had also shamed me into relinquishing my cherished possession. I became aware of my first stirrings of distrust in her.

According to a letter sent that same month, Mama had discovered that her cousin, Arthur, was a German prisoner of war in Camp 2781, near the Great Bitter Lake along the Suez Canal.

She wrote to her mother that she remembered playing with him when she visited her maternal grandparents in Gröna, near Bernburg:

```
Knowing that Arthur is in the vicinity
has made me truly happy. I wrote to him.
I comforted him. I shared his feelings
of being homesick. Shared pain is half
the pain. I took steps to get in touch
with him. Maybe I can manage to send a
package for Christmas.
```

Gretchen, grandparents & Arthur

Years later, in her eighties, she reminisced in passing of her infatuation with a blond German escapee, a prisoner of war from the 1942 El Alamein battle, claiming she was in some way in contact with the German underground. Many Egyptians had the furtive hope that German victory at El Alamein and German occupation of Egypt would lead to Egyptian independence from the British. It puzzled me why Mother mentioned this German liaison to me. I was speechless; such actions were treasonous and endangered the entire family. One morning in 1942 or '43, after Daddy left for work, a blond German escapee had come to the flat. I wondered if my fair features were not an anomaly, but were instead somehow related to such a person. The timing of the visit did not seem to fit with my birth in 1944.

Had she forgotten her near arrest by the British authorities in Sudan, with their intent of placing her into an internment camp together with other sympathetic Europeans for suspicious behavior? Had Baba's intervention with the British authority escaped her memory? Her romantic yearning for her homeland seemed to negate the danger to us. My father would have been alarmed at such risky, sentimental activities, not to mention immensely saddened. He remained profoundly loyal to her. I wondered if Mother truly appreciated him or even loved him, or if she had only been infatuated with his exotic Upper Egyptian background, one she perceived might facilitate her escape from her solid, working-class German upbringing.

After her death, when Gulnar and I discussed Mother's life, Gulnar confirmed these liaisons in a matter-of-fact way, explaining, or perhaps defending them, saying she may have been homesick and suggested that Mother had had a number of affairs beyond marriage. Once more, in the back of my mind I wondered if I was truly Abdel Aziz's son.

With the war over, Baba must have discussed with her the opportunity of accepting an appointment to the Arabic Department at Manchester University, England. She was encouraged that her confinement in Egypt would soon end and his promise to her would finally be fulfilled. In a letter to her mother in May, 1946, she shared the elaborate machinations of her plans for her children once back in Europe. Her letters show no sign that she discussed these plans with my father.

Cairo, May 1946

The children would attend the school with you in Wedel or in Hamburg. When they're older, it would be a wonderful experience for the children, and I do not at all intend to come for just a short stay. The horrible isolation that we helplessly had to endure year after year will now come to an end. It would almost be challenging fate and prophecy if we now would postpone a get-together to a later point in time.

They need to learn German thoroughly and correctly, giving them a solid basis right from the beginning. In addition to my speaking German with them, Meguid speaks English to them. Meguid will have to teach them classical Arabic, although they speak the colloquial language. . .

Had she shared these plans with Baba? He clearly had different ideas about my education than those expressed by Mama to her parents in her last letter to them.

Starting in December 1948, he sent me to a private Arabic preschool three mornings a week; the son would follow his father's academic mastery of Arabic. Lessons were in my native tongue, including math, hygiene, drawing, religion, and music. My report card reflected the teacher's assessment of my efforts in these subjects, as well as my play with the other children. Most of my grades were "good," a few "excellent." Baba signed my monthly reports, always admonishing me to do better. Mother's education plans, as outlined in her letter, closely followed a lengthy Germanic education trajectory. Why would Baba have wanted to send me to an Arabic school if my limited time abroad would only be considered as an interruption of an Arabic educational route?

Family home in Giza 1947. First left door to Mother's
"Sewing Room" where her Olivetti was in constant use.
Second left door goes to Daddy's study.

My last report card arrived in May 1949. By then, Mother, who had been in Egypt for ten years, was ready to force the issue of going to Europe for her education. In June, three custom-made, wooden sea trunks appeared. They stood end to end along the wall of the entrance hall, each having individually fitted, cotton-filled seats with the fabric hanging over their sides, camouflaging their true purpose. Tea chests also appeared. Since Bakhita took me to school, Mama was freed up to pack, telling us, "We are going by ship to visit your grandparents, *Mutti Martha* und *Vatie Wilhelm*." I heard what she said, but I could not really grasp that I had another set of grandparents in another world, referencing it in the framework of my caring and warm Egyptian grandparents.

The house bustled with preparations for leaving the flat. The spacious living room, Mama's typing retreat, Baba's oasis, and our bedroom had to be whitewashed. Mama packed the steamer trunks, and Baba's books disappeared into the tea chests. He had obtained a teaching appointment in England, at Manchester University and was preoccupied making final preparations.

After the painting was completed, Mama retreated behind her glass door, Baba into his writing refuge. Gulnar pushed me on the scooter around the room. I held a crayon against the newly painted walls, making a straight blue line with my outstretched arm along all four sides. We laughed with delight at the decoration. Seeing Mama's image grow as she approached her frosted glass door, Gulnar disappeared. Mama walked in, gasped, and clouted me. The walls were repainted.

Shortly before our departure I accompanied Baba to his publisher, *Dar El Maaref*—the House of Knowledge. During a tour, I saw the presses, cutting machines, and stacks of unbound books. "These are your father's," I was told by a voice bursting with admiration. When Baba and his publisher disappeared, I sat in a conference room with paper and crayons. Sometime later, when the publisher reappeared, he asked me what I had drawn. My answer elicited a smile. "I started to write a story."

———

One night in the late summer of 1949, we boarded the train at Cairo's rail station. From a lorry, porters unloaded more than a dozen heavy chests, trunks, and suitcases and deposited them awkwardly on the platform, where passengers climbed over them to rush to their carriages. During the chaos, my father helped my uncles supervise the collection and corralled the porters to ensure that a precious trunk did not disappear in the confusion —a common occurrence. We settled into our compartment, waving goodbye to our uncles as the train eased out of the station.

The promise that we were going together as a family on an adventure conjured up an unknown mirage, which like a balloon was half full of optimism, half full of excitement and goodness, yet mixed with uncertainty and apprehension. I wanted to believe what lay ahead was wholesome. What was I to anticipate otherwise? Leaving the only known routine, the young tendrils of our connection to life in Cairo, my grandparents, the aunts and uncles with whom I was forming relations, the negotiations of life's connection to my surroundings—where I stood relative to my growing world—weighed momentarily on my mind as the train pulled out of the station. What lay ahead was unknown.

After a couple of hours, in the late afternoon, we pulled up to the docks in Port Said. Baba successfully persuaded the customs officials who were inspecting the heap of piled baggage not to open each trunk, instead to merely sign their clearance to avoid a delay as mother hustled us into the waiting launch, the sun setting in our eyes facing west. In the station platform maelstrom, I was surprised to spy Tante Mustakima, Tante Souad, and Tante Sanaa waiting quayside with bouquets of flowers and a box of Belgian chocolates. I loved seeing them again for they always fussed over me. This time they brought a big bouquet of flowers for Mother and chocolates for me and Gulnar. We said our farewells and cleared customs, with Mother complaining about carrying the extra gift parcels. I wanted the chocolates. I loved chocolates. Mama told me I could not have them because they were stale. "Imagine, burdening us with these items—flowers and a box of chocolates when we're traveling," she complained as she unceremoniously chucked them into the Suez Canal in the dark of the early night. I was indignant at the dismissive treatment of *my family*. She always treated my aunts and uncles with disrespect and arrogance. I hated her for these reasons but at age four I was unable to verbalize my inner anger.

Our motorized launch chugged out into the dark waters of the Suez Canal. The lights of Port Said and their reflection diminished as the vague hull of a British transport loomed into view. The launch came alongside and sailors helped us onto a bobbing platform in the semi-darkness. We were ushered up a steep wooden gangplank onto the deck of the barely moving ship.

Baba and I stayed at the rail. With his arms around me I sensed his sadness as we watched the lights of Port Said become distant and fainter, while the cool sea breeze passed over our faces and I tasted the salt of the sea. He didn't talk to me. The tenseness of his embracing arms gradually relaxed with the dimming coastal lights.

Once the vessel got underway, we had limited access to the decks because the ship was filled with demobilized British soldiers from India and Iran. The troop transporter steamed through the Mediterranean, crossing the rough Biscay toward England—peace in Europe assured. Gulnar shared Baba's upper bunk, while I lay with Mama in the lower one, comforted by her body's warmth and yet confused, anxious, sucking my forearm to soothe my fears.

Had we left our loving Egyptian family because of Sit Nazifa? All I knew for certain was that uncertainty lay ahead. It unsettled me. I could not imagine what Mother had in mind. Perhaps Gulnar understood, and in her usual way did not share what she knew with me. I drifted off to sleep, in rhythm with the boat's gentle yawing, as we were carried away from warm, comfortable Egypt to an unknown Germany.

PART II

1949-1956

Some say abandonment is a wound that never heals. I say only an abandoned child never forgets.
—Mario Barotelli

We always deceive ourselves twice about the people we love—
First to their advantage, then to their disadvantage.
—Albert Camus

12

A STRANGER CALLED MUTTI

1949

Abdel Aziz graduation & young Mother

When we are no longer able to change a situation—
we are challenged to change ourselves.
—Viktor Frankl

L ife seemed to take place in the dark. We boarded the ship in Port Said at night, with a whiff of oil as slicks floated by, disembarking ten days later in Liverpool in the late evening gloom, engulfed in a blanket of ocean fog with pillows of sooty industrial smog that I could taste. Gulnar and I wore heavy overcoats with scarves, all new to us. The train was already quayside. Intermittent cones of station lights barely pierced the swirling murkiness, setting the ghostly coaches a-shimmer.

Mama hoisted me into an English train and guided me along its corridor to an empty compartment, which we entered and occupied. She sat by the window, her back to the hissing steam engine, and I lay with my head in her lap, stretched out along the seat. Baba and Gulnar occupied the seat opposite—he by the window and Gulnar stretched out in the seat. Our family reflection, mirrored in the window, disappeared when Baba dimmed the compartment lights.

Along the length of the train doors slammed, disembodied voices reverberated, a whistle blew, and the train began to jerk, nudging out of the station. I fell asleep, lulled by the accelerating clickety-clack of the wheels and the swaying car, waking hours later, disoriented and cold as we pulled into a poorly lit station. Baba rose to open the compartment's small ventilation window, searching in vain for the station name.

"It looks like Cadbury again," he told Mama, referring to the prominent chocolate adverts. Station signs had been removed during the war to confuse any German troops who might have landed. Where they had been replaced, they were in small lettering and swamped by the surrounding billboards.

We reached Manchester in the middle of the night. Baba took his bags, kissed us good-bye, and left us without an explanation. Or was I too disoriented and drowsy to take in what he said?

We sleepily changed platforms and stations, eventually boarding a packed Harwich-bound train. Every seat in our compartment was occupied. Strangers sat in silence as we dozed in our seats. My apprehension grew. Why were we going to Germany without Baba? Was he following us or even coming back?

In the overcast dawn of Harwich harbor, we boarded another troop carrier laden with tanks. I was excited seeing the guns. We were the only civilian passengers, and we were banned from the open deck and confined to our cabins. Two days later, we arrived at our destination.

My first glimpse of Hamburg stunned me. Frightened and shocked, I took in a panorama of total, incomprehensible devastation. It was a wasteland of bombed-out buildings, vast areas of debris, empty lots, sunken ships, and cheerless people on the wharf. Everything was dull and grey, bleak under the feeble, intermittent sunlight. I held Mama's hand tightly as we disembarked. What was this place of destruction?

A squat, elderly couple in dark clothes, the only people meeting the ship, moved hesitantly toward us. They received Mama coolly, calling her Mutti, but she greeted these strangers with enthusiasm. I picked up a few German words, such as "*Guten Tag.*" They bore no presents or flowers and spoke no Arabic.

"Where is my little brother?"

"Working, of course," came the reply.

"Working?" Mother repeated, perplexed.

They embraced guardedly, despite not having seen each other for years. She faced two weary, aged parents, whose souls had been drained by deprivation, terror, and near-starvation—the second major conflagration of their lifetime. The war had decimated Hamburg and changed her parents, irrevocably. My mother never spoke to me of her impressions when she arrived that day in Hamburg. Setting foot on German soil that dreary morning, she must have immediately understood that her memory lived in a country left in the past. Time, in her mind, had fossilized in pre-war 1938. She still considered herself Martha and Wilhelm's daughter, not Abdel Aziz's wife, or the mother of two demanding and bewildered youngsters. In a 1940 letter typed to her mother, Mama had written:

```
Many times, I travel to you in my
thoughts, I see myself in my imagination
running up the stairwell, all of a
sudden stopping at the door to take in
for a second the familiar smell that
defines our home. Then as a habit, I
would take a short walk through all the
rooms just to make sure that everything
is still the way it's always been. . .
```

Mama told us these were our new grandparents, Opa and Oma, with whom we would stay. This was very confusing. I already had grandparents who we left in sunny Cairo, and did not understand who these people were. We were bundled into a black taxi, sitting between Mama and the elderly woman called Oma, whose occasional chatter passed over my head in a warm German tone as the trip progressed. Opa sat silently next to the driver. We drove along the ruins, following a road along the Elbe toward Wedel, occasionally catching a glimpse of a ship's super-structure as the boats were sailing out of the harbor on the river toward the North Sea. As we traveled, the clouds thinned, letting through patchy rays of sunlight.

By late morning, we reached Oma and Opa's Hamburger Electric Company housing on Galgenberg Street, surrounded by agricultural fields, on the periphery of Wedel, Holstein. They lived in a two-story brick house with two flats on each floor. Our footsteps echoed as we climbed the central wooden staircase to the second floor. I heard a barking dog.

While Oma opened the door, the neighbors on the opposite landing came out to greet Mama. Once inside, we met Onkel Gerhard, her younger brother, who had come home for lunch. He was in his late twenties, and unlike my Egyptian uncles, he did not embrace us but greeted us with a grunt and cool nod. Gerhard was seventeen in 1938 and had seen service on a U-boat naval tender in the Mediterranean theater. Near the end of the war, he spent time as a prisoner in southern France; maybe it helped account for his gruff demeanor.

Oma put on a generous apron smelling of fried onions and cabbage, and busied herself in the kitchen. Opa expected lunch punctually at noon. I was hungry and, seeing a bowl of green apples in the middle of the parlor table, climbed up onto a chair with my shoes on. Onkel Gerhard immediately pointed to my shoes and the clock. Although I did not understand what he bawled, the harsh tone of his voice said it all. The dog that sniffed at me was frightening, and I would not climb down from the chair until Onkel Gerhard called him away. I picked out from the garble of his command that the dog's name was Bobby.

During lunch, eaten hastily and with purpose, the adults barely spoke. Mama tried to ask many questions, each of which elicited a curt reply from Oma or a grunt from Opa, discouraging further inquiries. Once we had eaten, Onkel Gerhard went back to work and Oma washed up, with Opa and Mama drying the dishes.

When they finished, we toured the flat—our new home. I saw a front bedroom facing the street with a view across fallow fields to the Elbe. In the distance rose the *Hamburger Elektrisitäte Werke,* the HEW, where Opa had toiled shoveling coal into boilers to generate steam for the turbines until he retired to vacate a place for a returning soldier. In the front bedroom there were three separate beds. Next to our room was the carpeted front living room, or parlor. It had a sofa, table, an armchair, a reading lamp, and Opa's side table on which stood a big pre-war radio. Hanging above the sofa was a framed oil painting of a fishing trawler in heavy weather, reminding Opa of his younger days at sea, when he shared ownership of a boat with his three brothers, Hermann, Friedrich, and Gustav. Friedrich had died in an accident at sea in 1929, while they were all together. After that, they sold their ship.

Hermann lived in an adjoining complex of company flats a mere 100 meters away. Opa never socialized with him or his family, nor acknowledged them, while we frequently visited with Tante Else, Gustav's widow. Two of Hermann's sons, Mama's cousins, had emigrated to the United States during the Depression, married, and found work as miners in Pennsylvania. I never knew them, or whether they had helped Oma and Opa during the war before the United States of America entered it. In Egypt, we had interacted with all our family members, so this new dynamic was strange to me.

On the wall opposite the couch was a photo of Baba taken at his London University graduation a decade earlier. It hung next to one of Mama taken during her last visit in 1938. Dominating the front room was a grandfather clock that chimed every 15 minutes and seemed to set the pace of my new grandparents' retired life. The parlor led into a linoleum-lined hallway, off which was a bedroom facing the woods at the back, where my grandparents slept in side-by-side twin beds. Next to their room was the toilet with an old-fashioned water heater over a free-standing bathtub. Facing the front door on the left was a large white-tiled kitchen with a cast-iron coal-burning stove, a larder, and a kitchen table next to a china closet. All the rooms had large windows, almost the length of the outside wall. Radiators beneath each windowsill were heated by a coal oven in the corridor. Since coal was rationed, only the parlor was heated during the winter, and the heat of the wood-burning stove warmed the kitchen. A closed door contained each room.

I could not grasp why we were with these strangers in this strange land. How long would we be here? That night I did not want to sleep alone in a big bed, I wanted to share Mama's. Neither Opa nor Oma, who joined putting us to bed, approved, so to avoid further tension with her parents, Mama acquiesced. I continued to fuss and was repeatedly shamed and intimidated by Opa raising his voice and threatening me to stay in my own bed. Forced to do so, I sucked my forearm for comfort, crying and wondering when we would go home.

They insisted on calling Mama by this other name—Mutti.

Once they addressed her as Mutti she transformed into a different person, and in the following days, she seemed to change. The word Mutti lacked the warmth, the familiar scent, and the closeness or the familiarity of Mama. Instead, she was very distant. A few minutes after breakfast each day, this Mutti person made in German what sounded like arrangements with her mother, which I could not follow, and then she departed to catch a train to Hamburg, leaving us behind. She never kissed or hugged us goodbye or told us when we would see her next. She barely spoke to her father, whose presence at the kitchen table was difficult to ignore; he occupied one whole side, while we sat around the other three.

I would cry out on hearing her footfalls down the wooden stairs, and Opa would bark, "Stop making that noise." Gulnar would slink away to the front parlor, watching our mother walk away down the road.

The day was lonely without her. We had nothing to do without cousins, playmates, toys, or books. We could not speak Oma and Opa's language nor understand what they said to us, and they barely spoke to each other. They went about their routine without structuring ours. I languished in a constant state of anxiety and apprehension, sitting in the living room waiting for Mama, uncertain what behavior or action would elicit a reprimand. Time passed slowly.

Soon after we arrived, I needed a haircut. Opa said he would take care of it. He arranged an armchair in the front bedroom and laid a board across the arms for me to sit on. He said little by way of explanation, and tied a barber's bib around my neck. I kept turning my head to see what he was doing. My last few haircuts in Egypt were scary, but Baba was always by my side. Opa opened a small wooden chest containing an impressive array of scissors, clippers, and one comb. I started to whimper and he harshly chastised me; the only word I could pick out was "baby." I began to writhe and Opa barked—this was more torture than haircut. He pushed my head about with his left hand, wielding scissors or huge dull clippers that pulled more hair out than he trimmed. Finally, with bits of hair sticking to my tear-wet cheeks, he lifted me off the board and pushed me away.

Occasionally Oma took us through a cool, damp, dark cellar and then along a path at the back of the house to her garden, separated from Galgenberg Street by a high beech tree hedge. She unlocked the garden gate and re-locked it behind us, telling us to stay on the paths and not to tread on the flower and vegetable beds, which led to a hen house. I was too leery to enter the chicken wire enclosure but Gulnar did, and soon came out smiling with a couple of warm eggs.

It was autumn. It grew dark early and the world around me became a series of variations on grey—grey skies, grey grass, and barren trees with black branches on a dreary backdrop. By supper, precisely at six, it was pitch black, and Mama had not returned. There was minimal conversation during the evening meal consisting of bread, herring, cold cuts, sausage—foods I was unaccustomed to and disliked. We ate the cold meal off a wooden board, as there were no plates in the evening. I would furtively try to give my food to Bobby under the table. Opa would yell at me, ordering the dog to his corner crate. When I wanted to drink a glass of water with my meal, as I had done in Egypt, Opa took the glass away, saying that water was bad for the digestion and would dilute the stomach juices.

I wanted to stay up waiting for Mama, but preparations were made to put us to bed. I refused. Opa raised his voice, harshly insisting that children had to be asleep by eight. He bullied us into lying down. I lay struggling to remain awake in the dark until Mama came, hearing the tick of the clock—sounding slower than usual—and the agonizing chimes as the night progressed.

I was fearful that something terrible must have befallen her, preventing her from ever coming back to me. I worried that I might have been a bad boy in some way I had not understood, and her absence must be my punishment. In my sorrow and fear, I promised myself to be better, without a specific aim. I dared not get up or Oma and Opa, sitting in the parlor listening to the radio, would yell at me. With every slamming front door in the stairwell, with every footstep climbing the wooden stairs, my heart filled with joyful anticipation—she was coming back to me! But then the front doorbell would not ring, Bobby would not stir, and the steps would enter another flat. The anguish of abandonment filled me with panic. When the clock struck nine, the parlor light seeping under the bedroom door ceased, leaving me in total darkness.

Finally, Bobby's faint barking announced Mama's late arrival. When I heard the front door open, my anguish evaporated. She would sit in the kitchen with her mother, chatting in murmurs, further delaying her return to me. In the dark I waited, and waited, and waited. When she finally entered our bedroom, I wanted her to kiss me, stroke my hair, and tell me she loved me —that I was a good boy. Instead, she quietly undressed and went to bed with a sigh. The occasional times I gathered the courage to call out to her, she would snap, "Go to sleep." Cocooned in my feather eiderdown, I heard no warmth in her new Mutti voice. What did she do all day in Hamburg? She never came back with shopping bags. Many years later when we were adults recalling those fearful, painful times, Gulnar confessed that she had feigned sleep but was also waiting. She had shed quite a few secret tears of hurt, too, hoping to be tucked in and kissed goodnight by Mother, as she used to be in Cairo. I never learned what she did in Hamburg, one of the unanswered mysteries of her life.

A couple of weekends after our arrival, we went in the evening to the local autumn fair. Onkel Gerhard and his fiancée, Tante Irma, tagged along with Mama, Gulnar and me. During the day there were cattle and pig shows, and contests for who had grown the largest cucumber or tomato or squash. Oma went during the day to the flower show and on her return praised the bouquet of colors.

That night the light of the fair set aglow the low, heavy clouds. We walked about amidst buoyant multitudes, organ music, flashing colored bulbs, delicious-smelling sausages, and cotton candy stands. The air vibrated with the noise, the whirls of carnival rides, and the screams of fear mixed with hoots of laughter of the riders in the jovial atmosphere.

Surrounded by these sights and sounds, I was excited, as I had not been since we got to Wedel. I looked forward to riding a carousel or even the Ferris wheel, to throwing coconuts at a stack of milk bottles to win a prize—perhaps the giant stuffed teddy bear that seemed to smile at me, beckoning. Maybe I would get some colored candy floss. When I badgered Onkel Gerhard or Mama for something—a ride, or food—they made excuses for why I could not have it, or that it was not worth the cost. Why had we come if I could not have a treat or a ride? Did I not deserve to have fun like other children? Was I bad? I knew my Baba or my Egyptian uncles would have let me have fun. As we walked through the merry, laughing throngs, I grew more dismayed.

We passed a tower where men were goaded to test their strength. Tante Irma teasingly challenged Onkel Gerhard, saying that he could not do it, that he was too weak, too old. In a great flurry, Onkel Gerhard stepped forward. I watched as money changed hands, money that somehow could not be used to amuse Gulnar or me. He swung the heavy mallet, hitting the pad, and launched a small puck up a track in a tower. He swung with such strength that I expected to hear the bell ring at the top, but his puck rose feebly, barely a short distance, to the taunting jeers of his fiancée. He looked sheepish; his face reddened as he pushed her around without saying much. I watched the spectacle in annoyance. I did not like my uncle. He ignored me and did not think I was special like my Egyptian uncles did.

I shared this incident with my father a few years later, when I was about ten years old. He told me that when they first met, Onkel Gerhard was struggling with his high school math homework. Mama asked Baba to help Gerhard, maybe hoping to seal a friendship between them.

"What would you primitive Egyptians know about math?" Gerhard had retorted to my father's offer.

"You have a point, Gerhard," my father asserted softly. "We only built the Pyramids, invented algebra and devised the zero." With that, Gerhard agreed to Baba's help. When he told me this I had to laugh.

As we resumed our amble through the crowds at the fair, Onkel Gerhard took my hand. The spooky noises from the various venues and the swirling music fascinated me. I pulled away from him to stop and stare at the House of Horrors. Hordes of youngsters climbed into cars that entered at one end of a darkened tunnel. They came out the other end, yelling, screaming, and saying things I could not make out. I wanted to be part of that excitement. Suddenly I realized I was alone, standing by myself in the dark. People were rushing by me. Where was Mama? Where were the others? I ran in all directions, between people, amid legs, through small groups, yelling, "Mama, Mama," trying to be heard above the crowds. People approached me, asking me questions I could not hear over the noise, and did not understand. A woman took my hand and walked me around in circles. The whole episode may only have lasted a few minutes, but to this day when I think of it, it seems endless. Suddenly my Onkel turned around and saw me. He grasped my hand, laughing as he passed me over to the comfort of Mama, and we left the fair. I was glad, yet disappointed. We had not gone on a ride, or seen the Holstein cows, nor had we eaten cotton candy. I recognized that my German family had a mindset of frugality and lacked the ability to enjoy a special occasion. I was too young to understand that the war had impoverished them spiritually. In Egypt, Giddi had always taught us, "Give without remembering, take without forgetting."

———

Snow fell late one winter morning. Bundled up, Gulnar and I went outside to enjoy this miracle for the first time. Fluffy snow was already up to my ankles as I ran about trying to grasp the flakes or catch them on my tongue. I wondered what the flakes tasted like. The wind started to pick up and it grew bitterly cold. I was having a wonderful time, even with my feet growing increasingly numb and wet. By the time Oma called us to come indoors, my lips were blue and my fingers and toes frozen. I shivered in front of Oma's kitchen stove. She stuffed our wet shoes with newspaper to dry them as we pried off our soaking socks. Suddenly, I got a tremendous right earache. I cried with pain, unable to explain what I was experiencing through my tears, merely cupping the side of my head until Mama came home some minutes later. They called Herr Dr. Soeltner, our family physician, who advised them to drop warm oil into my right ear and put me to bed. I promptly fell asleep feeling soothed and cared for. When I awoke, it was growing dark and my earache was gone.

———

Gulnar was required to go to school, which left me alone with Opa and Oma during the day. Soon after Gulnar started school, Mama announced that she was leaving to join my father in Manchester. Everyone else seemed to know she would go alone, but I did not understand and she did not explain why we were not going with her. Perhaps this attitude towards children was what was done in those days.

She left early one morning when it was still dark. The taxi's headlights reflected off our bedroom blinds as it stopped outside the house. I could hear her talking softly to Oma in the next room where she had packed her suitcases, thinking they were out of our sight. Opa remained in bed. I was certain Mama would come to us before she left. I wanted to feel her and smell her face once more. Instead, I heard her footsteps going down the wooden staircase to the waiting lights. There was a pause. Then car's headlights on the blinds faded away. She was gone. I was alone.

13

THE GERMAN STRIPES

Wilhelm Steinbach (Opa) & Martha Henning (Oma)

I wish I could tell you how lonely I am.
How cold and harsh it is here.
Everywhere there is conflict and unkindness.
I think God has forsaken this place.
—Sandy Welch

After Mama left, things changed. Our lives became more rigidly regimented and disciplined. Accustomed to our lush Egyptian culture, here we lived in an emotional desert: no hugs, no kisses, no treats, no touching, no toys, and no books. Following Mama's sudden departure, I cried bitterly for hours, feeling helpless, utterly rejected, unloved. Opa threatened me with corporal punishment if I did not "stop this nonsense." Weeks turned into months of anguish. An autumn of longing became a cold, desolate winter. In the first year of Mama's absence, homesickness and worry were my permanent state. If there was any word from either Mama or Baba it was not transmitted to us. Not one letter. It was my hope I would wake up one morning, the whole scenario having reversed itself, and I would be back among my Egyptian family.

Gulnar reacted to Mama's leaving by becoming even more solemn. At age seven, she started to wet her bed. She cried out when Oma slapped her. I can see her tears and pained face as she begged in Arabic, protesting the beating. Despite the punishment she received in the morning, the problem continued at night. Opa threatened her with having to walk to school with the wet bed sheets hung around her.

One day in late autumn, we sat on the linoleum floor under the kitchen table, hidden by the oilcloth. Gulnar whispered in Arabic, "I'm going to run away. I hate this place. These people do not care for us. Their food is terrible and they always punish us. I want to find our father and mother. Will you come with me?"

As she spoke, looking at me with her solemn face, her words roused in me a deep anxiety and agitation. Would Opa beat us if he discovered us under the table plotting in Arabic? The sound of the language was very comforting; it reminded me that we belonged together, and that we were captives of these German strangers. I doubted they were really our grandparents. At the same time, each word that came tumbling out of her mouth—

run away, hate, terrible, punish, father, mother—increased my pain and confusion. My throat tightened. "Where will we go? How will we live?"

She pointed in a direction. "I stole a five Mark coin from Oma's purse so we can buy food," she whispered, searching my eyes, seeking approval of her daring.

"Stealing is wicked." I was alarmed. "They will beat us." I also wanted to run away to find our parents, but I hesitated as thoughts swirled through my mind. The weather was getting colder, and we did not know where Manchester was. Might we end up just wandering lost out there? Just like the abandoned Hansel and Gretel? I had a brief flash of kind people finding us before we found our parents. We would be handed over to Opa, who would punish us terribly.

The idea of running away to find Baba and Mama—people who loved and cared for us—was clouded by my deep sense that I could not fully trust Gulnar. She had stung me, betrayed me, too many times in the past. I imagined having to continue stealing food from shops or at farmer's markets. Gulnar would give me the food and walk away, leaving me to be caught and she would then disavow me. "No, I will not do this," I said slowly, uneasily. She had already stolen money and I knew we would be disciplined for that.

"*Gibaan*," she hissed in Arabic in my face. "You are a coward," she repeated in Arabic, and crawled from under the tablecloth.

While she did not run away, she continued to steal money and jewelry from my grandmother. She gave it to her school friends or simply threw it away. She hated our grandparents. Oma asked me if I had taken any money from her purse. I denied it, not letting on that it was my sister, trying to protect her from a certain beating.

Gulnar was right. We were left with people who never cuddled, who never kissed, who spoke a harsh language, who ate horrible food. Where were the bananas, oranges, mangoes, watermelons, guava, and grapes we were used to? How were we to adjust to Germany's post-war diet of cabbage and turnips with pork belly? They boiled everything. We had to eat boiled potatoes, when we wanted only rice. Boiled cabbage stank up the small flat. We ate tasteless boiled whitefish with pears and canned beans, when we were used to lightly sautéed vegetables, onions, olives, Feta cheese, and Moses fish grilled with garlic and lime.

The main meal was at midday. Food was rationed, and we were forced to sit at the table until we finished everything on our plates. I did not understand my grandparents' repeated mantra of "we had no food in the war so you must eat this; that's all there is." Opa reinforced this point by leaning a carpet beater against the kitchen cupboard and threatening to beat us. I would eat a few mouthfuls only to heave it up, and then have to swallow it again with a slap from Oma. In the guise of dessert, they fed us apples, which I did not like. Apples, apples, apples, no other fruit, only hard green apples.

I learned to conform to the autocratic expectations of Opa, always issued with the threat of the carpet beater in the corner. The efforts to domesticate us drove Oma to weep silently during our difficult and confrontational meals. I would find her huddled in a darkened kitchen after supper, crying softly to herself while Opa sat in the parlor stinking up the room with his pipe or cigar. She must have felt a keen sense of failure in a situation where she was doing her very best to raise two challenging, traumatized youngsters.

During the day Opa sat in silence at the window all day, taking measure of the neighbors, smoking his pipe or his cigar, speaking rarely, watching the ships move up and down the Elbe in the distance, and occasionally listening to the 1 p.m. news. His day was punctuated by rigidly observed meal times. Opa always demanded and was served his meals punctually: breakfast at 8 a.m., except Sundays when it was at 9 a.m., lunch at noon, coffee at 4 p.m., and supper at 6 p.m. My poor grandmother was a slave to my grandfather's regimented, rigid life.

As a child, I failed to grasp their financial condition. Did they have little money? Were my parents' sending funds from England? They had survived the war, losing neither property nor their son; were they poor or just fearfully frugal?

Some mornings, Oma rode her bicycle to the bakery for fresh rolls. If she was five minutes late in returning, Opa grumbled. In the evening he undressed and laid out his clothes for the following day in the rigid order he put them on. When I asked him about this ritual, he explained that during his times at sea—in the Navy—it allowed him to rapidly dress in the dark in case of an emergency.

There was a melancholic lullaby that either Opa or Oma would sing to us as we prepared for bed. The first verse was:

So good evening and good night,
With roses bedight,
With lilies o'er spread,
Snuggle up in your nest.
Tomorrow morn, if God wills,
You'll awake once again.
Tomorrow morn, if God wills,
You'll awake once again.

Far from lulling me to sleep, the words frightened me. I begged them to stop before the stanza that if I closed my eyes I might die. When I protested, wanting to climb out of bed, they initially laughed telling me it was a song—famously written by Brahms. Terrified to tears, I did not want to sleep and persisted to rise. They got angry that I disobeyed at bedtime. I lay awake scared stiff. I did not want to die. I wanted to go home. I wanted my mother.

Opa bossed, yelled, and threatened us with corporal punishment—setting a big stick next to a carpetbeater along kitchen wall—until we inevitably fell in line with the household routine, which included getting up early. Opa could not stand others sleeping late. While Oma was cycling to the baker to get the rolls, he would come into our bedroom and yank off our covers, exposing us to the cold air. "*Auf! Auf! Sagt der Fucks zum Hasen, hörst du nicht der Jäger blasen?*" he'd say. "Get up, get up, said the fox to the rabbit, can't you hear the hunter blowing his horn?"

Weekdays were strictly disciplined. Monday was washday, which took place in the communal cellar. At one end was a brick fireplace on which rested an enormous copper cauldron with a wooden lid and a paddle. The four families in the house pooled their clothes, linens and towels, and placed them into the kettle. Opa lit the fire at six in the morning, and by eight, the water was boiling with soapy bubbles from their combined rationed detergent powder. Two housewives, working in pairs, would stir the boiling water, sloshing about the steaming clothes with the huge wooden paddle. Next to this cauldron sat a wringer. The other two women would rinse the suds and wring out the laundry, hanging it during the cooler months on row upon row of lines strung from one wall to the other. In summer, laundry hung in the back yard. Children were prevented from going into the cellar on laundry day, but I peeked in from time to time.

By noon, when Opa expected his meal—usually boiled potatoes, fish, and garden beans rendered grey by canning the previous year—Oma would be struggling to stay on his schedule. The afternoon was more restful as the laundry dried. Years later each flat acquired its own washer and dryer.

Friday was the day for Opa to do thorough housecleaning. Mama's and Bakhita's joint efforts at cleaning paled in comparison. The place became spotless; he banished dirt of any kind, and disarray was not tolerated. We learned not to get in his way. It mystified me how much energy Opa put into this endeavor. Had he learned to be that scrupulous in the naval barracks? Opa's seasonal routine included the clipping of the hedges about their garden. He would perform maintenance of the water heater and clean his radio's vacuum tubes.

Twice a year there was a makeover-cleaning day. Furniture was moved, mattresses hung out and beaten, and everything was replaced in its rightful, orderly location. Saturday morning Oma spent shopping at the co-op for a loaf of rye bread and a Sunday roast. Saturday afternoon was the weekly bath.

On a late November morning, shortly after Oma cleared the breakfast table, I helped her in what became the pleasant annual ritual of making the Christmas Stollen. Standing on a chair, I kneaded the ingredients on a well-used, floured wooden board. She chopped and added in a variety of candied fruits and nuts while we worked. I licked the bowl when we finished. Oma wrapped the dough in cheesecloth and left it to stand at the back of the kitchen stove. When it had sufficiently risen, she shaped into a loaf, and as it baked, delicious aromas wafted through the kitchen. By engaging me in this activity, she helped me feel useful, accepted for the first time, and for a moment the pain of Mama's leaving diminished. Each week for the next month, Oma unwrapped the baked loaves, poked holes in them with a wooden skewer, and delicately trickled some brandy into the bread, licking the drop at the mouth of the bottle.

Toward the end of November, Oma told us that St. Nicholas would soon be coming. We had to write out a list of presents we would like and place it in one of our shoes. During the night, St. Nick would collect it. If we had been good, he would leave a little present in our shoe, and if we had been bad, he would leave a piece of coal. Oma helped me write my list, sitting together at the kitchen table. I wanted only two things. The first was a toy car like the one I had given up in Cairo. Oma printed out the word "auto," making me learn the word and the letters for it in German. The second thing on the list was my mother. Oma hesitated, looking at me sideways; she told me that St. Nicholas did not bring people. She suggested that he might bring me a train set. I insisted my mother was to go on the list, and learned to spell the German word "Mutti."

With much excitement, Gulnar and I set our shoes with their notes at the door. The next morning, in exchange for the note I found a small, wrapped chocolate Santa Claus, which I was not allowed to eat until after breakfast—and then only a tiny bite at a time, one each day, starting with his feet.

We learned of Advent with our first Advent calendar, opening one of its windows each day, curious to see the pictures. Gulnar and I took turns lighting one red candle on the wreath on the parlor table for each of the four successive Sundays leading up to Christmas. The season progressed with our growing anticipation. We learned to sing the Christmas carols played on the radio. My grandparents bought a tree, their first since the war, which we decorated with candleholders, red candles, tinsel, and round chocolate wreaths covered with sprinkles. It stood radiantly in a corner of the living room. My anxieties receded, replaced with a sense of belonging and hope.

A sparkling snow fell on Christmas Eve. Opa lit the wood stove. We were cozy inside, listening to carols as Oma baked cakes and prepared the potato salad and sausages that were their —and now our—traditional Christmas Eve fare. Just before 4 o'clock coffee, we lit the candles on the wreath and ate the last of Oma's delicious Stollen. Opa announced we would soon have a visitor. In my heart, I was convinced it would be my mother.

The doorbell rang and we heard heavy boots on the stairs. St. Nicholas opened the door and entered with his long white beard and his red coat trimmed with white, carrying a big sack. He strode into the living room, demanding to know where the good children were. Gulnar held back. Wrapped up in the moment, I stepped forward. "Me, me!" I said, expecting toys and goodies when St. Nick opened his sack. Instead, he pulled out crumpled newspapers and lumps of coal.

"You are a bad boy," he said. The last time I had been called a bad boy was when Mama had scolded me about Bakhita. I was a good boy—why was I being punished now?

My fate was obvious: St. Nicholas was going to put me in his sack and take me away. He lunged forward to grab me. Terrified, I got on my hands and knees and scurried behind the Christmas tree as he followed close behind. He grabbed my ankle and started to pull me back to his open sack. I let out a scream, and in our struggle the Christmas tree tipped over and the lighted candles licked at the boughs.

My grandparents snapped on the lights. It was only in fun, they told me. I was safe. St. Nick reached up to his face and pulled off his beard. Onkel Gerhard's face stared back at me. I hated him.

Santa gave me new boots and a toy car. My mother did not come that Christmas.

A month later, Oma slipped on an icy pavement and broke her right hipbone. After a few days in the hospital, which seemed like a long time without her, she came home with her leg in a plaster cast. She holed up in the back bedroom with the door closed. Tante Annie, Tante Irma, and other women in nurse's uniforms attended her. They told me to be quiet since Oma had to rest. Otherwise, no one paid any attention to me or told me what was going on. I worried.

Listening with my ear against the door, I could hear Oma wince with pain as they moved her about while giving her a bed bath. Tante Annie moved in for a few days and one morning I saw her carry in a bowl of warm water with a face cloth and a towel. She and Tante Irma brought fresh linen every so often. I was scared. Would she be all right? Would she die? The adults about me were solemn and told me to get away from the door. They would not let me see her. I only caught a glimpse of her lying in bed when they quickly passed through the door. There was a flurry of activity in the morning, at lunchtime and in the late afternoon. Herr Dr. Soeltner initially came twice a day, announced by Bobby's barking. Bobby too hung about Oma's door with me.

"Oma, I want to come in?" I cried. I could not hear the muffled reply. The bodies of her caretakers blocked my view as they rapidly closed the door. It took Herr Dr. Soeltner time to pass through the door, as he was carrying his black bag; that is when I would see her, sitting propped up in bed in a white night gown, her dark eyes following the doctor and catching sight of me. She did not attempt to wave or talk to me. I wanted to go in to see her, to kiss her and convince myself I would not be abandoned again. But even the doctor barred my entrance.

"She will be all right," he told me. "Don't worry." With that, he would lay his hand on my head and direct me away from the door to the living room where Opa sat, gaunt and helpless.

Neither Tante Annie nor Tante Irma would tell me anything about Oma. Opa's status vanished as he conceded authority to the women running the household. At night, I would lie in bed with my ear against the separating wall, listening to their muffled voices.

My fear of her dying was intensified by the disruption of our routines and the discussion I overheard about the recent death of a downstairs neighbor's mother. I feared death for it meant the loss of someone I loved. I would once more be alone in this world.

When I had to walk by the cemetery at the local church on our way to the train station, I would cross the street, fearing that ghosts and worse things might suddenly rise from their tombs and chase me.

In time, the activity around the sick room lessened. The nurse did not come, and Herr Dr. Soeltner's visits stretched out to once a week. When Tante Annie and Tante Irma visited and helped Oma from her bed into a tepid bath, I sensed with relief that all would be well. Gradually, the household returned to its normal routines. Even once Oma was up, I hung about, fearful of letting her out of my sight.

As the days grew longer, Opa started to help Onkel Gerhard build his one-story house; one of Opa's many skills were being a bricklayer. After breakfast he rode off on his bicycle and generally returned in time for afternoon coffee. One morning after Gulnar had left for school, Oma also prepared to leave. I was going to be left alone. I shadowed her down into the basement to get her bicycle. Outside, she told me that she was going to the co-op and to visit some friends.

"When are you coming back?" I asked. "Soon?"

"I don't know," she said. "When I've finished." With that, she tried to mount her bicycle. I stood behind her holding her back, clinging onto the rear rack. She nearly lost her balance. She chided me, climbed onto her bicycle again, and started to pedal away. I ran after her. Once more I held her back, and this time she nearly fell off. She scolded me, turning around to clout me. She pushed me away and pedaled off, leaving me crying in the street.

Gulnar's presence in my life diminished. She went to school for longer hours and stayed for after-school activities when she could. The equality among girls and boys strengthened her character. I was too young to attend kindergarten, so I had to fend for myself as best I could. I sought approval and validation during the tortured eight months from our arrival in 1949 until April 1950, when I had learned enough German to begin kindergarten.

A year later, as I was about to enter first grade, my Christmas wish came true: my mother came back unexpectedly for a visit. I was in the front parlor in the mid-afternoon when she walked into the room. By now she was almost a stranger—a woman I didn't recognize. Our greetings were formal, but still I wanted to be with her. She gave me a traditional colorful paper cone filled with pencils, rulers, and some goodies. Mama accompanied me on the first day of school. Glad as that made me, I was embarrassed by her presence, since she was wearing what must have been a very fashionable hat and a brown suit when most of the mothers were sporting simple spring dresses. I had never seen her in a hat, and brown was not a color that suited her. By now, I wanted to blend in with the other children and her appearance exacerbated my awkwardness. Even so, I asked her to stay with me when the other mothers departed and class started.

She sat with me in the first row as the lessons began. I tried to focus on what the teacher was saying, but felt anxious about Mama leaving. Every time she made a move, I grabbed onto her. After a while, the teacher suggested that Mama stand at the back of the classroom; I looked back every few minutes to make sure she was still there. Then I turned around to see she was gone. I ran out of the classroom calling her. Seeing her cross the play-

First day of school

ground, I rushed over, hanging onto her handbag, dragging her back. This tug-of-war went on for minutes, despite my being conscious of the gaze of my classmates at recess. Finally, Mama took me home early while shaming me for being a baby. The next day I went to school alone.

All I wanted was for her to hug me and comfort me, but she didn't. She resumed her pattern of disappearing in the morning and returning late at night. After a few weeks, Mama departed once more, on a freighter for England, again with no reassurances. While I felt the loss, I was not as upset this time. I expected her to leave me as she had done many times. I told myself it did not matter—I had Oma now. I had learned to loved her. She cared for me. She was my real mother.

14
RENATE

First grade at ABC School

This bud of love,
By summer's ripening breath,
May prove a beauteous flower,
When next we meet.
—William Shakespeare

I saw Renate on the first day of first grade in the autumn of 1950. The school was on ABC Street, next to a mature chestnut tree that overshadowed the small gravel courtyard. It was an old brick building dating from the Weimar Republic days, three stories high, with a red-tiled roof. I stood among the milling group of new pupils under the chestnut's draping canopy in the shade of the mid-day sun when Renate stepped into my emotional loneliness. Renate, a girl who liked me. Just me!

I wish I could recall her family name the way I do her blonde pigtails. It must have started with a letter in the first half of the alphabet, because pupils from the top half went to school in the morning, while those whose names began with the letters M through Z attended in the afternoon; the same teacher taught both groups. All the first-grade pupils mingled in the schoolyard during the transition. Although I was among the youngest, we were all about the same height and carried stiff, oversized leather satchels that rattled with a few pencils, a ruler, and a notebook.

Renate and I met face to face in the schoolyard and stared at one another, curious and fascinated; then she turned away, shy at our mutual attraction. Her blonde hair was parted down the middle, and her long braids were tied at the ends with red ribbons. She wore a red and grey plaid coat with knee-high white socks and carried a green satchel. She looked pretty—radiant, in fact, in the autumn sun. The bell rang, its shrill noise ending the moment. She started to walk home, then spun around to see if I was watching her. Reassured by my attention, she skipped out of sight. I climbed the stairs to the classroom, happy at the mere thought of her. The next day when we once more were mingling in the schoolyard, I asked her name. She blushed without answering.

A group of boys surrounded us. "Renate! Renate! Renate!" they shouted. So that was it: Renate. I was too embarrassed to tell her my name was Marwan, because Germans usually could not roll their r's, making it difficult to pronounce. Everyone seemed to know that I was from Egypt. I wondered: Was her first look at me out of curiosity? Or did she like me?

A half-flight of stairs led to the first-grade classroom. Rows of wooden desks, each with a fixed wooden seat, had hinged tops that lifted up so we could store our supplies. An immense blackboard with the letters of the alphabet stenciled above it faced us. The chestnut tree blocked the sunlight from beaming through the classroom's four tall windows.

Around noontime, the afternoon students congregated to play noisily in the schoolyard, awaiting the release of the morning group. The teacher came to the open window, telling us to be quiet, since we were disturbing the class in session. She closed it. My curiosity was piqued. I wanted to know if Renate sat near the window. I stood underneath, too short to look in despite my jumping up and down several times. I called her name. Getting no reply, I threw some pebbles at the glass, calling to her again. A crowd of boys gathered around me. They scattered when the windowpane flew open.

To my horror the teacher appeared. "What do you think you are doing?" she yelled at me. I asked her if Renate was sitting by the window. She ordered me to come into the class. When I did, she made me sit next to her. Renate, who sat in the second row toward the door, blushed and did not look at me. I sat stiffly, glaring straight ahead, as the other kids jeered. It occurred to me that I was not scoring points with my new love.

When the bell rang, I made my escape. I never knew how she felt about my escapade, and I did not see her for a long time after that. I did not know where she had gone.

The next summer I found other friends. Gulnar and I, along with some older kids from the neighborhood, all children of blue-collar workers, sometimes set up a big tent on the riverbank and spent the night there in sleeping bags. In the morning, we would make a fire using driftwood we scavenged, eating the meager sandwiches we brought with us. We would spend the day on the beach in the sun, swim in the river, and watch the freighters from around the world steam into Hamburg harbor. The bushes were our toilets. No adults watched over us. We had tremendous fun.

By October, when new teachers joined the staff, we were divided into two classes: boys and girls. During a break, I glimpsed Renate playing with other girls in the schoolyard. Renate! It had been so long! She looked around for me when I played with the boys. I was looking for her. After school, we walked home together in our own way; she hung around at the top of ABC Street, waiting. When I came out into the school-yard, she would turn the corner into the adjoining street to start walking. I hoped she would wait around the corner, but when I got there, she was always a hundred yards ahead of me. I would start running, my satchel bouncing against me. She too would run, keeping the distance between us. Why was she doing this? I wanted to be her friend.

I decided that when she saw me coming into the yard and took off around the corner, I would run as fast as I could to the top of ABC Street. It worked. When I rounded the corner, she was only a few feet ahead of me. On spotting me, she ran, increasing the distance between us once more. I had already made my dash with a heavy school bag; winded, I could not run any farther. And I still didn't understand her game.

The grayer days of winter arrived. My feet hurt when I ran because I had outgrown my boots. In late October, I told Oma about my aching feet. She replied that I would have to wait until Christmas when I'd get new shoes. Renate continued to run and I to chase, though my crammed toes hurt me. It seemed that I would never catch up.

Eventually the game entered a new phase: the distance between us shrank. Renate slackened her pace until one day we were walking beside each other—until she promptly crossed the cobbled street to walk on the opposite side. When I followed, she crossed again. Confused, I decided that she was rejecting me. Ignoring her would be my best strategy.

When I was six years old and in second grade, we walked home together, parallel to each other on opposite sides of the street. There was almost no traffic and I shouted across the road, "Why do you never wait for me?" I wanted to add, "I like you. You look nice. I want to be your friend. I want to play with you. I am lonely." But I did not have the courage.

She looked down at the pavement as she walked on without answering my question directly. Instead, she yelled, "Are there camels in Egypt?"

"Yes. I have pictures I can show you." She shrugged, walking on.

"Are there giraffes near your house? Have you seen hippos in the Nile?" she hollered. To me these were amusing questions. Blushing, she went silent when I laughed. But now, at least, she didn't run away.

During these homeward-bound walks, I eventually learned via our long-distance conversations that she was an only child. She wished that she had a brother or sister to play with. I told her that my sister didn't like to play with me. I missed seeing her during the summer break. I pictured her spending those months with her Oma in the southern mountains, expecting these months to be as hot as the previous summer of 1949—the hottest ever experienced. Oma told me that Renate's family had been refugees, part of an influx that fled the advancing Red Army from the eastern lands of occupied Germany.

Once Oma and Opa's apartment building had a clear view of ships sailing up the river into Hamburg harbor, or down toward the North Sea, but now a massive resettlement project blocked the view, with one set of row houses after another built between the house and the Elbe. I met new children playing in the street or in patches of woodland that remained undeveloped behind our building. I never missed Renate. I had become accustomed to the people I loved simply vanishing.

Gitta filled the emptiness of that summer. She was seven, with dark curly hair and a pretty, upturned nose. Her complexion was slightly darker, which made her look exotic. She and her family moved into temporary housing nearby. Oma called them gypsies. I knew it was not exactly a nice term. Still, Gitta appealed to me, and I was curious to get to know her.

The details of how it began are fuzzy. One afternoon she and I built a den in the woods with thick sage bushes. We broke branches off low trees to fill in the gaps. Around the sage bushes were purple flowers and some daisies, which made our den feel very homey. Catkins from tall silver birch trees fell around us. "All we need," she said, "is a doormat at the entrance." I told her I could get one. Knowing it was afternoon naptime and the grownups were asleep, I ran to our apartment block to take the neighbor's front doormat for the final addition to our new hideaway.

Safely inside, we reclined on a carpet of moss. She broke the silence by asking me if I wanted to play doctor. I readily agreed. She hitched up her skirt, raised her bottom, and slid off her white panties. Spreading her legs, she displayed her private parts. I ran my finger over her opening. She lay back with her hands under her head staring at the birch canopy. I picked the colorful flowers, laying their heads, like buttons, side by side along her exposure. It looked pretty. She was not impressed, brushing them away and slipping her panties on. Then she insisted on examining me, with an air of curiosity and enthusiasm that alarmed me. She wanted to place her mouth on my penis, something she had seen her parents do when they thought she was asleep. Frightened she might bite me, I pushed her away. To my relief I heard Oma call me home through the open kitchen window.

I too slipped on my underpants. Gitta noticed they had no fly—they were girlies, my sister's. She teased me because I had inherited my sister's underwear. I had objected but my grandparents insisted no one would know. At home, Oma wanted to know if I had seen her neighbor's doormat. I retrieved it, explaining to her that we had used it in a game of pretend. Gitta never spoke to me or played with me again. In my rejection, I agreed with Oma that Gitta was a gypsy, a bad girl. I was sure Renate would never have exposed herself like that. The insidious idea that there were two types of females was planted deep in my psyche: sweet girls like Renate and naughty, exciting ones.

The authorities bulldozed the temporary shelters shortly thereafter, their inhabitants moved into new housing as the patch of land in front of my grandparent's house became yet another building site. Despite my Oma's warning that they might not be nice children because they came with unknown backgrounds from somewhere east, I soon befriended the new kids. We formed gangs, played war games or cowboys and Indians in the remaining woodlands. Our passion was to chase the girls, who seemed to want us to pursue them. At first, we assigned girls, at will, to be our wives. They played a game I did not know called Spin the Bottle. Once I had to kiss a girl I did not fancy nine times. I kissed her left cheek, counting out every peck, to the disappointment of the boys, who expected I would kiss her on the lips. But how could I kiss a person I did not care for, and who did not care for me?

Renate was not part of the ever-changing combination of boys and girls; she lived too far away. But the following April, in third grade, Renate and I again walked home together, this time side by side. I cannot recall what we talked about, only my elation. I admired her braids and her red shoes with white socks. I wondered if I should tell her about Gitta, though I never did, thinking it might upset her.

One Sunday Renate boldly suggested that we go to a movie. She would meet me at 2 o'clock at the local cinema near the railway station. Oma was reluctant to let me go alone, and Opa categorically said, "No, you can't go by yourself." When the neighbor's grandchild said he was going, my grandparents relented and gave me one Deutschmark, the admission fee. I rushed off, late, to the theater. The main feature had already started. The usher showed me in. Instead of following her flashlight down the aisle to a free seat, I walked slowly, row by row, softly calling Renate's name. I never found her so eventually I sat alone.

The movie house was packed. The film was about an orphanage in which a boy about my age watched everyone around him get adopted except himself. He sang a song of longing to be loved and taken home, a song I can sing to this day. I sobbed my eyes out. I too wanted to go home. When the lights came up at the end, I was greatly relieved not to be sitting next to Renate.

Renate and I met once in a while, when she would come and beckon me over to her when I was playing cowboys and Indians in the woods with the other kids. I'd leave the boys and sit with her, chatting awkwardly in a clearing on the scrub grass on top of a sand mound. I wondered what it would have been like if Gitta had been Renate, and as soon as the alluring image of Gitta floated by, I chastised myself; nice girls like Renate wouldn't behave that way. Renate had grown taller. Sitting close I noticed that she had a pretty face, a beautiful smile with dimples, and white teeth. Her tender eyes seemed to sparkle. To break the spell, which I found overpowering, we rolled down the grassy hill, yelling all the way. She stopped a couple of times when I accidentally rolled into her. I continued trying to impress her by rolling down the hill as she watched. She didn't say anything. Suddenly she got up and left without even saying goodbye. She just walked away. Why? What had I done? I had no idea.

15

MINIATURE STEINBACH

Gulnar, Oma, Marwan, Opa, and Bobby

*Assimilation is really a psychological process
where you come to identify with a new country as yours.*
—Mark Kerkorian

M other had prophetically described me in her letters
to her parents in 1944 as "a miniature Steinbach." I
had paler skin than my sister, and Teutonic features
resembling Opa's. The thought that I might be the product of

Mother's liaison with a German prisoner who had escaped, and who she was trying to help, didn't cross my mind then, for Sister Röske hadn't spilled the beans yet about Mother's machinations about her pregnancy. The reality was that I looked more Germanic than my father or Gulnar. In 1948, and in the years when I lived with my grandparents in Wedel, my pale German genes came to the fore and expressed themselves in my attitude and identity.

By the time I turned six I felt very German; I played with German children, learned and spoke German, and repressed my native Arabic tongue. I sought and received acceptance and love, especially from my Oma—the other woman in my life. How did this transformation occur? How did I accomplish this conversion from being an Egyptian child, unwilling to accept Oma, rejecting and fearing her, to firmly bonding with her? How did it transpire that through the rest of my life I thought of Oma as my mother, with profound feelings of affection and concern? My own mother became a mere fellow traveler. My father faded into a gray image.

Opa bullied and coerced us into German ways through his incessant verbal tirades and physical threats. During that traumatic adjustment, Gulnar was rebellious, argumentative, and resisted Opa's control. She told me when we were adults that she had greater self-confidence than I did. Not only was she older, but relative to the oppressive environment for females in Egypt, she felt liberated in Germany. She said that I, being younger, had a less-formed identity and was more vulnerable since I hated being alone. I had lost my precious status and wanted and needed Oma's love. At least that was Gulnar's interpretation. "You succumbed to the pressure of intimidation and assimilation by a bully," she concluded. She was perhaps right, but my reward was the constancy of Oma's caring and nourishment.

Societal assimilation was difficult in a country buried in depression. In fear of retribution for Nazi atrocities, Germany was suffering from a national psyche of defeat and humiliation.

The aura of misery was alien to me, particularly in contrast to our boisterous Egyptian family life. I could not understand or relate to it; after all, Oma and Opa had survived the war. They suffered a mindset of austerity and making do, despite having lost neither property nor family. Still, the upheaval and mass migration of refugees from the east to the west, and into what had been the quiet *Hamburger Elektrisitäte Werke* (HEW) community, created food, housing, and job shortages. The national unease magnified my state of despondency. My self-denigrating mood varied from the gloom of being abandoned, to the guilt of enjoying a joyous occasion at Onkel Gerhard's wedding to Tante Irma. Perhaps it was part of my assimilation that I, too, felt drawn into the national culpability. The more German I felt, the more I related to their shared guilt.

There was also the uncertainty and vagueness of the de-Nazification criteria, and the common experience of guilt along with the eternal wall of silence about what had happened to neighbors and non-Aryans of all stripes. Years later, as an adult, I understood that silence was also a means of survival. It prevented the danger of children overhearing what they should not hear, perhaps re-telling it to strangers or officials, and helped to suppress unwanted memories. Nonetheless, I could never understand the collective national amnesia, including that of my grandparents. I was curious: what did they know, what had they done during the war, how did they protect themselves from Allied bombing when they lived so close to Hamburg's major electricity source, and had they been swept up or actively participated with the National Socialist Party?

Opa and Oma were retired blue-collar union members with meager pensions, now registered Social Democrats. They lived in a relatively secluded community of six HEW company houses built in the late 1920s in the midst of woodlands and fallow fields. Ninety km west of Hamburg, the HEW sat on the northern bank of the river Elbe, a huge edifice with four smokestacks making an inescapable landmark on the near horizon. It had miraculously survived the war, although grass-filled craters peppered the meadows and woods between their house and the power plant. Before his retirement, Opa had cycled 15 km to work in rain, snow, or sunshine. He spent all day shoveling coal into a furnace to generate steam that drove the turbines providing electricity to Hamburg and the surrounding towns. He had volunteered to retire early, allowing a returning soldier to fill his job. After the war, the fields filled with townhouses to accommodate new arrivals of evicted Germans who'd once lived in Eastern Europe.

Opa, at power plant, sixth from left

Gulnar and I intruded on their lives, and perhaps we suffered because of the burden and resentment Oma and Opa must have felt toward their daughter's current need to be child-less. There were no other children in the six HEW workers' houses. Looking more German than Egyptian to start with, I was more readily accepted in Wedel than Gulnar, who was much darker-skinned, and was often taunted by the schoolboys, who knew she came from Egypt, with cries of "negro, negro, negro." I had no cousins due to the great age difference between my mother and Onkel Gerhard. I was not encouraged to bring home the random kids I played with in the street or woods. I

had no constant friends. Most in our neighborhood were tran-
sients anyway.

Opa, christened Friedrich
Wilhelm Steinbach, was born in
Saxony in 1886, the second to last
of six children. His father was
elderly and a strict disciplinarian
of Prussian descent—a bully. His
mother called her son Willie. He
was a sensitive child, her favorite,
and loved music. With only

*Embroidered membership
certificate of the Neptune Club.*

eighth-grade schooling, he and his three brothers took up a life
at sea. As a young merchant seaman, he visited Shanghai under
sail, where he received an embroidered certificate on Chinese
paper that recorded the date and time that he had crossed the
equator and became a member of the Neptune Club. Further
voyages followed under sail and steam. Between journeys in his
mid-twenties, he worked as a groundskeeper, where he met
Martha Anna Hennig—Oma—a twenty-year-old domestic from
a nearby town.

Opa was a handsome man, as confirmed by his early photos.
He had a full head of hair and a square face with refined bone
structure, stern eyes, and a straight, patrician nose. I can easily
see how Martha Henning found him a charmer. She told me
years later that she could not remember when Opa first set eyes
on her, or why he came to the house, but she did clearly recall
how he stole a kiss at the bottom of the servants' stairs and that
his mother was the most domineering woman she had ever met.
When Opa's father died, they, along with his mother, moved to
Altona, an eastern suburb of Hamburg near the harbor. They
had a registry wedding when Oma was twenty-one and already
three months pregnant. Their son, also Friedrich Wilhelm Steinbach, died fourteen months after their wedding.

Some months after the child's death, Oma took the tram to
its furthest western destination: the terminal in Blankenese along

the Elbe, about 24 km away. She found a small flat, determined to free herself from her mother-in-law's yoke. To pay the rent she became a seamstress, although she loved to bake. Opa joined her.

The stories she told me in the kitchen after *Abendbrot* —supper—sitting alone, just the two of us in the dwindling light, helped shape my German identity. Yes, I was part of them, and they were not total strangers.

He was a proud man and not prone to smiling. His apparent reticence was in fact a cover for his limited education, particularly when discussing current affairs with family, friends, and neighbors. An industrious man, he held a certificate issued in 1903 by the German Association of Barbers, Hair Dressers, and Wig Makers, attesting to passing their apprenticeship. He worked as a barber before and during the Great War. In later life, he adapted to different lines of work, including co-captain of a trawler, and after retiring from the HEW, an occasional bricklayer.

———

During the time Gulnar and I lived with Oma and Opa, there was a continuous stream of refugees from Eastern Europe—a steady influx of outsiders to distrust. In the already insecure environment, this produced a general state of paranoia: a fear of strangers and talk of menacing East German agents approaching in dark cars as we walked home from school. We were warned of the threats from East German spies who kidnapped children, or of harmless-looking toys lying on the ground that were set to explode and maim hapless youngsters. Furthermore, since it was the beginning of the Cold War, if active hostilities started, Russian tanks would mercilessly roll into Hamburg and Wedel on their way to the North Sea. Such rumors heightened my fears, especially when Opa confirmed them with authority.

Adding to my anxiety were the daily radio broadcasts called

Der Suchdienst—The Search-Service—in which the broadcaster read out the names of individuals and soldiers last seen on the Russian front. There were pleas from mothers desperately seeking children from whom they had been separated in wartime. Opa listened to this two-hour-long program and it drew me in, too, as if somehow, I would hear my mother looking for me. Instead I found myself alone, frightened by my own desperation and the regular fear of Opa terrorizing me. The past was the currency of discussions that I overheard, not just on the radio but also when my grandparents talked to neighbors in hushed voices in the staircase, or occasionally to each other in whispers in the evening—conversations that would cease abruptly upon my appearance.

My anxiety increased on hearing the story during Sunday school of Joseph being sold by his kin in Egypt; I felt like this had happened to me. Like Joseph, I was stripped of my beautiful robe—my colorful, protected life in the land of my birth—only to be sold and forsaken by my own mother. I was further distressed at hearing the story of Hansel and Gretel, two children living with a nasty witch in a dark wood, similar to the woods that surrounded my grandparents' community: two lost children who were trying to get back home.

And yet life went on. Saturday and Sunday mornings, weather permitting, Opa took me along on his daily walks with the dog by the Elbe, which helped me adjust. Bobby trotted off the leash, contrary to county law, but no one challenged Opa. In my Muslim background, a dog was not an object of affection. Opa, on the other hand, was convinced that every four-year-old boy should have a dog, so when he heard that we had left Egypt he got the puppy. Over time, while walking with Bobby I learned that a dog could give me the unconditional love I yearned for. The three of us walked along the banks toward Wedel's harbor. Opa always wore his sailor's cap. He enjoyed telling me about the various types of ships coming into Hamburg or going out to sea, and their different national flags.

He told me about the meaning of the colored pennants that flew over the bulkheads, such as "pilot on board," or "illness among crew requiring quarantine." Once we reached the local harbor, he showed me the place he and his brothers had docked their trawler. They had a sailboat, *Möve*—seagull—which they had sailed on weekends along the river, always taking their dog with them. When Baba had visited in 1938, they had gone sailing together. I began to look forward to our walks. On occasion, he bought me an ice cream, and I started to recognize his softer, more generous side. By the time I identified myself as a miniature Steinbach, Opa was in his early sixties.

Oma reading the news — Opa walking Bobby

From time to time, my distant life suddenly surfaced as a deep ache, a vestigial longing as if I heard a call echoing from my Egyptian tribe. I would feel a yearning, wanting a home, a family, "my mother," with a fading memory of Mama brought on by the sight of a ship heading down the Elbe to some distant land, or by Sunday school picture books of palm trees, donkeys, and camels, calling me back to my previous world. Bedtime was when I most longed for the past; I missed goodnight kisses, tucking in, and book reading. My Egyptian family was demonstrative, always touching and kissing children, emotional expression that was not part of German culture. I never saw my grandparents kiss each other, hold hands, or touch with affection.

Sometimes Oma sat next to me at the kitchen table to supervise my homework. In one session, I had to learn to write the figure 8, not two circles, one on top of the other, but starting at one point and completing it in a swoop. When I managed to do that, she was pleased, but my eight leaned in all directions. She showed me how to write it once more, expecting me to follow her style, erect and proud. When she looked away, I cheated, again drawing two circles. She looked at the paper and clouted me, and with my ear stinging, I tried again. Finally, I got it the way she wanted. I got it right.

By the 1950s, my six-month school reports reflected my growing accomplishments and my success at assimilating into the German lifestyle, documented in cursive German hands by my various teachers: Herr Haase, Herr Helfs, Herr Baumgaerter, and Dr. Packross. Oma read each report aloud, with Opa listening closely. The now browning report cards on my writing desk reveal Oma's signature at the bottom of each card in a sure, steady hand. The teachers' notes reflect that I had "zealously embraced with verve my new school, my classmates, my new German life." Oma and Opa were gratified that their attention to my education was paying off.

Surely, their daughter would be pleased. Opa, who had had a difficult relationship with his daughter, was reluctantly proud that she had broken out of the laborer's lifestyle, the first Steinbach to attend university.

My grandparents' life, and hence mine, was dominated by our rigid adherence to Opa's daily and weekly routines, which I had to follow from the moment I rose in the morning, made my bed, and hung up my pajamas—imbuing me with compulsive traits. Following his daily morning walk with the dog, Opa sat at the living room window reading the socialist-leaning SPD daily newspaper. He folded it neatly for Oma to read it in the kitchen when he retired to the living room sofa to listen to the one o'clock news, grunting in response to an item worthy of his opinion. When it was over, he rolled toward the wall for an hour's nap. As he became more rotund with age, the living room table prevented him from falling off the narrow sofa.

If some unforeseen event necessitated a disruption to their meal times, Opa would grumble or go into a major sulk and fart, as if by polluting the air in the small flat he was making his discontent known. Nevertheless, after more than 50 years of marriage, Oma and Opa seemed content with each other.

Marwan, Bobby and Gulnar

16

SECRETS AND HABITS

*It's challenging to find an identity as a young person
if you don't have the sustenance of love,
because you're being shipped around.*
—Mary J. Blige

My grandparents' flat in Wedel had its own locked cellar and attic. While Oma and Opa rested in the afternoon, or when I was left alone, which seemed often, I would take the key off the rack by the front door and climb down into the damp, windowless basement, or up to the warm attic with its pitched roof and closed dormer window. I would unlock the door, close it behind me, and spend hours rummaging through boxes and drawers, trying to discover their secret lives, particularly during wartime.

The attic was dry and had the scent of the pinewood that formed its partitions. There were two made-up single beds, and occasionally Opa would announce that he was sleeping upstairs. I always joined him, although it never occurred to me to ask why he would undertake such a drastic change in habit; I simply saw it as an adventure. As I lay in my warm feather bed, Opa would tell me tales of his sea voyages: at first as a hand deck on the *Möve*, which despite its coal engine relied on its sails, then on the *Planet*, *Waldemar*, and *Graf*, each progressively becoming a coal burner. The trips were for commerce and mainly to Shanghai. Whenever he stopped talking, I would ask him what he had done during the First World War. He served as a mariner on the light cruiser of the Imperial German Navy—the *SMS Danzig*. He didn't see action near Heligoland but against the Russian forces in the Baltic Sea.

Towards the end of the war he became a naval reservist in the Division of Zeppelins. He had gone on numerous naval exercises, based in Wilhelmshaven along the North Sea near Bremen. Oma took up residence in a nearby village. Sneaking out of the barracks at night, he joined her in her rented room. Their adventurous spirits surprised me. She would take him lunchtime sandwiches made with *Kommisbrot*—the dark rye bread—she bought from the co-op each Saturday. I too love eating this bread, and to this day consume it with each *Abendbrot*, never failing to think of Oma.

I enjoyed hearing Opa's stories and believed everything he said, primarily because he spoke little, and seldom, about the past. When I asked about the years between the wars, he would feign tiredness saying, "The first person to fall asleep should whistle." I would whistle joyfully, relishing the sense of camaraderie with Opa. It was not until I used the same line years later, when camping with my son, that I realized it meant snoring.

Between the beds were two old steamer trunks piled with a number of aged suitcases and hatboxes waiting to be explored. I unpacked them with care. Layers of clothing reeked of the mothballs scattered between. I found Oma's simple wedding dress, and a corset with stays. I tried the corset on, laughing, thinking of her wearing it. I found two items I felt sure would be important in revealing their past: a set of empty ledger books, and a small box containing an Iron Cross dangling on a ribbon. Opa claimed he had the cross because he had served in the Navy during World War I; he did not expand on why he had this medal, nor could I draw him in to discussing it further. To this day the medal lies in its box in my sock drawer. He said he had no idea about the ledgers, that I should ask Oma.

Her explanation was very hesitant, as if she were wondering how much to reveal to a curious young boy. "It belonged to a traveling salesman during the last war," she started to tell me one night as she took off her apron. "He'd sleep in the attic whenever he was passing through. I suspected he was a black-market profiteer, dealing in stolen French perfumes and liquors. This activity was very dangerous." She stopped again, settling at the kitchen table, as I leaned against her china cupboard holding my breath.

"At first, he was nice enough, but he turned out to be a seedy character. He drank too much. Opa quarreled with him when he wanted to bring . . ." she hesitated once more, "not such nice women to the loft." She rose and ended her story, admonishing me for being nosy.

Cellar secrets were different from the ones that hid in the attic. The cellar was dark and cold. I wondered if they had used it during the war as an air raid shelter. It had a workbench, several adult bicycles, a sled, a sack of coal, a stack of drying wood, and rows upon rows of shelves with jars labeled in Oma's writing—the harvest of last year's bottling. I touched every one, reading aloud: beans '49, cucumbers '49, pears '49, strawberry jam '49, plum '49, raspberry '49, gooseberry '48, and rhubarb '49, anticipating when we would eat each one.

During one of my cellar-snooping trips, a few weeks before my sixth birthday, I uncovered a boat that Opa was making out of wood. It looked like a steamer, with a red-painted funnel and a white superstructure. He had used small nails set a little distance apart and had yet to wind a thread around to simulate its railing. At its stern, on a nail that represented a pole, Opa had made a small ensign, three horizontal stripes of black, red, and gold—the new post-WWII German flag. He had christened it *Möve*, the name of the merchantman on which he had sailed to China, and the old sailing boat that he and Oma, with a previous dog called Bobby running about the gunwale, had sailed in the Elbe during their youth.

It was hard to suppress my excitement at seeing the ship. I hoped it was for me. My parents did not believe in giving presents, not to mention celebrating birthdays. Their idea was to get us what we needed, usually clothing and shoes. Baba said a birthday is like every other workday. I was overjoyed to discover that after all of Opa's shouting and threats, he cared enough to make me a present! I carefully covered it back with the cloth.

My sixth birthday was on a sunny April 14. Oma surprised me with six red tulips in a cobalt blue vase with a golden neck. They glittered like magic when she placed them on the windowsill. She told me the vase was her mother's, and that if I liked it I could have it one day. I had requested frankfurters for my birthday lunch, and was allowed to eat as many as I liked. My eyes were larger than my stomach and I only managed to devour two of four sausages. What a birthday! All the while, I wondered what had happened to the ship I spied in the cellar. I was kept in suspense until the afternoon, when Opa presented the finished toy, freshly painted in white on that glorious day— my day. He was pleased with my delight. I discovered later that the paint had not quite dried by the morning and the tulips were Oma's innovation—a wonderful stopgap.

Oma also made a special cake. Though it was a Friday not Sunday, her brother Onkel Willie, his sweet wife Tante Annie, and their developmentally disabled son Bruno, five years older than me, came from Hamburg to celebrate at coffee time, along with Onkel Gerhard and Tante Irma. While the adults chatted, I played with Bruno on the carpet, my new ship declaring war on the vessel he had brought with him.

On such special occasions, Oma would spread a white cloth over the table in the parlor and set the cake in the middle, surrounded by her finest bone china and silver. Wearing aprons over their Sunday best, Oma and Tante Annie would huddle in the kitchen, Oma grinding the beans in the mill for coffee and Tante Annie whipping heavy cream with a fork, adding a spoonful of sugar. The same ritual occurred in June for Oma's birthday, in August for Opa's, and in November for Gulnar's. Each time I licked the whipped cream dish clean. When Bruno grew older, he brought his accordion and played it as the adults sang songs I didn't know. The music provided the homey warmth I had missed since coming to Germany.

Irma, Opa, and Oma at coffee table

Onkel Willie had worked at Hamburg shipyard as a welder and married Tante Annie late in life. She and Tante Irma were domestics, and Gerhard was an electrician at the HEW. I felt comfortable with them. They were honest members of the working class, striving each day to make ends meet. Tante Annie hugged and kissed me, calling me a nice boy, saying that I must be missing my parents. She was always knitting, making me scarves, gloves, sweaters, and socks. They had no airs or graces, no unrealistic aspirations or pretenses. They had much in common with my Egyptian family, despite the cultural differences. From each family, I acquired a dose of solid work ethic, determination, and ingenuity.

Playing with Bruno on the carpet, I was eavesdropping, as youngsters are wont to do. The grownups complimented Oma on her cake. Their coffee cups clinked on their saucers. Eventually the topic drifted to my mother's presence in England while her children were here. Various opinions were rendered about the soundness of her actions. How much longer would she leave her *kinder*

Tante Annie and Onkel Willi

in Wedel? Childless Tante Irma, the young bride, said her sister-in-law was expecting too much of her elderly parents. In a pious tone, she insisted she would never ask her parents to raise her kids. "No, I wouldn't do it," she stated to Onkel Gerhard, who looked sheepishly away, clearly hoping that his wife's comment would not antagonize his parents. Several comments followed, uttered in *Plattdeutsch*—a Low German dialect—distinct from Standard German that I could not understand. They were presumably unflattering, for an awkward silence descended on the group. It did not escape me that, like my Egyptian grandparents, my German grandparents spoke another tongue too—one I had not learned, whose words I picked up with time, but I did not let on that I understood.

Tante Annie, older, more thoughtful, mellowed by raising an intellectually challenged child, was gentler in her assessment. She added that she admired how her sister-in-law, Oma, was doing such a fine, decent job. She changed the subject, wondering in a wistful tone what would happen to Bruno when they were gone.

From there, as usual, the conversation came around to Gulnar. As observed by these conformist adults, she was a difficult child whose individualism and rebellious nature was troubling. Somehow, mother and daughter were always linked, each considered problematic; like mother, like daughter, was their general conclusion. Although my grandparents tended to agree with the general tone of the discussion, they also defended both their daughter and granddaughter. They attributed Gulnar's behavior to the special circumstance of her parents' absence. This analysis proceeded under the photograph of my absent father hanging on the opposite wall. Perhaps his academic achievements excused him from criticism or responsibility.

Oma whispered something to Tante Annie as they were leaving; I think she had received a letter from England, but no discussion followed. Maybe she thought that avoiding the mention of our parents would diminish our pain. Despite my searching everywhere, I could not discover where she hid my mother's letter; possibly she burned them.

Mother arrived a week later for my birthday and for Easter. Baba didn't come. Her short stay was not memorable except that sleeping past Opa's waking hour into the morning was a point of contention. When my mother finally rose close to lunchtime, he expressed his usual displeasure.

"Well, the best part of the day is wasted," he would say, addressing no one in particular.

Once rested, she returned to her usual habit of going to Hamburg immediately after breakfast and returning late at night without explanation. If Opa was aware of any improprieties that kept her late in Hamburg, he certainly did not discuss them in front of the children. Mama had brought me a Dinky toy truck, a replacement of what had been disposessed from me in Egypt. I cherished it. When she left my anxiety was not nearly as wrenchingly painful as it had been in previous years, as Oma and Opa supplied a sense of security. It would be a long time before I'd see her again.

Every April, Oma's routine included a visit to the cemetery on the other side of the train tracks. She would cycle past vegetable fields to the edge of town and buy a flower or two to place on a grave. Each time I would ask her whose grave she had visited, but her solemn answer was always vague. When I was older, she once replied, "Just someone who was important to Opa and me." Opa never accompanied her and I was not invited; I am not sure she wanted company. She would set off alone, at first cycling toward her secret, then in later years walking to the bus station—always dressed in reverent black. She never spent their hard-earned Marks on any flowers for herself or the house, only to place on the grave. Years later, long after she had been laid to rest in the same cemetery plot, I finally understood. She must have been visiting the child she had lost when she was a young woman.

Oma planned a mushroom hunt each springtime. She knew the different types of local wild mushrooms that were safe to eat. We rose before dawn, ate a hasty sandwich, then left on our bicycles, with Opa in the lead, Gulnar and I following, and Oma in the rear. We headed northeast, at first along the paved country road on the way to Hamburg, veering off onto a dirt track leading through plowed fields, grasslands, and finally arriving at the *Staatforest Kloevensteen*, a recreational forest with a large pond, in the adjacent borough of Rissen.

The early morning mist rose through the rays of the sun that penetrated the mixed forest canopy. The dawn chorus was at its crescendo. Perhaps it was my wonder at the magical beauty of nature or my short legs peddling on the soft dirt that slowed me down. Opa, expecting his troops to follow closely, receded into the mist ahead of us, unresponsive to our calls to slow down, or perhaps unaware of the three cyclists falling behind. In a burst of energy Oma passed Gulnar and me and, in a moment of spite, which made us giggle, took a sharp right along another path that led deeper into the darkened woods. As we cycled, we would hear a cuckoo call, or see an occasional deer. Opa reappeared, annoyed, if not angry at our seeming independence. Our reward for the mutiny was seeing Oma heading straight to the base of a mature tree. Dismounting, she fell on her knees in mystical ecstasy and brushed away a layer of last autumn's leaves. She had harvested their forebears the previous year. Producing a small kitchen knife, she cut their stalks deep below the level of black dirt. Oma inspected them with the intensity and affection of one admiring a cherished child before lovingly placing them into her woven basket, covering them with a kitchen towel.

"Yes, these are good," she always said to herself as we surrounded her on our knees, invading the privacy of her communion with nature. Opa would stand behind us leaning on his bike, hands in pockets, until unable to hold his tongue, he spouted out a series of warnings about the dangers of poison mushrooms—a flow of irritating, negative energy which she wisely ignored. Oma carefully restored the leaves to minimize her telltale presence. "I don't want others to come here," she said, looking up at us over her shoulder. "This is my secret place."

Pushing our bikes through the dry leaves on the forest floor, we headed to another tree or cluster of bushes, where once more she would fall on her knees, enraptured by another discovery. Joining her enthusiasm, Gulnar and I searched for edible mushrooms under other trees. None passed Oma's test—knowledge she had acquired during the war when mushrooms augmented the meager meat rationing.

Spring was the perfect time of year to collect wild mushrooms, and many Germans visited the woods. We never encountered others, though, primarily because of Oma's early start to the secret hunting grounds. We were usually home in time for breakfast at eight. For the rest of the morning a stream of delectable odors drifted through the tiny flat as she sautéed onions and bacon bits in lard, added the washed, trimmed mushrooms, chopped the parsley, and peeled and boiled potatoes, making her secret mushroom fricassee. On the back burner, she had prepared carrots or leeks—whatever appeared in the market. Bobby hung around the kitchen hoping for scraps until Oma said, "Out of my way. Go to your crate."

Oma preparing mushrooms

My job was to set the table. Opa, seeing the clock's hands approaching twelve noon, would put down the paper, stride into the kitchen, and seat himself in front of his plate in time to help himself to the steaming parsley-garnished potatoes and vegetables. Every year he announced that he had read in this morning's paper how the four members of a family died from eating poison mushrooms. . . and only yesterday. Oma, placing the pot of the fricassee with its rich, silky sauce on the table, looked at him and rolled her eyes. Yet Opa would be the first to help himself to the mushrooms. This repeat performance played out each spring. I wondered if she had ever had the urge to dump the fricassee pot on his head; however, she maintained her sweet disposition and we ate with pleasure.

The future looked progressively brighter. Rationing had ended, my self-confidence swelled, and with it, the self-esteem of growing up in an ascending Germany. The economy took on a sense of dynamism with the implementation of the 1948 Marshall Plan and the de-Nazification plan, beginning the slow, gradual process of breathing new life into Germany.

By late spring of 1950, the milkman would arrive mid-morning with his horse-drawn cart, ladling pints of milk into Oma's kitchen jugs. On a lucky day, his horse would dump in front of our house. My task was to sweep it up to add to the compost heap in Oma's garden. Gradually, butter, cheese, cream, and eggs appeared. Occasionally a broom salesman came by or perhaps the peddler with his large whetstone, ringing a hand bell to attract the housewives. Kids stood nearby gawking at the sparks from his wheel as he sharpened knives and scissors.

Everything around me was new: roads, buildings, street-lights, buses. The old school on ABC Street was renovated with fresh paint everywhere, new double windows to keep out the cold, brightly colored classroom doors, and new desks, books, and young, enthusiastic teachers. Shiny new cars filled the road-ways. When we went to Hamburg, we traveled on a new electric suburban train instead of the old steam engine. The expectation of achievement filled the air. Manufactured goods stamped "Made in Germany," like the reliable Grundig radio Opa bought, the sturdy bicycles Gulnar and I rode, and the electric train set that grew with each birthday and Christmas, radiated quality and pride.

Slowly, season by season, I began to feel more content, and believed that I belonged. Sundays without homework and structure were my favorite days. In the mornings, during a leisurely, peaceful breakfast, my grandparents listened to a program called *Haffenkonzert* broadcast from Hamburg harbor. Music was interspersed with commentary on the ships—their ports of origin, their tonnage, their flags, their cargo, when they would depart, and their destinations. I enjoyed listening, learning a great deal about shipping. As rationing ended, more ingredients became available. Much to my delight, Oma baked a greater variety of cakes to accompany the adults' coffee, adding a shot of schnapps on special occasions.

In the afternoons during coffee time, the once anxiety-producing program, *Der Suchdienst,* was replaced by a classical music broadcast. Symphonies and lyrical operas were as comforting to me as Oma's baked goods, which we ate while listening. In the early years the music was always by Germans— Bach, Beethoven, Brahms, Schumann, Wagner—with none by Russian or Slavic composers. I came to know full symphonies; piano, violin and flute concertos; and now including Jewish composers such as Mendelssohn and Bruch. We also enjoyed popular overtures or sung arias. The music added a new richness, a novel dimension to my life, replacing the remembered faint strains of Egyptian tunes and the chants of the Qur'an from my earlier childhood.

Dignified aging Oma and Opa

My grandparents listened in silence, quietly consuming their refreshments, exchanging only a few words between the compositions. If the song was "Der Linden Baum," Opa on the sofa and Oma in her chair never failed to lock eyes as if hypnotized. They sang along, a duet, their bodies swaying in unison.

> *Outside the gate's a fountain*
> *And an old linden tree*
> *Under its shady branches*
> *My dreams were sweet and free*
> *I carved in its old bark*
> *So many phrases dear*
> *In times of joy and sadness*
> *It always drew me near.*

It seemed to transport them to an earlier period in their lives, a time of tenderness, passion, and binding love. I cherished hearing them sing, and could feel the deep, enduring devotion of the parents I had adopted.

17

LAND OF HOPE AND GLORY

Without courage, all other virtues lose their meaning.
—Sir Winston Churchill

Cleaved from Oma's side, despite my protestations, I was taken to England. This consolidated Oma as the "other woman" phenomenon in my life.

It took me a moment to realize as I awoke that I was in Manchester. It was cold and damp. Stiff, heavy blankets covered the double bed. I missed my soft duvet.

The woman who *now* called herself Mummy lay beside me. To me she remained Mother. Gulnar lay on her other side and they murmured to each other in companionable German. The Mummy woman addressed me: "Now let's learn some English." Pointing toward the early morning, she pronounced, "Window." Beyond the filmy curtain, it was grey with rain. She nudged me. "Say: w-i-n-d-o-w."

Parrot-like I repeated it. Gulnar said it too.

"*Gut.*"

Pointing to the door, she uttered its name. We followed.

"Why do I have to learn English?" I said in German.

"You're going to school. Don't you want to understand your friends?"

Didn't she know I had no friends in England?

She'd visited Wedel at the beginning of summer, 1952, and informed us that we would be returning with her to Manchester. I heard the words, but her message was meaningless. Why would I leave Oma and my dog to go to England after the summer? What would this German boy do there? What was the sense of this, when I was doing well at school? I liked my teachers. I had gotten to know some of my extended family, Tante Irma and Tante Elsa, and Frau Beckman, our downstairs neighbor, who was a White Russian fleeing the communists. I was making some headway with Renate. Why would I want to leave all this? My mother must not understand that Wedel was now my *Heimat*— my motherland, where I belonged. Oma was my mother. I felt comfortable; I knew my community, language, traditions, the scents and sounds of this place.

Sitting on our hill I told Renate that I was leaving Wedel for Manchester. She drew up her legs, hugged her knees, and rested her head on them, glancing sideways at me. With a hint of disappointment in her face, she stared at me silently. The intensity of her gaze made me uncomfortable and I turned away. I told her that when I got to Manchester, I'd write a card, and that I would probably return to visit my grandparents for the following Easter, and that we should meet. She cheered up before departing. When we met next, her mother had neatly written her address out on a piece of paper, which she handed to me.

I had dreaded the Mutti woman's arrival; she intruded on my stable world, where she did not belong. When she came up the wooden staircase in Wedel, our curious neighbors who had not seen her for some time greeted her. I had wanted to hide under Oma's voluminous apron, hoping I would not be found—a fantasy. Thinking of Oma rekindled my sense of emptiness and longing.

I had not wanted to be taken away from the woman who had given me a reliable, stable home, who had cared for me, nourished me, tutored, and loved me. When I had a hole in my sock, Oma darned it. I cried bitterly when I had to leave my Oma. She had become my steady beacon, helping me realize the preordained mold—a miniature Steinbach. She had shaped me to become a proud German.

Even Opa had boosted my confidence. He taught me how to get Bobby to obey me, how to be his master. *Selbst ist der Mann* —a man relies on himself—was his constant mantra. It is from Opa that I learned to do tasks right away, not procrastinate. He would tell me, "*Morgen, morgen, nur nicht heute, sagen alle faulen Leute*"—Tomorrow, tomorrow, not today is what all lazy people say. It stuck with me for life: I became a doer.

In Manchester, I felt embarrassed asking Mother to address a card for me. I wrote "Greetings from Manchester," no doubt misspelling every word. Now looking back, I wonder if I should have written a fuzzier, warmer message to Renate. I really needed her friendship in every sense of the word then, when I was alone and had no friends, no close female in my life. Gulnar didn't seem to exist, always sullen and self-absorbed, and Mother's five-year distancing left me with a sense of resentment toward her. The opposite sex was and remained so important to me all my life. I found women more interesting to talk to and be around than a bunch of boys, and later in life, men.

Facing the challenge of learning yet another new language and culture, I felt an acute sense of anxiety; I would be an outsider again. I would have to make new friends. With a different school and language came the risk of academic failure. Perhaps these forebodings were the effects of being tired from the train and boat trip from Hamburg.

My eyes wandered about the room, taking in my new surroundings. I wondered what I was doing there. I resented the demands she was making of me. Why did I have to get to know her and to learn English? I hardly knew the absent man, the one we were to call Daddy. He had gone to Egypt to attend Sit Nazifa's funeral and would be returning with Tante Souad, his second half-sister, who was about 24 years old, and considered almost over the hill. She was coming to meet her fiancé, Mohamed, a student at Manchester University and my grandfather's nephew —the son of the *omda* of our Upper Egyptian village. Daddy and Souad's ship from Alexandria was due to dock in Liverpool in about a week.

My parents had rented a huge room on the top floor of the Islamic Center. It was in an old, decaying Victorian mansion in the Victoria Park Estate, Moss Side, surrounded by neglected gardens and similarly decaying mansions. Overgrown rhododendron bushes and climbing ivy hid the sooty facade. The lawn was more moss than grass, contained by a crumbling stone wall. If the wall collapsed, the turf would cascade like a mudslide onto the pavement.

I got the impression that the large, drafty room was my parents' residence while they both were at the university—she a student, completing her studies in psychiatric social work, he building a department of Arabic and writing a new PhD thesis. The Islamic Center was only a three pence bus ride east of the campus.

During the first few days we were together, my mother never ceased to complain about the smell of curry emanating from a small communal kitchen on the second floor. The majority of the Center's residents were Pakistani students, with an occasional Indian or Malay. Did it ever occur to her that they found the odious smells of boiled cabbage from her cooking distasteful? Mother had little tolerance for what she called "their muckiness in the kitchen." To avoid them, she cooked in her room on a set of gas burners.

She complained about the increased noise level echoing up to the top floor along the central, majestic marble staircase when the number of occupants—all young men—swelled each Friday morning as graduate students from around the greater

Manchester area congregated at communal mid-day prayers in the first-floor front room. Once an elegant parlor, it was now devoid of furniture except for a billiard table and a threadbare, crimson carpet. Following prayers, a fair number of those other students stayed with friends for the weekend, so the general activity, the banging of doors, flushing of toilets, and kitchen activities, increased. Mother grumbled as the cooking smells multiplied and the pervasive odors revolted her.

Daddy had rented a smaller room for his sister's anticipated arrival at the other end of the corridor facing the front of the mansion. It had possibly once been a former servant's room, and although narrow, it accommodated two beds. Souad would live there, eating with us, until Daddy could complete the marriage arrangements just before Ramadan.

The plan, Mother cheerfully related, was that once married, Mohammed and Souad would move into this large room facing the back of the mansion. It was divided in two by a mammoth curtain—one part a bedroom, the other living room/kitchenette. We, being a family once more, would move into a rental house, away from Victoria Park to the newer neighborhood of semi-detached homes built in pre-war Manchester.

Marwan with bobby pin

Since I arrived in early October after the school year began and did not speak English, I was held back, placed into second grade at Burnage Preparatory School. We did very little academics compared to the third-grade class in Wedel, and I was bored. The school was a six-pence, thirty-minute bus ride away. I always wanted to sit in the front row on the top deck, but feared missing my stop if I did.

I loved the school uniform; for the first time I wore a tie, making me feel grown up, although Mother's insistence that I use a bobby pin to keep my hair out of my eyes detracted from the feeling and added to my embarrassment, particularly when some called me a sissy.

The school building took the shape of a letter H, with administrative offices on the second floor of the central arm and classrooms on the ground floor. It was probably built before the war. The walls were made of blocks of glass containing embedded chicken wire to prevent shattering. I sat at a standard desk-bench combination in the second row with a wide view of the grassy playing field through the sidewalls.

Miss Hedwig, my teacher, was ancient compared to the young German teachers I was accustomed to, but she spoke some German, which endeared her to me. Like most elderly teachers at the time, she wore heavy, dark blue wool clothes with multiple layers because of the inefficient pre-war central heating. She was a head taller than I was, and wore long skirts, heavy stockings, and sturdy lace-ups with a heel, like Oma. The children had much more freedom to talk during class, and at recess played noisily, running about on a green sport ground the length and width of a football field—quite a contrast to ABC's gravel schoolyard. Miss Hedwig was kind to me, perhaps remembering how her parents had come to England from Germany after the Great War and she, too, had had to learn a new language.

On returning home from one of the first days at school, I was surprisingly upbeat, elated, and hopeful for the future. The children were cheerful, happy, and played readily with each other, unlike the pupils at the ABC school who seemed insular and restrained by discipline, probably since most were newly arrived and had not yet formed the bonds of community. At eight, I was the tallest and the oldest, and although I struggled with learning English, I knew all the math quizzes. During break, my new class acquaintances would approach me, asking my name and trying to introduce themselves, which left me puzzled.

I asked Mother, in German, why the children all had the same first name.

"What do you mean?"

"They come up to me and say, 'Call me Peter,' 'Call me John,' or 'Call me Andrew.' They're all named 'Call me.'" She laughed and explained what it meant. I felt silly but was pleased they seemed to like me.

School started early with our first break at 10 a.m. Most of the boys ate a sandwich and drank a mandatory half-pint of vitamin D-fortified bottled milk, for rationing still existed. The bottles were too cold, and I did not like the cream on top of the cold milk, so I replaced my bottle into the crate, only to have Miss Hedwig discover a full bottle. She scolded me, emphasizing its goodness, saying it was free, and in fact compulsory, and if I did not like it cold, I should put a bottle on the lukewarm radiator next to my desk immediately on entering the class. Warm milk tasted worse. I had not drunk milk in Egypt or Germany and did not like it—cold or warm. A tough boy named Roy, who sat next to me, was overjoyed at getting a second bottle, and guzzled it down in what looked like three to four gulps each day with his Miracle bread sandwich. This arrangement worked well until one day when Roy was sick and Miss Hedwig discovered two undrunk bottles. She made me drink my bottle in front of the jeering class. Nevertheless, I felt much happier in this school than in the ABC School in Germany; my new friends lived in the neighborhood, were sociable, and I could easily do the schoolwork, which I had already covered in Wedel.

I soon made a friend called Andrew. He was cheerful, inquisitive, and quick to smile. I got the impression that his contentment was rooted in his secure family life and lay in his confidence and thoughtfulness. He also seemed somewhat lonely, just like me. He always wore grey—grey shirt with a school tie, grey shorts with knee-length grey woolen socks, and a grey ribbed V-neck pullover with a tri-color border at the neck, which passed as the school uniform. He talked incessantly about Dan Dare, Pilot of the Future, who fought little green Martians about to conquer the earth, from the boy's comic magazine, *The*

Eagle. He invited me over to his cozy house after school to play, and often to stay for dinner.

After school, we would lie on his bedroom carpet poring over *The Eagle*, looking at the colorful pictures of Dan Dare, with Andrew reading to me about the exploits of the green Martians. *The Eagle's* centerfold had detailed, cutaway diagrams of World War II bombers, racing cars and other sophisticated machinery. Andrew explained that he was a member of The Eagle Club, showing me his membership card and badge. This was the first time I had seen a magazine specifically for children. I was envious. Andrew told me he bought it with his pocket money and it arrived every Friday. I too wanted to get a weekly comic. I too wanted to belong to the very exclusive boys' club. However, I did not get pocket money, so I did not think it was possible.

He showed me his set of Enid Blyton books, which actually belonged to his older sister who was at boarding school. This particular Blyton series was about four schoolchildren and their dog, and their adventures. The stories took place on an island and included a mad professor. Occasionally the children stumbled onto smuggler's tunnels or pirate's treasure. When he lent me *Five on a Treasure Island,* I learned English while catching up on the escapades of the four schoolchildren and their dog.

Andrew's portly father was a kind man, with a patient, smiling face. He made me feel welcomed and at home. Over dinner, I learned he was a bookie who ran an off-track betting shop, gambling on horseracing. Seeing my fascination, he explained his work in detail. It was the first time I had heard about another father's job. Sitting at the dinner table, I suddenly felt quite grown up being brought into his confidence. I saw Andrew often, forming my first comfortable boy-to-boy bond. I enjoyed having a close friend and it added to my gradual transformation into an English schoolboy.

Daddy and Tante Souad arrived. Instead of this being the joyous occasion we had anticipated, she was tearfully sniffling and had dark rings under her eyes. After cursory greetings, she immediately retreated to her room. Daddy explained that when they had arrived in Liverpool there was no fiancé to meet them. He had broken off their marriage. On hearing this, she had thrown her engagement ring into the Mersey.

"Why didn't you leave her in Cairo?" my mother asked. Daddy was taken aback. He repeated that he had only discovered the betrayal in Liverpool. Mother refused to believe him, cynically saying that his sister would be an intrusion, a burden, and he should send her back to Egypt. Daddy argued that Mohamed had probably just gotten cold feet. When he had a chance to talk to Mohamed, and when Mohamed met Souad, Daddy would be able to smooth matters out. Mother was contemptuous of Daddy's assertions and accused him of always putting his Egyptian family first. They argued.

Gulnar and I witnessed Mother's escalating attacks, hurled at Daddy in a strident tone; she was merciless—vituperous and hurtful. He became agitated and defensive. He tried to tone the argument down, embarrassed that the whole Islamic Center must be hearing their quarrel. Mother said something abusive and insulting about his sister, and his "useless Egyptian family." The hurt on Daddy's face turn into rage. She had crossed some cultural line. He slapped her, counter to all Islamic strictures against the beating of women, in this case more to bring her to her senses than to hurt her. She struck back, and in a flash picked up a kitchen knife, shrieking, "I'll kill you!" She repeatedly slashed at the air. Daddy grabbed her hair, holding her at arm's length.

Gulnar and I sobbed, imploring them to stop. We wanted to separate them, but we were afraid we would get hurt if we stepped between them. Mother threw the knife into the sink and pushed Daddy aside on her way to confront Souad. A loud banging started on the locked door. The Egyptian couple in the next room yelled, "Is everything OK?" My parents were both panting, Gulnar and I terrified.

"Either she leaves or I will! I am not going to live with her in our midst," was Mother's ultimatum.

With that, Daddy stormed out of the room, down the stairs, past staring faces, and out of the Center. I ran after him as he headed through Victoria Park south toward High Street. He was a stranger, yet he was my Baba. I was afraid to approach him, fearing his anger. All my old feelings of affection for my Egyptian family, with their aura of kindness and love, flooded over me as I chased him. I wanted to cry out to him that he was right, that I supported him, and that I understood how unreasonable Mother was, that I wanted him more than I wanted the woman who called herself my mother, and he should not desert us.

By the time I caught up with him, he was boarding a bus heading in the direction of the university. He never looked over his shoulder to see me standing there, gasping for breath. Why was I frightened of this man? Why didn't I keep distance between us or shout out to him when I was chasing him? I know he would have stopped and cared for me. Just holding his hand and walking with him to where ever he was going would have helped us both . . . I think.

I walked back in the afternoon's gloom, kicking the wet chestnut leaves covering the pavement. I passed the red mailbox where I imagined the letters to Oma had been posted, crying to myself because we would never be a happy family. I blamed my mother for her intolerance and discontent, and for the first time was conscious of how much I hated her.

When I re-entered the large room, a helmeted police officer was taking statements. Mother wanted me to support her side of the story. I refused and left the room, not knowing what Gulnar had said. That night Mother locked us all out. We slept in Tante Souad's tiny room. She and Gulnar shared one single bed while Daddy and I shared the other. I lay in Daddy's spooning embrace and fell asleep exhausted, comforted by the scent of his skin, the fragrance of his favorite Pears soap, only to be awak-

ened by his shaking body. It was the first and only time that I
saw Daddy weep. I felt a deep, sympathetic pain in my chest as I
ran my hand over his curly hair. He tightened his hold on me
and kissed my forehead.

How my parents made up
would be pure speculation, but he
moved back into the big room
while we stayed with our aunt.
During mealtimes, the atmosphere
was cool, with minimal exchanges
between my parents, not unlike
Opa's typical sulk. Tante Souad
claimed she was not hungry,
continuing to refuse to eat. She
sniffled, holding onto soggy paper
tissues. Mother, not believing

*Stressed Dad, Souad & Egyptian
guests, Marwan and Gulnar*

Souad's claim of "non-hunger," periodically raided her room
searching for food. She was convinced Souad secretly ate food
given to her by the Egyptian family next door. When she found
some, she would produce it at meal times as evidence of Souad's
conniving. She felt that Souad was undermining her authority
and insisted Daddy book his sister's passage to Egypt immediately.

My parents each kept their pent-up, wounded emotions.
Mother was haughty and sulking and maintained the attitude
that she had the moral high ground. Daddy walked about as the
righteous wounded party, never smiling, his entire face tense, his
eyes turned down. It seemed they had difficulty communicating
with each other in an effort to resolve their differences. I
detested the atmosphere and felt like banging their heads
together.

When Daddy entertained colleagues and friends from Cairo,
Mother left for the day, refusing to entertain her husband's
guests. It was hard for us to maintain the semblance of a happy
family when the tension in the air was thicker than Mancunian

smog, but we tried our best to pretend all was well. I despised Mother for her vindictiveness. Until my aunt's departure, Mother maintained a frosty attitude, a stress on all the family.

Souad was friendly and deferential to me because I was the son of her elder brother. I spent much of my free time with her re-learning Arabic. We reminisced about the kindness, love, and comfort I had once known in Sayeda Zeinab.

By Easter 1953, a passage became available. I was sorry to see Souad leave for she was a reminder of the tranquil life in Cairo before I had been taken to Europe. Furthermore, she had reawakened my vestigial connections to my Egyptian family, culture, and language and reminded me that in spite of my German pride, Egyptian blood also coursed through my body.

My sorrow extended to Souad, who would return to Cairo as "damaged goods," and perhaps a sullied reputation for she had been rejected for marriage. Daddy took her to Liverpool where she boarded a passenger ship to Egypt. On its way to Singapore through the Suez Canal, the ship would stop at Port Said—the same port through which I had exited Egypt that dark night long ago, not knowing then what upheavals lay ahead of me.

18
_____

A FAMILY ONCE MORE

1952-1954

Our rented duplex in Wally Range

All happy families are alike; each unhappy family is unhappy in its own way.
—Leo Tolstoy

The semi-detached house, above, in the Wally Range, a suburb of Manchester, was sparsely furnished. It was near several bus routes for easy access to the town center and to Daddy's university. Gulnar walked to the local high school wearing the distinct school uniform: a blue cardigan over a white shirt with a school tie, a grey pleated skirt, white knee socks, and brown walking shoes. I continued at Burnage Preparatory School. It was a longer ride, but I did not have to change buses.

The house had a stained-glass window in its front door. The entrance led along a narrow hallway to a kitchen in the back, past a parlor and the dining room. The parlor had a piano and a drafty bay window overlooking a rose bed, with a low wall separating us from the relative quiet of the street. In the dining room, another impressive stained-glass window overlooked a large garden with a small frog pond. Off the entryway, a staircase led up to three bedrooms and a bathroom. Gulnar and I each had our own room; I could shut my door, lie on my bed to read, or build model airplanes without interruption.

For the first time in five years, we lived as a family. At last I had a home, unlike the orphan in the film I had seen in Wedel. Home meant living with a sense of comfort, harmony, and established roots, not a transitional place like Wedel where I had sometimes felt anxious, fearful, and lonely and my parents were my aging grandparents even though I did feel Oma's warmth and love for me.

Now that Tante Souad was out of the picture, there was amity between my parents. Although Daddy was busy writing, he was interested in our home activities, helped us with our schoolwork, and tucked us into bed at night while Mother washed the dishes. He would gently help me brush my teeth and wash my face. Once I was in bed, he improvised a song in English about his precious children, how clever and how wonderful they were, using encouraging and positive adjectives, and emphasizing that I was his valued son. Leaning over, he would kiss me on my cheek and invoke the Lord's blessings as he wished me a good night, calling to mind the spirit of my Cairo family—belonging, warmth, and togetherness.

During school holidays, Gulnar and I visited the university museums, learning about geological formations and rare elements. Daddy took me to the university to show off his office, with books and papers crowding out his desk space. We ate lunch in the cafeteria, where I was treated to a Bakewell tart for dessert. I slowly nibbled it to prolong the joy of its sweet taste and his company, and to my delight, he did not attempt to pinch a piece or ask me to share. Needing his cup of tea, he led me across the campus to the staff's common room, where a sprinkling of faculty was reading the paper or snoozing in plush armchairs. Daddy sipped his tea and I sat in an armchair that nearly swallowed me up. When I did not understand the gold relief sculpture set in the distant wall, Daddy whispered the meaning of "Silence is Golden." I could never get enough of his attention or his casual touching, and I relished being alone with him.

Mother, like Oma and Opa, did not hug, kiss, or ever say "I love you." She occupied herself with shopping, meals, and purchasing new clothing for growing Gulnar and me until she found employment as a Psychiatric Social Worker for the Manchester City Council. She became animated when she read us excerpts from my dear Oma's frequent letters describing events in Wedel—a reminder of the distant world I had adjusted to but was now eager to forget due to the painful parts and the loneliness.

Returning from school one day, Gulnar brought home a kitten. Mother let her keep it despite Daddy's lack of enthusiasm for the stray, which Gulnar named *Kunterbunt*—calico, in German—although he stipulated that it could not sleep in her bedroom. One evening when Gulnar did not feel well, Mother persuaded Daddy to let his daughter sleep with her and he reluctantly took himself to Gulnar's bed. In the middle of the night Daddy awoke in a panic, shrieking with fright. He stormed out of Gulnar's room, yelling that someone had tried to strangle him in the dark. Kunterbunt had slinked into Gulnar's room, alighted on the bed, and plunked herself across Daddy's neck.

The cat was put out into the autumn night and Gulnar was put back in her own bed.

On my way home from school one day, I came across a hedgehog. I knelt on the pavement and studied it. He did not seem to mind my close attention; he stared at me kindly, his beady eyes studying me and perhaps wondering about my intentions. I was overcome with empathy and love for this beautiful creature. He was not a dog, but he could become my personal pet—Prickly, I would call him. I gently placed him into my school cap, and talking to him, I slowly walked home, admiring his dark eyes and little feet. Mother was not impressed, nor did she share my affection for the creature, as he nibbled on a salad leaf.

"No, you cannot keep him. They are full of fleas." With that, she placed him on a newspaper and took him out into the back garden. Despite my protestations, she released Prickly near the pond, depriving me of a pet who could have become a friend. I was angry and saw her actions as favoritism toward my sister. I would frequently go into the garden looking for Prickly, but never caught sight of him again.

Central heating was not yet a standard feature and homes were drafty. Cast-iron fireplaces in each room were modified to burn gas rather than rationed coal. An on-off switch controlled the rate of flow—the amount of heat. We had to feed coins into a meter box set in the hearth; once we heard the gas flow, we lit it with a long candlewick that caught with a whoosh and instantly began to radiate heat. Dressed in layers, and huddling as close as the four of us could get, our fronts and feet soon became steamy warm while our backs remained frozen, even when covered with several wool sweaters. Mother hung a heavy blanket from a rod across the closed door, which kept the drafts out, as did the heavy blanket roll at the bottom.

Apart from books and magazines, the radio on the mantle was our entertainment. During the week, we religiously listened to the six o'clock BBC news, a habit to this day. Unlike Oma, Mother did not bake and I missed the permeating aroma of fresh cakes. Nonetheless, at teatime we enjoyed an assortment of British biscuits and tarts. Late Sunday afternoons, we gathered cozily about the fire and drank hot cocoa, riveted to a one-hour serial enactment of *The Mill on the Floss* as we ate cold sandwiches from Sunday's lunchtime. Mother shifted the furniture around to better suit our lifestyle. She reversed the functions of the parlor and the dining room. The late afternoon sun shone cheerily through the stained-glass window into our new backroom parlor, which became the hub of our family congregation for warmth and activity. She also rearranged the furniture so it was closer to the hearth—the room's centerpiece.

Gulnar (12), and Marwan (10), with Daddy, preoccupied, irritable, and tense.

On several occasions, when Mother went food shopping, she returned to find that the landlord had rearranged the furniture to its original positions. When I came home from school, I had an eerie feeling, knowing that perhaps someone had walked through my bedroom, even touching my precious stamp collection or model airplanes. Unable to get him to stop, my parents took him to court for trespassing, and the proceedings became our first civics lesson. He had leased the property to us, we paid our monthly rent, and he was intruding. An injunction prevented him from entering the house and the locks were changed.

In Wedel, Gulnar had studied piano as a reason for staying late after school, avoiding Opa. The upright black piano, now standing to the left of our new dining room's bay window, led to Mrs. Polanyi coming once a week to give Gulnar lessons. At the initial visit, Mrs. Polanyi suggested in her slight Polish accent that we needed to get the instrument tuned, that Gulnar held potential, and with the right instructions and practice she had a promising future. She said I, too, was not too young to begin to learn—all very convincing news to Mother's ears.

After the piano was tuned, Mrs. Polanyi artfully arranged small busts of Bach, Beethoven, Mozart, and Haydn on the mantle as an introduction to these composers, and Gulnar's lessons began. I confessed I was not too eager, though I did not want to disappoint my mother. My protestations were overruled. It was almost as inexpensive to teach two children as one, and Mrs. Polanyi was a convincing saleswoman taking advantage of a mother's ambitions for her children. I reluctantly began, and with this came a maternal daily nagging that I practice, practice, practice. I did not mind doing the scales, but the musical pieces held a very low priority on the list of things I wanted to do. I would much rather be outside, playing by the pond in the garden.

There was no escaping Mrs. Polanyi. Piano lessons continued. She would play a new piece and I would repeat it. No matter how hard I tried, reading notes on the sheet music was challenging. I cheated by reproducing what I had heard, giving the impression that I was reading the notes. She was impressed at first, but by the spring of 1954 began to suspect my profound limitations.

Musical notation was just a jumble of squiggles—a unique language. It was the fourth new language I needed to learn in ten years, after Arabic, German, and English. When I learned

German, I forgot Arabic. This was particularly embarrassing to my father and to me, since Daddy's Egyptian friends came to visit and we could only converse in English. I was acutely aware of my inadequacy. When I learned English, I might have forgotten German, except that Mother spoke to us in a mixture of both, constantly refreshing my memory.

In German, every letter is pronounced. Why in English did certain letters not contribute to the sound of a word? It made spelling senseless. Music, too, was a language, a code. I had learned my fill, and my brain could not absorb any more at this time. After a while, and despite my difficulties, Mrs. Polanyi signed me up for the Grade I (Primary) examination in music for the Pianoforte at The Associated Board of the Royal School of Music. It had the desired effect: I practiced and practiced.

I was put to the test. I sat next to an examiner in a state of panic. For every ten-minute test segment—exercises, scales, broken chords, playing by sight-reading, and study and pieces from List A—I barely scraped through, averaging one or two points above the passing grade. The shame of publicly demonstrating my lack of skill was torture. Only in the aural tests did I get 18 points out of 18. My total grades were 113 out of 150, with a passing grade of 100. To my dismay, the examiner stated in his report that I was "...a very promising student," adding "but he must improve his sight-reading."

I was thankful when, after a few months, Mrs. Polanyi retired, because Mother was tired of nagging me to practice and Gulnar did not like Mrs. Polanyi's style of teaching compared to her instructor in Germany. For me playing the piano became history.

Once I had a reasonable command of English, thanks to the private lessons Miss Hedwig had given me, I advanced to a higher class commensurate with my age. In the spring term of 1953, I moved into Miss Jones's fourth grade. I immediately liked my new classmates; I was one of them, just as old and physically developed. The boys were rougher, played soccer at almost every school break, and although I frequently met Andrew on the playing fields, sadly, we grew apart. He tended to be a loner and was too shy to join my new friends. I did not miss Roy the Guzzler, because we no longer had to drink milk since rationing had ended.

*Marwan at Burnage Preparatory School 1954. Janet is
standing above him in the top row.*

After school, we formed a gang led by a different Roy, one who was tough and quick to raise his fists. We had rules and secrets, even matches and cigarettes. Roaming the alleyways and passages between the back yards of neighborhood buildings, we teased the most popular girls, including Wendy and Margaret, and chanted a ditty that Roy taught us:

> *She wears red feathers and a huly-huly skirt*
> *She lives on just coconuts and fish from the sea*
> *A rose in her hair a gleam in her eyes*
> *And love in her heart just for me.*

Singing while giggling made us feel like naughty adults. We roved about, looking for mischief, flexing our young muscles and feeling the strength of our numbers.

I fancied a tall, shy girl—Janet. Not only was she the prettiest, but also clever and knew all the answers. Janet had curly blond hair and two braids crowning a pale face with beguiling, inquisitive eyes and an inviting smile. I was too embarrassed to befriend her, fearing exposure of my amorous feelings, despite the fact that her gaze followed me about the class. She reminded me of Renate, though taller and thinner, more delicate-looking, and with the same alluring appeal. She was constantly on my mind, and when I mentioned her name at home, Mother said she knew her father through her work. He was the hospital administrator, and they lived near us. After that, we occasionally played together with Gulnar and Janet's older brother. I remained coy about my feelings toward her, hiding my longing to be close to her.

Her birthday party was on a warm, dry Saturday afternoon. The other children from our class were noisy as they ran about her garden. Every time I turned around Janet bumped into me. Her mother attempted to direct and regulate the activities, but the children, refusing instructions, were rowdy, raiding the table laden with food, helping themselves to the sandwiches and biscuits before the birthday cake, and playing games in a frenzy for prizes. Her mother would gaze at Janet in frustration while she continued to attempt to corral her visitors. Even with my reservations about her controlling mother, Janet's admiration of me added to my comfort at being in England.

My friends and I joined the soccer team. Mother took me to a sports shop and I tried on a pair of soccer cleats. They fit and I liked them, but they were relatively expensive. Instead of telling me so, she said, "Oh, you'll not use them enough," and, "You won't like playing soccer that much." Her statements angered me. I wanted to be worth the expense to her. Did she not want me to play my best? How was I to play soccer without cleats? What would my friends say? It evoked the memory of Gitta mocking me for wearing Gulnar's underpants.

It affected my self-confidence. I joined the team as quarterback, appearing in English plimsolls, a shoe with a canvas upper and rubber sole intended for beachwear. These did not allow me to generate sufficient force to kick the ball straight. In the middle of the first practice, I walked off, humiliated and angry with myself and with Mother for my ineffective participation.

On Sports Day, I had no suitable attire, giving the embarrassing impression that we were poor. The other children were fully decked out in sporting gear; some even had running shoes with spikes. Wearing my plimsolls and school uniform, I nevertheless came in first in the twenty-five and then the fifty-yard race. Each time I won three pence. I did not do well in the three-legged race with my friend Graham, or in the race where I had to balance an egg on a spoon.

The other children gathered with their families after the races, but mine had not come. Once more I felt let down, shamed that they did not value my activities sufficiently to cheer me on from the sidelines. With my winnings, I bought two Wall's ice cream cones, each with a chocolate flake bar stuck into the top, and slunk behind the school buildings to devour them.

Daddy was very proud of my promotion to the higher class. The downside was that he started to nag me to do my homework. My advancement and Daddy's momentary delight emboldened me to ask him for some pocket money.

"What for? You have everything you need," was his reply. I confessed that I frequently walked one bus stop closer to home from school because it reduced my fare by three pence. I jangled the coins in my pocket and told him that I occasionally bought sweets. We were standing in the hallway and he looked down at me strangely.

"Wait here." He came back with a blank white 5x7 card. We sat at the dining table. "How much do you want?"

"Half-a-crown." Two shillings and sixpence.

"Half-a-crown a month? What will you do with so much money?"

"I want to buy *The Eagle* every week, and join the boys' club

like my friends, and go to the cinema on Saturday mornings. . ."
I hated the quizzing. The old feeling, first experienced at the
Wedel Fair, of being unworthy gripped my stomach. Maybe I
did not deserve pocket money like all my friends. *It does not have
to be half-a-crown*, I thought, *just say you love me, and give me a
little bit of money.*

"All right," he said. Taking the card, he wrote on the top
line: credit. Beneath it, he wrote: half-a-crown. Then he flipped
the card over and wrote debit. "Do you know what this means?"

"No."

"It means that every month I'll write on the credit side half-
a-crown. That is what you earn, and every time you want money,
you ask me for it and I'll give it to you, and deduct it from your
credit. Just like the bank."

"But where is my money?" I said, holding out my hand.

"It's on the card," he replied.

I felt cheated. I wanted to hold the coins in my hand, to
jingle them about in my pocket while in class. He walked away,
undoubtedly feeling he had taught me something valuable.
Perhaps he had, yet I had no money. The 5x7 credit/debit card
never reappeared, but to my joy, some boxes arrived through the
post containing several series of Enid Blyton books, and also *The
English Oxford Encyclopedia for Children*. I loved reading the
former and thumbing through the latter, especially when the
weather was dreary.

Roy and his "lieutenant," a meek boy named Nigel, told the
gang that the following Saturday there was to be a military
tattoo in the park and we should attend, and that they would be
there. Daddy took me. It was sunny. A band played rousing
patriotic music under the cover of a raised gazebo, while soldiers,
airmen, and sailors in dress uniform marched about the grounds,
changing formations in response to loud, sharp commands. A
passionate voice announced over speakers each regiment and
their heroic past. The crowds clapped and cheered enthusiastically, waving small Union Jacks. I joined in, enjoying the elabo-

rate entertainment. World War II Lancaster bombers and formations of Spitfire fighters flew overhead. These were the very planes that had defended Britain in the air battles and conquered the skies over Europe. Reading about them I didn't feel a sense of Germanness, such was my need to seek a present identity A squadron of jet fighters followed. The audience was jubilant. I was proud to be an English boy, and hoped my classmates would see me waving my new flag, though the dense crowds prevented me from spotting them.

With the end of sugar rationing in February of 1953, sweet shops cropped up everywhere, often next to a newsagent's shop by bus stops. I entered my very first, clutching a sixpence with my friends after school. The appealing aroma of sweets and the jars upon jars of toffees, jellies, and caramels overwhelmed me. There were lollipops, chocolate bars, and heaps of loose sweets that I had never seen or tasted before. Which should I buy with my silver coin? Yes, a quarter of a pound of sweets, I knew that, but which ones? It was too much to decide, and I walked out without spending my money that day. My friends followed, chewing as many toffees and licorice as they could shove into their mouths. Gradually I overcame my awe, and when given some small change for chores, I spent it on a variety of goodies.

Unexpectedly, *The Eagle* began coming through the mail drop every Friday morning, along with Daddy's *The Listener.* With its regular arrival, I felt a new emotional bond to Daddy. He had not forgotten his son. Yet there were times that he sowed the seeds of mistrust, such as when he played the trick of making a credit/debit card instead of placing money into my hands. On the other hand, I was his son and knew he valued me. We would be friends and allies our whole life—I could not imagine being without his support, guidance, and advocacy.

I lay on the carpeted floor looking at pictures of my favorite candies and their prices shown on the back page. There were various Cadbury bars, Kit-Kat chocolates, Turkish delights, and boxes of licorice. I spent hours early Saturday mornings while my parents were sleeping calculating which combination would buy me the most sweets for twenty shillings—one English pound—if I ever had that much. Then, after breakfast, Gulnar and I would take the bus to the local cinema.

The neighborhood Odeon, or Empire, or Rex were local institutions where the seats were all one price. Hordes of yelling and screaming children packed the theater, only occasionally accompanied by one or both adults. Kids ran up and down the aisles with ice creams or rock candy. We would finally settle in our seats when the music started and the lights dimmed to the sound of our cheers. The standard fare was serialized Hopalong Cassidy, or the Lone Ranger with his horse, Silver, and friend Tonto, an Indian, who called him the Apache name *Kemosabe*. The theaters showed cartoons and occasionally mini-documentaries. It was two hours of sheer delight. When it was over, parents would collect their broods in the cinema's foyer or just outside. Gulnar and I walked home alone contentedly as we chatted about the program.

That summer we spent a week on a family holiday in the Lake District, staying in bed and breakfasts. Despite the relentless steady rain, the dampness, and the constant grey sky, we visited the sights and the various lakes, traveling by antiquated public buses. We ate tomatoes, cucumber sandwiches, and nibbled at cold pork pies, squatting under barn eaves to remain dry, and visited the crowded Wordsworth and Keats Museums.

One Saturday morning, Gulnar and I were dispatched to see *Seven Brides for Seven Brothers*. We found it boring, so Gulnar persuaded me to take the bus back to where we were staying. We walked into the room to find our parents both naked in bed. I was not accustomed to seeing them in the buff; however, I recall feeling mostly annoyed. Somewhere in my mind, an irritating voice from the past, sounding like Opa, nagged that they had squandered the best part of the day.

On our return to Manchester before school started, Mother, reluctant to leave me alone at home, dragged me along on her numerous shopping forays. She would deposit me in a cinema showing animated cartoons intermingled with Pathé newsreels. The patrons were elderly, or parents with children having a break from shopping, or like me, children deposited there while their parents were otherwise busy in and about the city center. I would watch Bugs Bunny, Mr. Magoo, and my favorite, Tweetie Pie and Sylvester. I would sing along, "I tawt I taw a puddy tat a-creeping up on me." Seeing "That's all Folks!" unravel across the screen at the end of the reel gave me a sense of satisfaction.

For Easter 1954, Mother made plans to visit Oma and Opa, as well as the rest of the Steinbach family in Wedel. Gulnar and I would accompany her and Daddy would stay in Manchester. I took Renate a packet of PG Tips, at Mother's suggestion. She wrapped the package, saying that since Germans drank coffee, a packet of Britain's best tea would be a welcome present.

Renate and I met on the hill once more—a few days after my tenth birthday. She had grown, but she still had her blonde braids. Her budding breasts made me think of my exploratory foray in the woods with Gitta. My repeated and casual glances at her chest made her blush with self-consciousness. We were both awkward and said little. I sheepishly placed the packet on the grass between us and pushed it towards her. "A small present from me," was all I said. She hesitated for a moment before picking it up. "Thank you," was all she said.

It would be ten years before I next saw Renate.

———

Back home in Manchester, Gulnar's school friend Joan, who lived a few houses down the street, had a TV. She invited us to watch the coronation and we eagerly accepted, watching the pomp of Princess Elizabeth becoming our Queen in June of 1953. The TV screen was round and grey and the pictures were grainy. Despite the lengthy process, and much boredom, we saw the crown, the carriage leaving Buckingham Palace, the cheering crowds along Pall Mall, the proceedings in Westminster Abbey, and finally the Coronation. I heard the thunder and saw the fly-by of World War II planes. When the congregation sang "God Save the Queen," I stood at attention, filled with pride, feeling patriotic and very British. Gone was any lingering German identity.

Mother signed me up for the Brotherhood of British Scouts in the spring of 1954. I joined the 2nd Wally Range Wolf Cub Pack. The very word "brotherhood" excited me, with its promise of purpose and belonging. As a Cub, I wore a smart green pullover with a triangular yellow neckerchief, shorts, and knee-length woolen socks. Mother did not think I needed a special Boy Scout belt, which all the other boys had and I wanted. Once again, I wondered whether she truly loved me. I proudly wore a Cub Scout cap, on which I pinned my awards, first one star, and then two. Sewn on the pullover were the distinctive insignia of my pack and the two achievement badges I had earned: the collector's and the house orderly badge.

My ten-year-old self greatly enjoyed being a valued Cub Scout member—part of a pack. We built campfires on weekend hikes and at overnight tenting. Saluting, we recited the oath, and when it came to, "I will do my duty as a scout, to my God, and Queen, and Country," my chest swelled with British pride. By actively incorporating Boy Scout values—working to be reliable, helpful to others, polite and obliging, friendly to animals, and self-reliant—I felt my character developing.

Daddy came home one day in early May, pronouncing that when school ended for the summer, our family would *permanently* return home to Cairo. Again, I did not want to understand.

Home, Daddy, home? England may not be your home, but it is mine, I thought. *My being, my spirit, my soul chooses England. I am not compelled to be someone else's child. I am doing well in school. I like my teachers, they like me. I have school friends who invite me over in the afternoon. I play with their dogs. I am invited* to stay for dinner. Yes, an English dinner, unlike Abendbrot. Dinner, a welcomed hot meal at the end of the day. My friends' parents chat with me. I have learned English. We play, read, and have fun in the ways families do. Germany has long ago ceased to be my home and Egypt is a very, very distant memory. This is my home, Daddy.

Late that same spring, Miss Hedwig asked me to assist her in creating two flowerbeds. I spent a sunny afternoon working, trying not to think of what uncertainties lay ahead. I wore my Cub Scout outfit. She told me that when the plants bloomed in autumn, she would think of the young boy who entered her class two years earlier, not speaking English. I was glad to return her kindness. In the bright sun, she took several photos of me working in her garden. Among the eight pictures she sent me, the one I cherish most is the image captured by a self-timer of us standing together, her arm about my shoulder, both smiling. I was now as tall as she was.

Miss Hedwig and I

19

UPROOTED YET AGAIN
JULY 1954

A bad word is like a bad tree, uprooted from the surface of the earth,
not having any stability.
Qur'an 14:26

Despite my repeated protestations, tea chests, trunks, and suitcases appeared. The packing ritual I had first witnessed in Cairo recurred. I repeated my claim that England was my home more forcefully. To strengthen my argument, I added that both Daddy and Mother had been educated here. Although my parents heard my assertions with sympathetic ears, preparations advanced unabated.

Our departure from Manchester was delayed when, in July, Daddy developed nervous exhaustion, warranting admission to the neurological ward at the Manchester Royal Infirmary. He suffered from general weakness, fatigue, and a burning in his left calf. A viral diagnosis was made.

Recently I had the chance to read his diary where he documented his symptoms during his ten-day hospital stay. His main complaint was left-sided body numbness, tingling of hand and foot, accompanied by a burning sensation and inability to walk or bear his weight on his left leg. The neuropathy flitted from one limb to another, to his face and lips, and made swallowing of food difficult.

Given that the event occurred in the wake of the polio epidemic, and that he had suffered from polio as a child, the symptoms detailed in his diary are consistent with post-polio syndrome. This condition had not become a recognized clinical entity at the time. Now we understand that the condition affects polio survivors' years after recovery from an initial acute attack of the poliomyelitis virus. Most often, polio survivors start to experience gradual neuropathies and new weakening in muscles that were previously affected by the infection. The patients present with slowly progressive muscle weakness, generalized and muscular fatigue and muscle atrophy. He was treated with bed rest, physical therapy and Vitamin B12 injections while in hospital and for four weeks after discharge.

Mother became helpless, drifting about the house unsure if she should continue to pack. Her ambivalence left me uneasy.

Daddy looked haggard, grey, and tired when we visited him. As he embraced Gulnar and me, his loss of robustness alarmed me. He held us for a long time. He tried to be cheerful, but his voice was feeble. Addressing Mother, the neurologist reported that all the tests they had done were normal and that Daddy's discharge was imminent. This news did not quell my anxiety. He looked sick—he was sick and perhaps he would die. I could not imagine life without him. He had overworked himself. He had wrapped up his five-year appointment at the university developing an Arabic department, while also successfully defending a doctoral thesis. On top of that, he tried hard to please his wife, who wanted him to find another job in England. Perhaps, too, the anticipation of returning to the uncertainty of life and career in Cairo, and the huge responsibility he bore to his family—particularly the aging Sheikh Amin, who had lost Sit Nazifa—weighed on him.

After Daddy's discharge, tensions between him and Mother grew. While Mother was eager to see her family in Germany before we would leave Europe, she was displeased about our return to Egypt, where he would resume the mantle of the oldest son; she did not like competition for his attention, and resented what she saw as his large family's overdependence on him. Plans to leave Manchester progressed quickly.

The tea trunks swallowed Daddy's books. Our stylish, 32-piece pink and grey dinnerware set from John Lewis was carefully packed. The six-piece Georgian silver tea and coffee set, engraved with "AM" for Abdel Meguid, also vanished into the trunks. Mother planned to use it when entertaining her foreign ladies for tea, despite that she drank only coffee. It was only when I raised the question of taking my books that there was a pause. Yes, the seven volumes of the *Oxford Children's Encyclopedia* would come; perhaps some of the Enid Blyton volumes, too.

"What about my subscription to *The Eagle*?"

"Ah! We will have to cancel that."

"It's my favorite comic."

"You'll probably get it in Egypt," was the reply. I was not convinced.

"And Kunterbunt?"

There was no reply.

––––––

The benefits of my father's book royalties were beginning to add comfort to our lives. A shiny, metallic-blue 1954 VW beetle awaited us on our arrival in Wedel. Built in Wolfsburg, it had magical Germanic properties in Mother's mind. She gently took her first car through its paces; she would be the sole driver. Daddy had had a secondhand Humber when he was a student in Exeter in the 1930s, but he no longer wished to drive.

Opa had mellowed. He was less assertive. Wearing his usual sea cap, he carefully attached a luggage rack to the top of the car, stood back, and then preached to my parents how to care for their new toy. He let his daughter and Daddy make packing decisions. His demeanor toward us, too, had changed. He no longer bossed us about. He had a greater degree of self-control in expressing his opinions and anger. Oma continued to abide by his mealtime schedule, and had to ask him to take Bobby out—a habit Opa sometimes neglected. He was slowing down, though at the time I did not understand it as a normal process, so the changes unsettled me.

My earlier feelings about Mother, of alienation and indifference almost to the point of hatred, seeped back as she took up her old habits. She became preoccupied and once more neglectful of me. She and Daddy went to Hamburg during the day, leaving me to do nothing in Wedel. She took my dependence as a drain, and my innate affection for granted. I continued to thirst for her attention, and sorely needed her warmth and affection. I saw her through a growing lens of bitterness, which incrementally magnified over time. Yet I could not defend myself against these intense feelings. I lacked an inner sense of having been valued inordinately by her at the start of my life—and even now in this time of stressfulness. Furthermore, the presence of my adopted mother, Oma, and the biological one—Mother, confused me emotionally. I drifted psychologically. Once more Oma provided warmth, comfort and food. Mother was a mere inanimate object whose social position demanded respect and attention. In *who* should I invest my emotions, my love and loyalty? And Gulnar? Well she just created her own world and went her own way without me.

Perhaps Oma said something to my parents about my moping about and missing them, because on their next excursion, both Gulnar and I were taken along. Once in the center of Hamburg's shopping area, we seemed to wander from one shop to another. I did not know what they were looking for, nor could I decipher a plan, but at least the sun was shining. We walked up and down Mönkberg Strasse toward the *Rathaus*, or City Hall, and back, darting in and out of shops. They were trying to buy last-minute items in Europe before returning to Egypt. This pointless mission went on for hours. I began to complain of hunger and tiredness brought on by the lengthy stretches of purposeless walking. My complaints were ignored, as if to say, "That will teach you to want to come with us." I became crankier. We continued aimlessly window-shopping, crossing from one side of the street to another, dodging the trams.

They promised that if I stopped complaining we would go to the Berg Strasse Kaffeé—Mother's favorite coffee house and hangout, where I could have a cake or an ice cream. We got there shortly after three and there were no sandwiches left. I wanted an ice cream sundae like the picture in the menu.

"It's huge. You will never eat all that," both my parents claimed after they ordered coffee and a modest piece of cake.

"I am hungry and thirsty," I replied.

"It's too much for you. You will be sick. It's so expensive."

"You promised," I said.

"Well, you will have to eat all of it," Mother said.

When the small Everest was placed in front of me with a long teaspoon, I grinned with delight—I had always wanted one. Gulnar gazed wistfully down at her small scoop of ice cream, regretting succumbing to my parents' pressure. While my parents scarfed down their tiny cake, they kept eyeing my prize. I ate slowly, wanting to savor each bite and let the pleasure last.

Soon the harassment started. "Oh, look how slow he is eating it . . . it's too much for him . . . his eyes are bigger than his stomach," and so on. I resented these comments, but worse was to come. Soon spoons dived in from left and right, swooping down on my reward. I protested and whisked my glass away from the aerial attacks.

The outcome was that I never again accompanied them on their indecisive shopping trips. As an adult, I do not like sharing my food. If you want what I am eating, order it yourself. Lastly, I find purposeless shopping tantamount to torture.

My Oma—My loving mother

Since I no longer accompanied my parents on their day trips, I spent progressively more time with my Oma, re-establishing our close relationship. I was then Oma's height, and stole kisses from her on impulse when she was cooking or otherwise unable to fend me off gently. She had soft, full cheeks that felt delicious against my lips, and I sensed she truly loved being close. All she would say in protest was, "*Ach Junge, muss doch nicht,*" which translated roughly as, "You mustn't," which I took to mean, "Stop it, I like it." I think she adored having her grandson around again.

I had a profound sense of love for the warmth and steadfastness of the woman I considered my true mother. She always watched out for me, even when Mother was present. She darned my socks, ironed my shirts, sewed on my buttons, and washed my clothes, removing stubborn grass stains. Oma continued to give me unsolicited guidance about this or that. When I felt low, she remembered my sweet tooth and raised my spirits by slipping me my favorite sweet, or cake, or marzipan chocolate.

Mother & Oma in upstairs flat window

Before we left Wedel, Oma organized a Sunday afternoon coffee with Onkel Gerhard, Tante Irma, and their baby son Wolfgang, along with Onkel Willie and Tante Annie. There was the usual gorgeous spread of cakes, whipped cream, and strawberries, with coffee for all and tea for Daddy, accompanied by the strains of a soporific symphony in the background. The general discussion

concerned our route of travel south along the Autobahn across
Germany, through Austria to Salzburg and Vienna, and across
the Dolomite Mountains to Genoa to catch the *Esperia* to
Alexandria. I did not want to go, but there was no stopping us.

Shortly after the traditional 8 a.m. breakfast, and with the
car packed, the suitcases hoisted on the roof rack and covered by
a tarpaulin against the rain, Gulnar and I squeezed into the back
seat surrounded by cases, food baskets, and pillows. Only Opa
stood on the pavement to see us off. Oma stayed upstairs in their
flat, claiming that the situation was too emotionally over-
whelming.

Leaving her again was not easy. It seemed that I was always
leaving her, when in essence, I wanted her and needed her
emotional support and love. Deserting her reopened raw
wounds, and I was wretched at the separation.

The packed car and Mother with Opa

She, like the neighbors, looked out of the window while I
shed a silent tear. Opa waved goodbye and repeatedly yelled into
the open VW window *Gute Fahrt*—have a safe journey—
making me snicker because he did not know the English
meaning of fart. Waving our goodbyes, we set off on a trip our
parents called a great adventure.

Mother drove south on the Autobahn heading some 620 km
toward Landstuhl, near Frankfurt, where we planned to stop for

a few nights as guests of Onkel Hansi and Tante Trudel. Trudel was one of the young girls who had gone to England in the early 1930s and become friendly with my mother. They had remained in contact over the years. The stopover was a reunion, and a chance to meet Onkel Hansi.

Neither Onkel Hansi nor Tante Trudel were blood relatives; both the German and Egyptian cultures dignified my parents' friends with these lifelong titles. I found this practice comforting. Uncle Hansi, a lawyer, had been conscripted into the Wehrmacht's 6th Army legal unit. He was a captain when the Red Army surrounded it in Stalingrad in November, 1942. As a prisoner of war, he was pressed into forced labor until his repatriation in 1948.

When he returned, he was emaciated from the chronic starvation diet; he barely weighed 45 kg (slightly over 99 pounds). He had mild hepatitis and TB, and also suffered from several hypovitaminoses including Vitamin A deficiency, causing him night blindness.

In the years following Onkel Hansi's restoration to health and the resumption of his law practice, he exchanged his Mercedes-Benz every year for the latest model. He had built a new house with the compensation he received, consisting of full officer's pay through the end of the war, compensation for each month in captivity, veteran's benefits, and his pension that included the number of years he spent as a Soviet prisoner of war.

Onkel Hansi's office was on the first floor; his clients were mostly U.S. servicemen from the Ramstein airbase in nearby Kaiserslautern. During our visit, he did not think twice about driving us to his favorite restaurant, Le Coque D'Or,

Onkel Hansi, Tante Trudel

just across the French border. There, he ordered the best dishes and the finest wines. Even at home, they ate the freshest seasonal fare.

On occasion, his older brother Walter, who had been a Junker Ju-52 transport pilot, accompanied us. He had volunteered for the increasingly dangerous relief missions supplying the perilously besieged 6th Army stranded in Fortress Stalingrad with fuel, ammunition, rye-*Kommisbrot,* and tins of *Leberwurst* (hog-liver sausage) in worsening winter weather and fierce blizzards, as the Russian noose tightened around the entrapped army. He knew his younger brother was in the *Kessel*—the cauldron of the encircled army—but he could not know that he would not make it home for nearly a decade after the war.

Unlike Opa or Onkel Gerhard, Onkel Hansi was not reluctant to answer my numerous questions concerning his life during the war. I was fascinated, listening to the tales, and I admired how he forgave his captors, letting go of past suffering, hatred, and pain. "If I don't forgive, they'll constantly live with me. That's too great a burden." I admired his attitude towards the Russians and towards life. How many times I wished I could forgive Mother.

With a lightened heart, he was always jovial and unfailingly pronounced each day "a great day." He had an enviously infectious attitude, and Tante Trudel, infinitely supportive of him, never failed to spoil me with my favorite candies or cookies. I loved being with them in that very positive atmosphere. While the adults chatted throughout the day, I worked on building my model airplanes. Through the open window, I could hear the jets taking off from the nearby U.S. airbase. I would rush to the window with my camera, and could identify most of the jets flying overhead.

After a few days, we headed southeast along the Autobahn to Salzburg, then on to Vienna. I remember little of Mozart's Salzburg, only that we had to walk a lot. Although it was early summer, my recollections of Vienna were of a dreary, grey, cheerless city under post-war Soviet bureaucracy, full of army trucks belching black exhaust. We stayed a few days in a pensione. I ate yogurt for the first time with a layer of jam on the bottom of its glass container and saw Strauss's *Der Rosenkavalier* at the old Staatsoper Haus. More importantly, after the dark days of Manchester, in Vienna my parents were relaxed. They seemed young to me. I sensed their love for each other. They casually touched one another or briefly held hands, even if it was just crossing the street—little signs of affection I had never seen before. The regimented domestic routines orchestrated by parents during a busy workday were absent. For once, my father's nose was not in a book, nor was he writing one. Best of all, he was not nagging me about doing my homework. There was no tension, only harmony, in an otherwise dull Vienna. No doubt, Daddy was happy to have this family respite before he returned to Egypt.

Traveling across the Dolomites, on the other hand, was a frightening experience. The winding roads over the mountains were very narrow and hewn out of the hillsides. Fortunately, we started the crossing on a perfect late summer day. Mother drove our tightly packed VW cautiously. The engine groaned when she shifted into first or second gear. Italian drivers, more familiar with the terrain, frequently overtook us, blowing their horns, regardless of blind spots ahead, or plowed down in the opposite direction at reckless speeds. Our destination that night was an inn in Genoa. The following morning, we planned to leisurely embark on a modern passenger ship, the *Esperia,* which regularly plied the Mediterranean between Italian ports, Alexandria and Lebanese ports.

We crawled up the last mountain road leading to the Genoa plain at about two in the afternoon. The sheer white rock of the cliffs crept slowly by me, barely six inches from my backseat window. I was peering nervously through the windshield between my parents, trying to see beyond the next curve ahead, when a heavily laden farmer's truck came barreling out of the blind spot, clipping our left front end, smashing the bug-eye light and ripping off the front fender. Seconds before the crash, I had watched the expressions of the Italian driver and his passenger—joy and laughter, almost singing—change to expressions of horror. They swerved too late to avoid the impact. Rammed backwards, our car stalled and skidded across the curved road toward the cliff's unprotected edge. Mother slammed on the brakes. We continued to skid backward from the force of the impact across the road with its oncoming traffic, coming to a jerky stop a mere foot from the cliff's edge. Looking out the back window, I was certain death lay below. Beneath the vertical drop—a long way down—there was a miniature Italian village and the shimmering Mediterranean.

Daddy got out to inspect the damage, as did the speechless Italian driver, who placed rocks behind our rear wheels to prevent us from sliding over the edge. Daddy popped his head into our car to say, "Do not mention tomorrow's departure." Mother got out of the car to begin photographing the accident scene, including the black skid marks. This alarmed the driver's mate. Traffic piled up behind our crippled cars, eliciting a sonata of car horns and unsolicited advice from fellow drivers. Serious haggling started between Daddy and the truck driver, who begged us not to call the police. Gulnar and I stayed seated in the car for fear of the passing traffic. Daddy returned holding several million Italian Liras flapping in the afternoon breeze. Mother started our engine. Plenty of hands pushed both vehicles onto the appropriate sides of the road. We resumed our creep from the scene with our engine whining up over the mountain.

Daddy looked over at Mother saying, "It's a good thing you took those photos. That shook them up quite a bit. We got cash to repair the car." After a moment, she looked back at him and said, "There was no film in the camera." He smiled. The advantage of a damaged "new" car was a significantly lowered import tax to pay in Alexandria.

On the *Esperia*, we traveled first-class because of Daddy's status as a government official. The night before we reached

Alexandria, there was a fancy-dress ball. Some passengers gave us their paper hats and masks, and we collected the discarded ones, loving these novel toys. On our final arrival in Cairo, Daddy made us give them up as presents to our Egyptian cousins.

It never ceased to bother me that the concept of possessions held little meaning for my parents. Could it be that they held few "treasures" as they grew up, she in post-WWI Germany, he in the scarcity of Upper Egypt and then

Daddy & friends at stern of
Esperia

during life in a madrasa? Books were his treasures—his cigarettes, as he used to say; as other men bought ciggies, he bought books.

The objects they so lightly, so frivolously parted with, however, didn't belong to them. Instead they belonged to their children. Particularly in my case: my toy lorry at four, my ice cream at ten, and now my party favors. In her adulthood, Gulnar also lacked the respect shown to other people's trinkets. She helped herself to the objects of others that caught her eye and equally easily parted with them by giving them away.

20

DEADLY SHAME

1954-1955

The desperate man has no native land.
—Albert Camus

I n Cairo, Daddy resumed his full academic schedule. We recommenced our weekly ritual of visiting my grandfather in Sayeda Zeinab—sans Mother. Gulnar, approaching thirteen, occasionally accompanied us, since Sit Nazifa, who had died, was no longer a threat. Sheikh Amin's daughters, Tante Souad, and my youngest Tante Sanaa remained unmarried at home, caring for my aged Giddi, who was frailer than I remembered. Giddi's personal hygiene had slipped. He was clean but unshaven, with untrimmed mustache, nasal hairs, and fingernails. He had lost weight and his vitality had diminished. Life without his wife was not worth living, he told me in his low voice with his hands trembling slightly. The atmosphere was more subdued in the absence of the cheerleader, while the flat seemed less cared for—an absence of spirit.

Many of the uncles and aunts had married and moved out. They and their young families were dispersed about the greater Cairo area, dictated by ever-rising rents and the limited availability of flats. The increase in Cairo's population and the resulting overcrowded public transportation meant that they seldom attended Friday's once joyous congregation. Friday meals were now a shadow of the previously lavish and festive affairs. The selection of dishes was meager, particularly those containing meat. We consumed unleavened bread in greater quantities. Because the cost of living had risen substantially, Daddy supplemented Sheikh Amin's paltry pension, which together with Tante Sanaa's teacher's salary, was the household's sole income.

Tante Mustakima, the eldest, was absent. Tante Sanaa took me aside and in a low tone told me she had a son, Ali, the product of an *urfi marriage*—a contract marriage of limited duration.

"Married? Does Baba know?"

"Yes. He approved it. Her husband, Mr. Muharram, is a wealthy Sunni Egyptian businessman. He traveled to Europe and met your father in England. She and Ali live in their own flat in Shubra. He already has a family, but your aunt is nearly thirty-five so she accepted his one-year marriage offer. He is very kind and takes good care of them and helps Sheikh Amin, too."

"She delivered a healthy son. *Al Hamdulil Allah*—Praise Allah. Marwan you have a new cousin—Ali. You will like him. Take care of him as he grows up." The news stunned me.

Evidently, Mr. Muharram got her some pills on his European trip for her nausea and vomiting during her early pregnancy, and Ali was born with no left hand. "His arm stops here." She pointed to her mid-forearm. "Don't show surprise when you see him." She added that Mr. Muharram would raise Ali like a real son, and take care of his mother.

Giddi no longer attended mid-day prayer at the mosque; negotiating the stairs had become difficult. We performed our ablutions, praying together in the living room facing Mecca, each on our own prayer mat, accompanying the broadcasted service. Unable to remember the Arabic, I shamefully mimed the liturgy, hoping this charade would help me be accepted.

I loved seeing him on a weekly basis. Giddi wept with joy

whenever we arrived. I was sorry to be unable to converse freely; Tante Souad translated our words of affection and mutual support. He insisted I sit next to him in the parlor and at the table. He held my hand, lavishing kisses on me, then murmured what I interpreted as pleasantries by the tone of his voice.

During such visits, I felt closer to him than to my father. I felt my whole past family lineage, all the way back to our village, to the adobe hut in Beni Harem in Upper Egypt, and our Assiut identity. It was clear he had missed us, and he was invariably saddened when we left in the late afternoon. Our departure elicited a stream of tears, with repeated requests for us to stay a bit longer. He gave praise to Allah to guide our safe journey home and prayed for our speedy return.

At first, his tears frightened me. I did not understand why he would weep. Half a century later, their profound meaning is clear to me. I, too, become emotional and shed a few tears when I part from my son and daughter, who live their lives thousands of miles away with families of their own. I cry tears of joy when they honor me with their visit. Tears of gratitude they have not forgotten me. Tears of pain on seeing them depart. Tears of hope the Lord continues to bless them. Tears, for I will miss them. Tears of self-pity, for I will be alone. Tears of fear, for should I die we may never meet again. Yes, die I must. Please Lord, will it that I go before them—according to nature's order. I could not begin to think what I would do were they to depart this life sooner than I. Yes, dear Giddi, yes, dear Sheikh Amin, it is only now I understand those bittersweet tears of yours.

Beyond our Fridays in Sayeda Zeinab, it became more difficult to visit the growing branches of our Meguid family tree. We occasionally visited my various relatives in their disparate corners of growing Cairo: Heliopolis, at the northeastern fringes of the desert, in new developments near the Pyramids, or in the southern suburb of Manial Rhoda. We ate heavy, greasy lunches, more carbohydrates than vegetables and meat. I had many cousins, and we always came bearing gifts for them.

My cousins did not speak English with confidence. Given the language barrier, it was difficult to share personal aspects of our lives. I, who should be the future patriarch of our clan, could not converse with them in any meaningful way. They had grown up during my absence, and our cultural references differed. With time I began to speak broken Arabic, still not nuanced enough to chat about anything other than current topics. We failed to form bonds that would carry us into adulthood.

Daddy registered me in a private, all-boys Arabic school near our new flat in Zamalek for the autumn term of 1954. The school uniform was a black blazer with long grey flannel trousers. The prospect of going to an Arabic school made me feel incredibly vulnerable, since I had no Arabic language skills. Looking back, it makes no sense that my father would have enrolled me there. Was this an act of faith or folly? I could speak German, but was most comfortable as an English-speaking British schoolboy. I think my father gave insufficient consideration to my school placement; this assumption was misguided. He thought that sinceI had spoken Arabic until I was four that it would easily come back to me. However, we didn't speak Arabic at home and Mother spoke no Arabic. We conversed in English. By contrast, Gulnar attended the English School Cairo, continuing her education with minimal interruption.

What did my mother have to say about sending me to an Arabic school? I discovered her views in a letter to her parents written in German:

```
Arabic language? Which donkey has
created this language? It is extremely
old and nobody even thinks about
cleaning thoroughly in that vegetable
patch.
```

Had she forgotten, as she hammered out these words on her

typewriter, that Daddy earned their living as an Arabic word-smith? That he invested his academic life in reading and writing in Arabic and propagating Modern Standard Arabic? Indeed, as she had typed to her parent's years before, when living in Sudan:

> Meguid had published an article in one
> of the monthly Bakht El Ruda magazines
> which generated two pounds income. He
> gave these to me with a note that
> stated: 'As a sign of my gratitude for
> you not disturbing me while working!'

Perhaps Daddy thought that since I had picked up the other languages by cultural immersion, somehow the same process of osmosis would lead me to relearn Arabic. The headmaster and a few of my new teachers were his former students, so maybe he expected they would encourage my progress or cut me some slack with homework, and one of his students would tutor me weekly. Ironically, we started with my father's textbook intended for first graders. The illustrated primer's first line read, "The fox jumped over the duck." This quirk of fate—being unable to read my own father's work—shamed me immensely.

Three versions of Arabic were taught simultaneously: collo-quial, everyday spoken Egyptian Arabic; Modern Standard Arabic (MSA) in textbooks and newsprint; and finally, the clas-sical and venerated Qur'anic Arabic. MSA was taught in school, although the discussion during the lessons—be they history, geography or math—was in the Egyptian spoken dialect. The Arabic language system was difficult to learn, because while the spoken colloquial is derived from the MSA, much of the vocab-ulary and the pronunciation is very different. This was the state of affairs among the three hundred and eighty million in the Arab world, living in twenty-two contiguous countries in the Middle East and North Africa. In each country, the inhabitants spoke their distinct dialect that was not necessarily understood by other Arabs. Most Muslims worldwide understood Qur'anic Arabic, although it was not commonly spoken. MSA was the common tongue spoken between Arabs, which Daddy promoted in his writings.

Had we stayed in Cairo, not gone overseas and been exposed to two different cultures and not knowing if I was ever to return to Egypt, then by eleven I would have known the 28 primary letters of the alphabet. I would have been fluent in cursive Arabic writing, would have known which letters connect with a preceding or a succeeding letter, and that all primary letters have conditional forms depending on whether they are at the beginning, middle, or end of a word. My script was that of a five-year-old learning to connect letters. I struggled to write my name from right to left in a straight line.

Any educational progress was suspended. Most of the time I had no idea what the teachers and students were saying during class. I followed crowds of boys into recess and to lunch without knowing what was happening next. Unable to communicate, and with my German looks, I made no friends. I was an outsider in a society measured by interpersonal connections. It was a blighted time for me, filled with anxious confusion and shame. I had re-entered Egyptian school life as the son of Abdel Aziz, Professor of Arabic, author of Arabic textbooks read in every classroom in Egypt and across the Arab world. I was failing to live up to everyone's expectations.

To gauge my progress, Daddy grilled me about what I had learned on my return from school with an intensity that could have matched the Inquisition. There seemed no letup in his nagging to do my homework and practice reading Arabic out loud. He had no idea of my degree of isolation, embarrassment, shame or the humiliation of my inadequacy. It seemed all eyes were on me, watching me fail. Worse, there seemed no support and no escape.

I confessed to my parents that I was not doing well. What else could I say not to disappoint them? My problems eluded their comprehension. They did not seem concerned, and told me to give it a chance. There was little emotional support. My spirit preferred injury to cowardice. I could not understand the lessons, nor convey to them the extent of my distress. When I got home, I retreated to my room, closed my door, lay on my bed, and lost myself in my English adventure books or in making a model airplane. In Daddy's eyes I was shirking my responsibilities and being lazy.

Egyptian nationalism under President Nasser was reaching its height. The British were tenaciously hanging onto Egypt and the Suez Canal, while songs like "Egypt Our Motherland" and *Allahu Akbar*—God is Great—blared from every radio. I wanted desperately to belong, but was perceived as a *Khawaga*—a foreigner—a derogatory term for an outsider: not one of us. I could not alter my looks, but how I wished with all my heart that I spoke fluent Arabic. I would be able to relate to my Egyptian family and be genuinely engulfed in their love, and be accepted into my surroundings as an *Ibn el Balad*—a native son. Language was identity. I took refuge in the local mosque, despite the men who looked at me suspiciously when I entered. I prayed to Allah to help me learn the language.

My acquisition of colloquial Arabic increased rapidly. The other two versions lagged behind, particularly my ability to read. I had to learn how to pray by reading English instruction books provided by Tante Mustakima. Daddy continued to nag me relentlessly to utilize my after-school time doing extra Arabic reading. The idea of tutoring me himself seemed not to occur to him, and progress with the once-a-week tutor was agonizingly slow. As far as I was concerned, we had returned to Egypt and to my cultural roots for good. This was where I would live out my future. Unlike Germany and England, Egypt was not a rest stop in my life. It was where I was to be and live.

To my surprise, Daddy, the compulsive worker, began to travel once more to "lecture overseas." At least this is what he told his children and the Meguid clan. In reality, he was at interviews in Geneva for a new job with UNESCO, no doubt encouraged by Mother. We would once more live abroad, possibly in Beirut, where I would go to an English-speaking school—probably the American school. During his absence, he wrote almost daily. To Gulnar, he wrote in English. In the same envelope he enclosed a copy to me, written neatly in MSA. He must have assumed I could read it. I could not, and I was angry with him for his lack of sensitivity. Why did he make a distinction? It was a tacit admission by Daddy that I was different. I wonder what Gulnar would have done with such a challenge, for she could not read Arabic either.

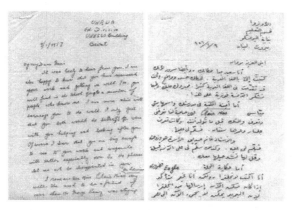

Daddy's letter to Gulnar in English & me in Arabic

After several weeks abroad, Daddy came home and gave me my first camera, a Brownie Kodak Box with two rolls of film. I loved this camera and started photographing everything, everywhere. I took it to school and photographed my school friends. Daddy had ulterior motives.

"If you became a cameraman or producer in the new, fast-growing TV industry you'll always have a job—one independent of your command of Arabic," he said, almost talking to himself. I was not enamored with his idea, wanting to be a pilot or a surgeon. The Air Force had just acquired Soviet Mig-15 fighter jets, flying them over Cairo to boost nationalism. I was sufficiently impressed to dream of becoming a fighter pilot, although my interest in medicine was piqued by reading the biography of Albert Schweitzer. I had no clear idea of how to achieve these goals and no one to guide me. Emotionally I lived in limbo, worried about prospects for my future—one never elaborated on by Mother. She did not raise the issue, nor did I try to discuss it with her, knowing I first had to complete school. Daddy wrote regular letters to Mother from Beirut. In one, he included a typed letter in English to me:

Last time I saw you I noted that you had become a big boy. I felt proud of you, and am praying to God to preserve you my only son. I also feel that you are getting steadier and more understanding. Of course, it should be like this, otherwise I could not rely on leaving you without supervision. I know you are doing your best, but I am not sure you are receiving the help you want. We shall soon decide whether to live together in Cairo or here in Beirut. We feel the need of being with each other.

Do Sonny let me know your difficulties at school. Don't you find teachers helpful? Why not ask them privately to solve your problems? Or else ask friends and older pupils. I am anxious to know about your work. I hope you are pleased with your camera.

Love and blessings from your Daddy.

All of his suggestions were impractical for an eleven-year-old boy. Most of the teachers had been his students at university. How could I reveal the extent of my lack of competency without embarrassing us both? How could they help me? I was already maxed out learning Arabic. I knew from learning other languages that there is a time when, like a volcano, one's vocabulary and syntax grows quietly, until it finally explodes into the open, when one can begin to put sentences together, reading with greater ease. I was not at that stage, only getting there.

Finally recognizing my unhappiness, depression, introversion, and lack of educational progress, my parents decided to yank me out of the Arabic school. Being transferred was akin to acknowledging that I would never learn Arabic in these circumstances, that I would always be stigmatized as a *Khawaga*—that I had failed. Moving to another school was a huge relief for me.

They applied to the English School Cairo, whose motto on the school crest was "Led by Love of Country." Gulnar was a day pupil, and were I accepted, I could resume my education in English. The spring term in 1955 would start in a few weeks; in the interim, I was to continue with my Arabic tutor and my self-directed religious studies.

The junior school headmistress, Miss Savage, and the class mistress interviewed me and found me capable of doing the work. Given my checkered schooling, the teachers decided that I should be set back a year and enter Miss Freemantle's class. Mr. Leighton, the English School's headmaster, gave the green light for my acceptance, and my parents forked out the hefty £E60 per term school fee for both Gulnar and me.

In the remaining few weeks of the 1954 autumn term, Mother placed me in the German School. I had to adjust once more to convoluted German thinking, and German punctuality, and to re-learn the language. Compared to the Arabic school, the German pupils were highly disciplined, always standing up when being addressed by a teacher, never talking during class, and not rushing about noisily during recess. Mother somehow expected that I would easily fit into the German sixth grade. I

did not, renewing the whole cycle of
learning and performance anxiety, and
rekindling my identity crisis.

I walked across Zamalek each
morning in the opposite direction to the
route I had taken to the Arabic school. I
was sure everyone who saw me would
know I had failed there. Once in the
German School, I was lost, disoriented,
and confused: neither German, nor

School motto "Led by Love of Country"

English, least of all Egyptian. The German children in my class
asked many questions about my past. I found myself inventing
stories, exaggerating my triumphs at track and field, which they
did not have, to make myself important just to be accepted. I
would go home loathing myself for lying. I swore that I would
stop, asking God at the 4 a.m. *Salat el Fajr*—dawn prayers—to
forgive me and guide me toward truthfulness. I could deal with
reality no matter how painful—as I had done in Germany and
England. But could not deal with the web created by my lies. I
could not wait for term to end to escape my predicament and
enter the spring term at the English School Cairo.

On January 26, 1955 Mother wrote to her parents:

We have finally dropped the idea of
moving to the Sudan for good, and as I
mentioned before, the idea of going to
Libya too will fade away. It would be
easier without children, but their
future is important.

The entire family is sitting here in
around the table. Everybody is working
like bees; father between the two children, very earnest and strict. Gulnar is
learning Arabic with Meguid, and I am

learning Orthography (the art of spelling), geography, or any other schoolwork
with Marwan.

We work like this on a daily basis;
Marwan now has started with French. If
someone comes to visit Abdel Aziz,
Marwan immediately takes off to play.
Marwan must work hard during the three
months school holidays, to be finally
caught up with studying the material he
did not learn while he was at the Arabic
and German school. Marwan's experience
at the German School was torture
for him.

Gulnar, at the English School, came
second in her class. She has already
jumped up two grades, I'm only afraid
that her cramming so hard may soon
become too much, but her father is very
proud of her: his daughter!

In 1955, Egyptian nationalism reached a hysterical zenith.
Nationalism, and the feeling of belonging abounded. Later that
year, in early May 1955, Mother wrote a note to her parents:

Meguid expected a student at 4 o'clock.
I put a table and chairs on our large
balcony, determined to have the place
look upscale. I noticed that there was a
thick layer of dust. Secretly, I mopped
the balcony, being careful not to be
seen by the riffraff. Who is the
riffraff you ask?

Everyone that is serving and who does
not belong to the "ruling class." This
includes the servants of different rank
and status, chauffeurs, garage caretakers, car washers, housekeepers etc.,
etc., everyone who stands up or curtseys
once their masters walk in. Gulnar does
fit into this milieu.

As for Marwan, it was difficult for him
not to relate to the riffraff. He just
cannot yet keep his distance from the
riffraff. He is a people's man.

It also took a long time to convince him
that his class could not deliver newspapers. He wanted so much to increase his
pocket money.

This letter, as with all her letters to her parents, reflected her superiority complex befitting a German who came of age during the National Socialist era. Throughout her life she would manifest such attitudes which embarrassed me intensely. Whether it was to our servant girls, my Egyptian family members, the Arabic language or everyday Egyptians that she came in contact with, she clung to her complex. After all, didn't she refuse to visit my family for Friday lunch? And whether in Cairo or Balteem, didn't she congregate with ex-pats? I'm surprised it didn't bother Daddy more.

I hated, no, despised such an attitude. I never asked our servants to clean my shoes. I did so myself, to Mother's annoyance. Yes, I was proud that she considered me a "people's man." That she thought of me as loving and being one of the "riffraff." Perhaps my attitude toward my fellow humans steered me toward becoming a surgeon.

Mother's letter of November 10, 1955 to Oma and Opa shared information I had not picked up. Perhaps I was too involved with my new friends. But more likely my parents did not discuss their plans with me or Gulnar. Mother wrote:

I am particularly interested in Meguid joining UNESCO. This will increase our possibility of travel, to Europe. A hint of a likely move and the children declared in unison that they would not want to change school again.

Meguid has been selected as the one most suitable candidates for this position at UNESCO (United Nations): these are highly desirable jobs. Meguid is quite interested, and it would be very posi-tive career move for him.

His first assignment would be in Beirut, Lebanon, from where he can "work" the Arabic speaking countries via airplane, and which might take him to Geneva under certain conditions. Before all the formalities with UNESCO are finalized, it might well be spring, if not summer 1956. I will stay in Cairo because the children must stay in their English School. After a year, we can once again revisit our decision if they should be schooled in Beirut. We would once more live abroad where Marwan would go to an English-speaking school—probably the American school.

My parent's plans were formalized and were shared only with Sheikh Amin, my aunts, Oma, and Opa in Mother's last letter of the year—a year full of uncertainty and impermanence. The letter was dated December 10, 1955 in which she wrote:

```
Our father has been offered the job by
UNESCO. He will be the consultant for
technical professions in the Arabic
speaking countries of the Middle East.
Such a job would not have been avail-
able, if he had gone to Sudan or Libya
immediately after our return from
England.

He leaves for Beirut in January 1956.
While father is busy, winding down his
job at the University and preparing for
his new position, the children do their
work at school; Marwan is second of 36
pupils in his class.
```

It always mystified me why they did not share these plans with their children. It would certainly have made me less apprehensive and more accepting of my new life. Egypt would have become another stop in my life and the learning of Arabic a less serious matter. My whole being—shame, introversion, embarrassment, lies, humiliation and self-loathing—would not have existed. I would have been or become a very different person. While living in Egypt I would no longer have lived in life's no man's land but would have been given a sense of belonging. My feelings would have been mellowed and I could have rationalized that I was back where I was conceived and born—a true *Ibn El Balad*.

21

SETTLING DOWN

Unless someone like you cares a whole lot,
Nothing is going to get better. It's not.
—Dr Theodor Seuss Geisel

I n January 1955, before I started the English School Cairo, my parents left thirteen-year-old Gulnar and me without a babysitter for the first time to attend a dinner. The late afternoon sun was leaching away the day's heat. Feeling unwell, I had taken refuge on a chaise lounge on our balcony overlooking the Nile, seeking the comfort of a cool breeze; the muezzin's entreaty to the faithful for evening prayers wafted across the water from minarets on the opposite bank. My mother phoned often, concerned about having left us unattended. As the evening progressed, I vaguely remember the calls becoming more frequent, no doubt in response to Gulnar's unease about my worsening stomachache.

Later that evening my mother appeared on the balcony, where I'd fallen asleep in a fetal position. I awoke to glaring lights, seeing a stranger standing next to her. He was balding with grey temples and wore a dark suit. He told me in a soft but authoritative voice to roll onto my back. Then he started to prod my bared abdomen.

My parents' dinner host was a surgeon. He had accompanied them home to examine me. Proclaiming, "It is definitely appendicitis," he swept me up in his arms and carried me down to the back seat of his Ford. My father sat in front as the surgeon drove to Papaioannou Hospital.

My next recollection was of being wheeled on a gurney into a white-tiled, brightly lit operating room. The pre-anesthetic shot hurt and made me dizzy. Noises echoed in my ears. The room smelled of a mixture of borax soap and medications. Hands moved me onto the operating table. A doctor placed a black mask reeking of rubber over my nose and mouth, which I tried to fend off. As I struggled, the overhead operating light started to sway and voices faded out.

I awoke from an anesthetized sleep around 2 a.m., smelling and tasting ether, which made me vomit. A saline-filled glass bottle sat on the counter beside my bed, containing my gangrenous appendix. I marveled at it in my post-operative misery.

A nurse sat at my bedside. I was confused to wake up without my parents. Mother did not arrive until early afternoon; I had expected her sooner and was angry at her tardy appearance. To my further dismay, she told me that Daddy had left that morning for Beirut. She explained he had accepted the position with UNESCO, who had seconded him to UNRWA— United Nations Relief and Works Agency. I returned home after ten days in the hospital. Daddy was gone.

Mother began to share more of their thinking and planning with Gulnar and me. Instead of living in the dark, I now lived in a state of apprehension and uncertainty. Daddy was to head up an international team to develop an education program for the children of the displaced Arab refugees who lived in camps along the Israeli border, specifically in Jordan and Lebanon. His main office would be next to the King David Hotel in Old Jerusalem,

Jordan. If his program was successful, they would offer him a lifelong contract and we would possibly move to Beirut. In his absence, we never went to Sayeda Zeinab, we never called on my numerous uncles and aunts, nor did I see my cousins.

On the first day of the new semester, I proudly donned my new school uniform, a blue blazer, white shirt, and grey flannels. Eating a hurried breakfast of scrambled eggs, toast, and marmalade, I rushed to the corner, fearing I might miss the blue school bus. Gulnar, being a senior student in Junior High took an earlier bus. I sat quietly on the bench behind the driver, Ibrahim. After picking up students at various stops in Zamalek, the full bus traveled through central Cairo, past the main train station, and out into the suburbs to Heliopolis—new parts of town to me. The trip took nearly an hour.

When we reached school a few minutes before 9 a.m., I discovered there were numerous buses, all dropping off students. As I wondered which I'd have to take home, Ibrahim told me that he was the 5th bus in a convoy that would be lined up waiting. Disembarking, I and the rest of the students rushed to our classes.

I sat in the second row at my own desk, paying keen attention, happy once more to be in an English-speaking environment. At 10:30 a.m. we had recess, during which I roller skated about the rink outside my classroom, going faster and faster as I became more confident, feeling better on skates than on my feet. Others joined me, and I made friends. We started to bash a tennis ball against the concrete wall of the squash courts, chasing the returning ball. Frequently sweating, we resumed classes half an hour later. I was immediately comfortable. I was in my element.

Lunch was served at noon in a huge dining room, resurrecting memories of school lunches in England: tasteless food consisting of dried peas, mashed potatoes, and some form of ground-up meat in a sauce. As unhappy as I had been in the Arabic school, I now missed their delicious lunches, which consisted of rice, beans in a tomato sauce, and usually a piece of lamb—much more to my liking. We could not hang around after our meal because the senior students began to appear and squeezed us out.

Following afternoon classes, we caught the 4 p.m. early bus. I counted five buses and found Ibrahim waiting in the driver's seat. There were seven other buses lined up behind mine, each going to different suburbs of Cairo. The second fleet of buses left around 6 p.m. after the various sport activities had ended, and included those after-schoolers who had to remain behind as punishment.

The private English School Cairo was located in the north-west suburbs of Heliopolis, on the arid outskirts of the city. Established in 1913, it was the first co-educational school in Egypt, and became known as the Eaton of the Middle East. It was set in well-tended grounds, with its own playing fields and a roller-skating rink for the juniors. The grounds also included squash courts, a fully equipped gym, track and field facilities, as well as a cricket pitch, all encompassed by manicured English lawns and groves of eucalyptus trees. The compound had sepa-rate areas with buildings for junior school and senior students. Set between these was a memorial garden for the staff and students killed in both world wars. The school emulated the British public-school model, and was a jewel set in the middle of the politically and military tumultuous Middle East. Outside the walls of this thriving English colony was the sprawling, baking, dusty desert.

The school's charge was to educate the sons and daughters of the colonial staff that ran Egypt via proxy of the Egyptian royal family. Its unspoken mission was also to educate successive generations of elite Egyptians who would enter the civil service, the arts, medicine, and commerce, and who would harbor sympathy for the British status quo. It had boarders—children whose parents lived throughout the Middle East—and day pupils who belonged to British, foreign, and affluent Egyptian families living in Cairo. The student population was primarily British, but it also was very international and reflected the spectrum of ethnicity and religious beliefs throughout the Middle East. I met the sons and daughters of royal aristocratic families, of diplomats, owners of large estates, and tycoons from the Levant, whose children were driven to school in chauffeured limousines and whose homes had the finest furniture, china, and crystals—exposing me to luxury, exclusivity, and opulence.

Boys lining up in the morning according to house

Students from higher grades were organized into houses similar to fraternities. I fully expected to be promoted to the Junior High School and became acquainted with its routine from Gulnar. Each house separated the males from the females, and in addition to illustrious names such as Sir Walter Raleigh and Sir Martin Frobisher, each house had its own color— Raleigh purple, Frobisher red, and so on. The houses were designed to enhance competition in academics and sports and to foster group loyalty.

On Parents' Day and at graduation, prizes were awarded to the winners in various team sports, individual achievements, and in an array of academic subjects.

The primary spoken language was English. Arabic was compulsory and students had to select a third language—usually French, which was new to me, as recognized by my French teacher in my end-of-term examination. I scored 36%. I could live with that. My headache remained Arabic, in which I got 16%, shaming me once more, despite my teacher remarking, "I find that he is progressing." These two scores weighted down my overall exam scores; even so, I landed up in the eighth position in a class of more than thirty children. Miss Savage, the grade school headmistress, concluded her report writing, "Marwan has gained a well-deserved and very good place in class." Mr. Brandon Layton, the headmaster of the entire school, signed the report, and the concluding note was that the next term would begin in early October. I had worked hard and looked forward to three months of summer holiday, free of nagging about doing my Arabic homework.

Not so for Daddy. Through his letters, it seemed there would be no escaping my trials and tribulations. Despite the glimmer of light that I saw in my Arabic teacher's remark, Daddy found my grade unpalatable and lectured me accordingly. I wanted to become fluent in my native tongue for many reasons; the motive now became one of living up to my father's expectations. He designed for me an intensive Arabic reading curriculum. I continued with my private lessons, increased to twice weekly, and a weekly French lesson was added. Despite my desire not to disappoint him, I resented this intrusion into my vacation. The badgering to do my homework continued, becoming a battle of wills. I retreated into my room or focused on playing with the American twins who lived next door.

My friends Jamie & Jeffery

Jamie and Jeffery Johnston were adopted and, born relatively close to each other, deemed twins by their mother. When I first met them, they were seven years old and attended the American school. Their adopted sister, Jennifer, nearly four years old, showed signs of delayed mental development. Rosemary Johnston was from Illinois, while her husband, Stuart, came from California; I never once saw Stuart Johnston or discovered what he did, except that he was in Egypt under President Eisenhower's Seven Point Plan. Rosemary was the daughter of James Kemper, the founder of the Kemper Insurance Company in Chicago. Since both my father and Stuart were chronically absent, Mother and Rosemary became fast friends.

The Johnstons lived next door in the apartment's penthouse. Each Sunday, Mrs. Johnston invited me to join her and the kids to visit a different archeological site around Cairo. Neither Mother nor Gulnar participated. I had never seen anything except the Giza Pyramids and the Sphinx, and loved escaping from the house and my eternal homework. We would leave early in the morning in their huge Ford station wagon to beat the heat, following desert roads to a Pyramid or some historical site, meeting up with other American families. We hired Egyptian guides to explain the archeological ruins. I cannot recall much from those visits, not being interested in archeology. I spent the time playing with Jamie, a calm kid who was not easily frazzled, and Jeff, who was high-strung, often provoking his brother, or physically attacking him. Perhaps it was the sun or the heat, but each outing ended with Jeffery crying and needing comfort from his mother.

I had a nasty shock at our first lunch. Sitting in the cool sand of a pyramid's mid-day shade, Mrs. Johnston handed us Wonder bread sandwiches made with peanut butter and jelly that dripped from the edges due to the heat, and cups of warm Kool-Aid. Both were revolting. Where were the German, British, or Egyptian sandwich spreads to which I was accustomed? It was my first introduction to American food. Being hungry, I consumed as much as I could stomach, and gave the rest to Jeff, who seemed to relish the extras.

Both boys had hardy, thick-tired Schwinn bicycles. We dreamed of riding them over a ramp and gliding through the air. Luckily, at the very northern tip of Zamalek, the island where we lived, there was about 100 square feet of Nile mud forming a triangular area. We built a bicycle track with a ramp having a three-foot drop. Jeff eagerly volunteered to go first. He whistled around the track, gaining speed, and rode up and off the ramp. We imagined him soaring into glory. With the weight of the bike and the insufficient speed, he dropped like a stone, tumbled into the dirt, and cried. I consoled him. Next was Jamie. Triumph—having gained more momentum, he flew for two feet or so before crash-landing. I did not try. We decided the bikes were too heavy and abandoned our fantasy. Learning physics in action like this was much more fun than sitting indoors studying French or Arabic.

During the summer holiday, we visited Daddy in Lebanon and lived some weeks in the suburb of Ras Beirut, Lebanon, looking at potential flats. The rest of the time we stayed in a villa outside Old Jerusalem, where we met Daddy's team members, a physical educator

At UN function in Jerusalem

from Holland, an English teacher from London, a math teacher with his wife and two daughters from Finland, and a Frenchman with his mistress.

"Daddy, what is a mistress?"

"A future wife . . . they didn't have enough time to marry before they came here," was the answer, which satisfied my curiosity.

We dined with local Jordanian and Palestinian dignitaries, as shown above, enhancing my belief in Daddy's importance. Lena, the youngest daughter of the Finnish family, was a cute blonde of nine. At eleven, I began to feel the early stirrings of my masculinity. Gulnar and I often played basketball with the two sisters. I tried very hard to impress Lena with my dismal basketball skills, spoiling it when I accidentally farted trying to jump and get the ball into the hoop. The play stopped as they pointed at me with laughter. We went on guided tours, seeing the border between Israel and Jordan, the misery of the refugee camps, the Church of the Holy Sepulcher within the old walled city of Jerusalem, and the Stations of the Cross. I found none of these sites as interesting as Lena. It was a pleasant holiday, where in addition to playing basketball I built a plastic model of a French Mystère fighter jet with Israeli insignia.

Despite my best intentions, and Daddy's constant, tortured reminders to do my assigned Arabic homework, I did not get much done. He did not tutor me, which would have helped greatly. When Daddy came home from his office, he spent time with his wife, or we had various functions to attend. From conversations I overheard between my parents when eavesdropping under their open bedroom window, it seemed that we were going to leave Egypt imminently and live in Beirut. They discussed the prospect of their children going to the American school, and visiting Daddy in Old Jerusalem during our holidays. They thought I could attend the American University Medical School if I wanted to become a physician. Plans for Gulnar were vague. The entire scheme was contingent on Daddy being offered a permanent appointment to the United Nations —a decision, he thought, that depended on the initial success of his program, and one that would be made in the near future. After the summer, we were to return to Egypt. He would stay behind and would visit us as often as his work took him to Cairo.

Marwan, Gulnar, Dutchman, Mother, and Daddy in Jerusalem

By now, we had UN passports. I was a citizen of the world, and I imagined a united world where all people were citizens of the United Nations—putting an end to war. This naïve fantasy was soon shattered. Our return flight to Cairo was on the white DC-3 Dakota with the distinctive blue United Nations name and logo. I had a window seat. Halfway through the flight, several Israeli Mystère fighter jets buzzed our Dakota, forcing it to land on a grass field in Gaza. We piled out onto the field. A UN car collected one of the VIPs on our flight and took him to Gaza City while the rest of us stood around in the shade of the plane's wing in the mid-day heat. A couple of hundred feet from us was a farmer plowing his field next to a barbed wire fence that separated us from Israel. The fence reminded me of the ongoing political turmoil of the cold war, in which the Middle East was a pawn. Naively, I had thought the UN was immune from politics.

We learned, when the car returned, that a formal complaint had been lodged against the Israeli government. We piled on board again and the Dakota took off. Twenty minutes later, the Suez Canal was clearly visible as a dark blue line across the pale desert. The Canal carried crude oil from the Middle East to Europe and was of strategic importance to the British and the French, who owned it via the Universal Company of the Maritime Suez Canal.

———

On the first day of the autumn term, I shared the front bench of the school bus with a handsome, dark-skinned boy my age. Asad Karim Khan had black hair swept sideways with coconut oil. He was soft spoken and thoughtful in character, the son of the Indian Ambassador to Egypt. He was so smart he hardly ever had to study. In contrast, I studied incessantly. His older sister, Minu, entered in Gulnar's class.

He boarded and alighted from the bus one stop earlier than I did. He lived above the embassy—a lovely villa with well-tended lawns that flowed down to the Nile. With each bus ride, we got to know each other more, and talked about airplanes or his attempts to bribe the corpulent embassy chauffeur with chocolate so he could drive the embassy Cadillac along deserted streets in Zamalek. His ultimate aim was to drive a stretch along the Nile's corniche. He felt to achieve this goal would require much more chocolate and he would also need to become accustomed to power steering, power brakes, and the lack of a shift stick.

On the morning trip to school, we kept a watchful eye on a Greek first-grader sitting a row behind us who had the propensity to motion sickness. Kristos would stand up, giving us fair warning. Asad and I barely had enough time to move apart before the stream of vomit would project forward, bisecting us and cascading into the aisle. The children who sat near us would stand up and give vivid and loud descriptions of what poor, pale Kristos had for breakfast, yelling, "Ooh! Scrambled eggs, tomatoes . . ." Ibrahim would pull over and clean up the mess, but the stench persisted, despite opening our window.

As we became more acquainted, Asad invited me to come to the embassy after school. He took me to the visit the kitchen, since there was going to be a diplomatic function that evening. He persuaded the cook to give us some of the desserts being prepared. I nibbled at delicious *jalebi*, pretzel-like warm dough baked in oil and covered in sugar syrup. The cook was busy making one of Asad's favorites, *rasogolla*, a dessert made from cottage cheese, deep fried in oil and soaked in sugar. Eventually the cook showed his irritation. We beat a retreat when he complained we were feasting excessively on the delicacies and that there would not be enough for the function. Asad showed me the laundry, the parlor, and pointing to a closed door, his dad's office. We climbed to the top of the villa using the servant's stairs to reach the radio room. Our intrusion caused consternation to the wireless operator, and once more we beat a hasty retreat, escaping into the garden.

The morning after the diplomatic event, Asad produced two large aluminum cigar cylinders. He thought that if we stuffed them with cotton wool soaked in lighter fluid and lit the base, we could make a rocket and fly them like the Germans. The question he pondered was where to launch them. I knew the ideal spot. A few days later, he got off at my stop and we walked to the end of the island. We carved a ramp and laid one cylinder on the mud. He worried that lighting the soaked cotton might result in an explosion. We concluded that in the absence of TNT there could not be an explosion. I watched him light the cottontail and run. At first, it burned like a cigarette lighter, but the flame petered out.

"If you could steal a bullet from the policeman guarding the embassy, we'd have some gunpowder. That should launch our second rocket," I suggested.

"The problem is the police have old Lee-Enfield Rifles but no ammunition," he replied. This ended our effort to launch a rocket.

A young girl named Cynthia Gardner also stood at my bus stop each morning. She lived in a villa around the corner, and came from New Jersey, USA. She was shy and reserved.

At the beginning of term, our teacher, Miss Freemantle, recognized Asad, a new friend Hassan, and me as three eleven-year-old potential troublemakers sitting at the back of the class. She moved us forward to the second row to keep an eye on us. Cynthia sat in front of me. Her fair braids dangled into my black inkwell. I gently tweaked one or the other when my view of Miss Freemantle was blocked, bringing Cynthia to tears, which mystified me. They were only tender tugs, after all.

Her father was my imagined archetypical American: tall and thin, with button-down collars and rimless glasses, like some American movie stars. He was kind and soft-spoken, with the voice of a man who knew life's joys and suffering. When he occasionally picked Cynthia up after school in his WWII Willis U.S. Army Jeep, Hassan and I climbed all over it in awe. It was the genuine article, similar to the one that Audie Murphy, our current hero, had driven during the war and in the movie *To Hell and Back*. He had bought the Jeep in Greece before he transferred to teach at the American University, Cairo, where Dr. Gardner had met my mother. Sometimes he gave us a ride, usually with the front windshield down. We felt very grown up riding in his Jeep, scarcely paying attention to Cynthia who sat at the back with her legs dangling over the jeep's chassis, apparently enjoying every moment.

On weekends, I often cycled to their villa. Cynthia's little brother, James, was about seven. He cried in protestation when Cynthia and I went cycling around the block without him, or when we excluded him from our other play. Her older sister Lucy visited during her college fall vacation. On that occasion, I was invited for Sunday "brunch." What exactly was brunch?

I sat at the far end of the dining table, next to Cynthia, while Lucy sat next to her mother at the other end. Lucy had blonde hair, was tall, wore a lovely pale flowered dress, and looked like an American film star. I could have fallen in love with her. Instead, I fell in love with their mother's exquisite waffles, which I soaked in maple syrup. I added a heap of cottage cheese and a slice of watermelon to my plate. Brunch was a heavenly delight, and beat German boiled lunch or my mother's perpetual scrambled eggs. I wished my mother served waffles. Lucy did not hang around with us after brunch, disappointing me.

22

THE GLAMOROUS MISS FREEMANTLE

1955-1956

No fewer than seventeen eleven-year-old boys were in love with you.
I am proud of my service in that army.
—Andy Selsberg

At the beginning of the 1956 autumn term, my teacher, Miss Freemantle, was in the prime of her womanhood, stunning with pale, freckled cheeks and flaming strawberry hair. Yet it was not her face, or her fine, tall form, or even her perfect, full buttocks that occupied my friends' and my attention. It was her breasts, which overflowed her tight blouse.

Having moved Hassan, Asad and me into the second row—"To keep an eye on us," she said—our adolescent imaginations were inflamed as we kept an eye on her. Miss Freemantle's high-riding breasts jiggled ever so slightly under her red blouse with each movement of her arms as she stood in front of her class of thirty-nine fifth graders. Hers were truly mesmerizing, majestically so: the very model of glorious distraction to the seventeen pubescent boys who followed her every movement. Asad and Hassan were ardent wiggle watchers too, totally riveted to their task, afraid we might miss one because our views were obstructed by the heads in front of us. Each wobble was stealthily marked into our notebooks for comparison at recess. Any discrepancies caused heated discussions.

Could we focus on our lesson?

Hardly.

We were too preoccupied with our visual vigilance. Under her blouse were two large mysterious pyramids . . . no, more like Himalayan peaks rising from the flat Egyptian sands, shrouded in silk. When she climbed the platform to the chalkboard to emphasize some relevant point, we exchanged brief glances, shaking our heads in heavenly disbelief. Oh God, what a beauty. School couldn't get better than this.

She seemed tall to us. During class she stood on a platform in flat shoes, but during her break—recess duty—she wore high heels. And because of the bright sunlight, she also wore Polaroid sunglasses. We took turns agonizing among ourselves about what questions we might come up with to ask her, merely to be close to her. When it was my turn I'd think of any rambling question as my eyes gawked upward through the shady valley of her breasts and I preened myself in the reflection of her sunglasses. It was difficult to pay attention as she leaned down to seek clarification of my gibberish. I would catch only a word or two from her red-lipstick mouth, while mesmerized by her utterly beautiful, radiant woman's face crowned by a glorious mass of blazing hair, gently fluttering in the breeze that swooped out of the western desert. My faithful compatriots, Hassan and Asad, would stand speechless by my side, each lost in their own fantasies. Asad's mouth would hang slightly open, perhaps secretly counting each tremor, particularly when she leaned towards me to better hear my prattle.

We'd compare our numbers, arguing over missed or miscalculated wobbles as if comparing the results of seismic jolts from an earthquake. After a while I noticed that she became suspicious of our questions and cut us short, although she had a soft spot for Asad, the most charming and handsome among us. Perhaps she was impressed by his status as the son of the Indian ambassador. He was blessed with the astonishing gift of controlling his wandering eyes. Instead, he glanced in a stealthy fashion, discreetly trying not to be noticed gawking.

Creative Hassan, pensive Marwan, and cricket sage Asad

Miss Freemantle was a confident woman who exuded the essence of womanhood, perhaps somewhat aware that her influence extended to the awakening eleven-year-old boys' young desires, yearning, lust and ardor, all still protected by naive innocence. We were totally absorbed in our infatuation, and I in my undying love for her!

Our observations of her were fueled by our suspicions that we shared her with Mr. Woolf, a middle school teacher who, as rumor had it, was her boyfriend and more, although the "more" was a mystery. I knew with a schoolboy's certainty he was messing with my idol.

Slimy Woolf oversaw the live-in boys and Miss Freemantle was in charge of the boarding girls. The teachers resided in staff quarters above the administrative building. She had a green and a red bulb over her door; the red light forbade students from disturbing her. I imagined that at those times the despicable Woolf was in her room. When his parents were in London, Hassan was a temporary boarder—our insider eyes and ears. Each morning he shared the latest rumors. What my friends whispered they might be doing alarmed me. "Never," I said adamantly in her defense. "Miss Freemantle would not!"

Meaningful insight into the "more" came a few months later during Wednesday sports lessons. The boys' teacher, a short, muscular, ex-army type, started the hour-long pre-lunch class by having us run in circles about the gym. Breathless and sweaty, we lined up at the far end and he threw a hard, red cricket ball in our direction, randomly yelling a name to indicate the intended recipient. When my turn came, my hands smarted from the ball's force. It had once hit my right temple, stunning me.

He would set the wooden horse in the middle of the gym, placing heavy jute mats on one side. I managed to jump over the horse, landing on the prickly mats, but others had difficulty clearing it. He bullied them mercilessly, calling them sissies; the same unathletic boys were always the target of his abuse. Soaked with sweat, we would file out through the boys' changing room door and strip down, happy to shower in the cold water.

The girls' instructor was a slim, olive-skinned Greek woman who took the girls out to the sports field. An hour later, she would troop them into their changing room at the other end of the gym.

One day the boys' gym teacher mysteriously locked the doors, leaving the girls' instructor and him in the gym. A boy peeking through the keyhole cried out, "Hey, look!" We rushed to the door, shoving one another aside—the sweat-drenched, the semi-undressed, and the freshly showered boys—all wanting to get a peek. Our frenzy rose on glimpsing a few seconds of real sex. The one glued to the keyhole provided a running commentary.

"They're kissing!"

Another boy yelled, "He's pushed her onto the mats."

The next murmured, "Still embracing . . . still kissing," followed by a series of "wows," and "gollys," as more boys shoved to get a view.

A voice declared, "He's moving between her legs."

We agreed each had five seconds to sneak a look. Bunched up around the peeper, we chanted one thousand one, one thousand two . . . until shoved aside by the next eager peeker. We were noisy in our excitement. The instructor pulled up his shorts, hobbling to the door, one shoe on, one off, unlocking it as we scattered and yelled, "Shut up, get out or you'll all get walloped." We had fled into the showers. The door banged shut, the lock turned. The brave among us rushed back to peek again. They resumed—we resumed; a very excited boy disbelievingly whispered, "They're fucking." Someone said it was a dirty word.

We saw him lean her against the wooden horse and attack her from behind. It was like two dogs I had seen in Cairo's street. I couldn't see too well, but fucking was the predominant word whispered loudly by some of the very excited boys.

I never for a moment equated what they were doing with the loathsome Mr. Woolf and the pure, wholesome Miss Freemantle. She remained the angelic Madonna I drooled over, the Madonna with the fantastic, dreamworthy breasts.

23

FRIENDS & THE STORK

Hassan and Derek, Asad

A faithful friend is the medicine of life.
Ecclesiasticus

H assan was witty, funny, wise, poetic, smart, and very
thoughtful, making our friendship more cerebral
than other friendships. On occasion, I slept over at
his flat for the weekend. I admired Hassan and wished he were
my brother. We talked about the latest Egyptian jets flying overhead. At creative moments, we invented witticisms. He taught
me Marx Brothers songs, and we changed the lyrics to make
them funnier. During the Christmas season, when we sang carols

during assembly, we chanted, "While shepherds washed their socks by night/All seated round the tub/A bar of 'Sunshine soap' came down/and they began to scrub." And, "We three Kings of Orient are/Selling soap at two pence a bar/Fag ends at three pence/Match sticks at six pence/ Following yonder star." We laughed at our daring and silliness. He taught me some dirty ditties and limericks I still remember, and my favorite aphorism was, "I've had a perfectly wonderful evening. But this wasn't it."

He introduced me to the judicious use of water pistols and peashooters, aimed for fun at the girls during class, teaching me how to hide them when we were in danger of discovery. During recess, we played Frisbee in the classroom with the girls' berets while they rushed between us screaming, trying to retrieve them. These activities were punishable offenses if caught by a teacher or the prefect.

Asad and I lived in the same district in Zamalek and took the same school bus. We sat behind Ibrahim, watching him drive. When it rained, the windshield wiper flicked steadily, and occasionally, in a brief burst, it flicked uncontrollably fast. Asad suggested that when Ibrahim noticed a pretty woman, he got excited, making the windshield wipers move faster. We chuckled at the absurdity. The topic led us to compare our rudimentary knowledge of sex and our speculations about Miss Freemantle's sex life.

I never believed the German story that a stork brought babies. When I asked my mother where babies came from, she pointed downward, saying, "From a little hole down there." For the moment that had satisfied my curiosity. Now, in our relentless drive to learn the mysteries of sex, I made no connection to Gitta's garland-encircled private openings, or to Bakhita's breasts, or to finding my parents naked in bed. I told Asad what my mother had said. He laughed, convinced my information was wrong. He confessed with great awkwardness that he was mortified to learn his mother was expecting. How she got pregnant preoccupied him. He shook his head. "Can you imagine having a baby at her age? It's embarrassing. What will the embassy staff think? What will my friends think? How will I be able to face them?"

Weekends we sometimes lay on the embassy roof with binoculars to peek into the room of a neighbor's daughter, hoping to spy her. We never succeeded. At other times, we played cricket in the large embassy garden. He showed me how to eat green mangos with salt. Sometimes we practiced shooting with his air gun, aiming at the huge statue of the Indian Lion, pockmarking it. Occasionally, Hassan joined us with his newly constructed slingshot, impressing us with his accuracy in hitting squirrels. No matter what we did, Asad's agonizing thoughts returned to his mother's bulging belly.

"I found a book in the embassy's library," he told me soon after sharing the pregnancy news on the school bus. "I'll have to get it very carefully. I do not want the staff to see me looking in that book." Instructing me, he said, "Get off the bus with me. Use the servant's stairs to sneak up to my room. I'll smuggle the book up."

He entered his bedroom, locked the door, and then produced an old book hidden under his pullover. We lay on the floor thumbing through it. It was a general health manual. One of the diagrams showed the internal and external male and female anatomy which elicited his "Ah-ha" along with a self-conscious little laugh—one part of the puzzle. He blushed, lighting up his olive-skinned face.

I was too embarrassed to confess I had accidentally seen a similar view when I glimpsed my mother exiting the shower. She grabbed a towel to cover her front, turned around and then bent over to pick up the bath mat, exposing her external anatomy, albeit upside down, before shutting the door. What I glimpsed in those few evocative seconds, combined with the male and female diagrams in front of us, and what happened in the gym suddenly seemed to make sense of how things could possibly fit together. They failed to shed light on how his mother got pregnant, though.

One day Miss Freemantle instructed me in an unusually crisp tone, "Take the late school bus today." Was I in trouble? After the last bell, I made my way to homeroom, Miss Freemantle following close behind. She climbed the platform. On her desk were two stacks of papers. A girl walked in. Miss Freemantle ordered her to close the door. She stared down at us, solemn as we stood there a few feet apart. She held out our last homework assignment, mine in her right hand, the girl's in her left.

"You were to write about Alexander the Great." The pitch of her voice had risen to match her angry face. "You both wrote the same thing and drew a similar map of his empire with the route of his army's advance." She paused and the implication sank in. Turning to me she asked, "Did you copy Carol's work?"

"No." I was puzzled.

She turned to Carol. "Did you copy Marwan's homework?"

"No." Carol looked over at me. A pause followed.

Miss Freemantle surveyed us. "Do you ride the same bus?"

"No," we replied in unison.

There followed a longer pause, after which she asked, "Do you know each other?"

"No."

Exasperated, she took a step forward. "Carol, where did you get your information?"

"The *Oxford Children's Encyclopedia*."

I answered the same question, indicating I'd used the same source. We were dismissed.

Our unfamiliarity with each other did not last long. Carol sat next to Cynthia in front of me and Hassan. Emboldened by the recent vindication, Carol would turn to chat. I liked her bubbly manner.

The following Saturday night things got serious. The rotating strobe dimly lit the gym; the night was airless and the windows

were wide open. Nervous boys and girls stood along opposite
walls, bunched together chatting, apprehensively eyeing the
opposite sex while the music teacher played the latest hits on the
gramophone. The gym teacher yelled "girl's choice," encouraging
them to pick a partner. A few couples shuffled awkwardly
around the dance floor. Carol approached and I began to
perspire. She selected me from among a group of my friends,
took my sweaty hand, and pulled me into the middle of the
gym. My pals snickered. What had started as a fast dance, Bill
Haley and the Comets, became the Platters' slow "Smoke Gets
in Your Eyes." Carol continued to hang onto my hand. She
moved right into me, placing her cheek against mine. The boys
along the wall laughed, pointing at me. I was mortified. If only
the dance floor had opened to swallow me up. At the same time,
I felt grown up. I liked her cheek against mine. Curious feelings
of warmth rose within me—ones that would last through our
lifelong friendship.

Carol Ades

Carol was the only child of affluent parents. She told me that
her father, a merchant from Aleppo, had married a French
woman so they spoke French at home. He owned a very
successful upscale clothing shop in downtown Cairo. She lived
with her parents, but Lilly, her nanny, raised her. Carol had
attractive eyes, rich brown skin, and semi-curly black hair. We
became firm dancing partners. I found her ponytail, her
constant smile, and her forward personality attractive. Her easy

laughter was infectious, adding to her charm; the scent of her body was alluring. Like me, she was highly competitive. During recess, she would join a group of boys playing tag ball on the hedged croquet lawn. She was a fast runner and a swift ball thrower. Following her example, gradually more girls from our class joined the almost daily ball games. It made the boys and girls more comfortable with each other.

One afternoon, Hassan and I met Carol by chance at the prestigious Gezira Sporting and Jockey Club in Zamalek. We waged a bet that a girl could not climb the surrounding trees higher than a boy could. Accepting our challenge, she started to climb, wearing her leather school shoes and uniform. She was an impressive climber. The higher she went, the more easily we could look up her skirt at her ribbed white cotton panties. We giggled, and Carol suddenly recognized our game. Her demeanor became frosty. She descended rapidly, walking wordlessly away. We smiled at one another sheepishly. "What did we do?" we called after her innocently.

———

One Friday, Miss Freemantle asked Asad and me why we were in class past 4 p.m. We were co-captains, discussing strategy for a late afternoon cricket game against the boys from Victoria College, he told her. "You can't stay here. I am locking the room to go to a conference with the headmistress. It is too hot outside. Go up to my rooms to plan in comfort."

We entered her flat, uneasy yet elated, like two lowly priests intruding into the secret sanctum of our revered goddess. We looked at each other. We could not miss this opportunity. We locked the door, decided against switching on the red bulb, and headed straight to her bedroom. All reverence evaporated on finding her bras and knickers in a drawer. I fingered them, sniffed, enveloping myself in her body's scent, breathing the air of our idol. In that instant, she was mine alone. Not Woolf's—

all mine. We ran our hands over the cups of her shiny satin bras with curious wonder. Her deep drawers had an endless supply of undergarments, all types. We dropped them on the floor in a growing heap. Which ones did she wear when she was close to us? Which did the smutty Woolf fondle? I found a brownish bra and put it over my head. The cups covered my ears. In the mirror, it looked like a WWII bomber helmet. We laughed at the sight. Asad swung one over his head pretending to catch butterflies, simultaneously bouncing on her sofa bed. We rummaged with ebbing excitement. Disappointingly, there was nothing frilly or fancy. Fearing she might return shortly to discover our intrusion, we quickly folded what we had taken out and unlocked her door. I fancied that, with her approval, I had come very close to her. For the remaining quarter hour, we sat on her beige sofa with its magnificent view of the cricket pitch, the playing field, the waiting team members, trying to focus on our match strategy.

———

Hassan and I continued to share interest in airplanes, admiring the pictures in the *Observers Book on Aircraft*, building static models, sharing books about the daring feats of RAF and Luft-waffe pilots, gradually displaced our obsession with Miss Freemantle.

At mid-term, October 1956, Miss Freemantle prepared us for the eleven-plus examination. This evaluated our relative apti-tudes in the arts or the sciences. Depending on the outcome we would enter the science stream or the classic stream once in middle school. The results of the exam would become our end-of-year evaluation.

Mother kept all my school records, among which I found a letter handwritten by Miss Freemantle, mimeographed, and sent to all parents. She claimed we were an exceptional class of 39 children. Each child attained a high score—none less than 65%

—a perfect class. Ranked first with a score of 89% were Carol Ades and Cynthia Gardner. The second highest was Marwan Meguid with a score of 88%, while Hassan attained a score of 86%. Under Miss Freemantle's tutelage, I had moved to second position. I was extremely pleased, but I didn't receive accolades from Mother. My new decision—founded on my Dad's letter—to seek, strive, and not yield until I had mastered a subject was, I believe to this day, my way of showing him that I was worthy of being his son.

Suchitra, Gulnar, Cynthia, Hassan, Marwan and Asad with guide on top of Cheops Pyramid

We celebrated Cynthia's twelfth birthday. Her class friends and I followed a guide and her father to the top of the great Cheops Pyramid. The view was breathtaking, stretching across the luscious green Nile valley to the grey Mokattam Hills on the eastern edge of the delta. Cynthia's father took a photo of the small band of smiling youngsters leaning against the large blocks of granite on top of the Pyramid. It hangs on my study wall. We were at peace, blissfully ignorant of the coming calamity.

Shortly following mid-term, at dawn on October 29, 1956, disaster struck: the Suez War started. It was a war that forever changed our lives to a degree we could scarcely envisage. When the fighting stopped, Egypt's cosmopolitan intelligentsia—the large, international community of British, French, Italian, Greek, Levantine, wealthy Egyptian, Christian, and Jewish families that formed the middle class—and with it the multiethnic and multireligious society in which I had been raised—had been expelled. With it went many of my friends, among them close school friends with foreign passports, although they had been born in Egypt. Their departures added to my underlying sense of insecurity, rekindling the legacy of my early childhood. Was this my fate, *maktoob*, that closeness to people I cared for in my life led only to loss, pain, sadness, and emotional emptiness?

Miss Freemantle was evacuated, along with the entire foreign school staff, as the war erupted. We, her pupils, were the victims of Middle East politics, the consequence of the colonial past. She left without saying goodbye to her "exceptional class." Would I ever see her again? I would have shaken her hand, adding, "I'll wait for you, my darling, my sweet idol."

Fourteen years later, in the autumn of her years, Miss Freemantle and I would meet again.

PART III

1957-1960

We are each of us angels with only one wing,
And we can only fly by embracing one another.
—Luciano de Crescenzo

24

LETHAL LETTER
1957

If you would only recognize that life is hard,
things would be so much easier for you.
—Louis D. Brandeis

Daddy was due to arrive in Cairo from Beirut during the last week of February 1957. His self-described "duty complex" induced him to squeeze in a hurried visit to inspect the curriculum in a small primary school at a Palestinian refugee camp before boarding the United Nations plane. The school was high up in the northwest Lebanese mountains along the border with Israel. Due to the altitude and wintery conditions, the area was nicknamed the Switzerland of the Middle East. Unfamiliar with the climate, Daddy

Last picture of Daddy

traveled wearing a light anorak. The weather was freezing with blowing snow. Two days later, he returned to Beirut feverish, with a hacking cough. He was admitted to the American University Hospital on the 4th of March, 1957, and penned a brief one-pager to Mother, on hospital letterhead, informing her of his confinement to bed rest. His physicians had started him on antibiotics for a diagnosis of pleurisy—inflammation of his lung lining. He promised to write daily about his status. The letter came in the mail to Cairo the following morning.

Mother lived for these letters. He did not disappoint her. Beginning with their courtship in 1935, they wrote to each other regularly whenever they were apart.

She loved reading selected portions of his Beirut letters to us, particularly what she called the "messages from your father."

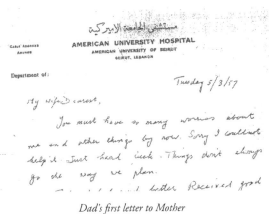

Dad's first letter to Mother

Mother ordered us to sit down after our evening meal. By now, Gulnar was fifteen; I would reach thirteen in a month. With Daddy's letter in hand, she stood in front of us, demanding our undivided attention. We obeyed, anxious for news about Daddy's health. These sickbed missives, written on both sides of airmail paper, were one sheet long. According to Mother, they were directed at his children. Gulnar and I were skeptical about the validity of Daddy's "messages," suspecting that she concocted or embellished them to reinforce her disciplinary control. Daddy would hardly be writing about these trivial domestic issues. One concerned Gulnar's repeated infringement of her 6 p.m. curfew, warning that she risked tainting her reputation in a conservative country and imploring her to abide by the time limit. Another was about what he perceived as my apathy regarding my Arabic homework. He instructed me to be more diligent. He would have had to be clairvoyant about some events to which she referred since the letter was in transit when they transpired.

"Pay attention. This is important," Mother would insist. I felt that some of Daddy's comments about my scholarship distorted the facts and could only have originated with her. She would not let us read the letters on the premise that they contained private comments addressed only to his wife. Further, we were not privy to her responses. Every day another letter would arrive, chronicling Daddy's hospital stay, his symptoms, their progress, what his team of doctors had said, the various tests done, their results, the treatments he had received, and the colleagues who had come to visit.

On reading his correspondence almost sixty years later, I found no specific paragraph titled "messages from your father." The letters, however, reflected a compulsive man on a mission to prove himself, driven once again into exhaustion. He had simply worked too hard to demonstrate that he could do this job. He held himself to an unreasonably superlative standard, seeking the rewards of a life-long contract with UNESCO, which came with a generous pension on retirement.

He was depressed at being alone, feared sickness, and downplayed his condition by withholding from his physician a critical symptom—the persistent burning of his left leg. He feared it might affect the ultimate employment decision. The description of his symptoms reminded me of his previous illness in Manchester—the utter exhaustion and weakness he had experienced two years earlier. In his medical history, Daddy had avoided reference to polio as a child, and his hospitalization in Manchester. Could he have had the second bout of the symptoms described as post-polio syndrome?

The pleurisy progressed to pneumonia, which he attributed

to the unaccustomed cold mountain weather. In addition to the antibiotics, he described receiving oxygen and having a morphine drip. He welcomed the prolonged bed rest and the pain-free sleep.

His March 6th letter was more cheerful. The doctor had tapped off accumulated fluid in his chest, which diminished his pain and eased his breathing. At that time, he mentioned to his physician that he was having a burning, aching, heavy sensation in his left calf. Since the muscles in this post-polio leg were underdeveloped, it would have been difficult to detect swelling of the leg when compared to his right one. His physicians attributed the calf pain to muscle strain from attempting to ski in the mountains.

———

At the beginning of the term I had managed to eke out 33% on my Arabic exam, reflecting the loss of learning during the Christmas holidays when there was no consistent tutoring. This dismal result would have displeased Daddy had he been in Cairo. Unbeknownst to me, Mother must have transmitted the poor grade to him. The news may have been delayed by some weeks as he was traveling. With the resumption of regular home lessons, I scored a passing grade of 65% at mid-term before Daddy arrived home. This grade would surely please Daddy on his return. The news of this better grade didn't reach Daddy perhaps because he was hospitalized.

In his letter to her, he enclosed an undated personal handwritten note to me. When I came home from school, Mother handed it to me, and stood in front of me as I read it:

My dear son,

I am very disappointed; I hear you only scored 33% in the early term Arabic

exam. Such results, especially after I
doubled your tutor's lessons and your
Arabic reading assignments, show you are
making no effort.

*Life is too easy and too comfortable for
you. If you had no father, you'd not
only make an effort, you'd have to
struggle, like I had to as I grew up,
and your life would be different. Conse-
quently, you might do better in school
and in your life.*

Meguid

Meguid? Why had he not signed *Daddy?* Was I not his *Dear son?* I was stunned. *Only if I had no father would I do well in life.* What sort of threat was this, based on one test result? I knew that his promise of dying was only figurative; nevertheless, the gravity of his message was in his formal signature, which emotionally distanced him from me. As I read and re-read his letter, I felt defenseless and utterly vulnerable. Mother had dumped me when I was four. Now that I was nearly thirteen, was my father abandoning me, too?

Mother had given me the open note, so she knew its contents. I hated her manipulations—payback for what? She was hardly a role model when it came to Arabic, for she made no effort to learn the language. Her persistent failure to see my Egyptian family during Daddy's absence sent me subliminal messages that they, and learning Arabic, were not important. "We," or at least she, was superior to them.

Did my father really know his wife, and had he considered these points before angrily scribbling his sentiments? I was boiling inside. I did not respond but instead remained stoic, not wanting to give Mother the satisfaction of seeing how profoundly Daddy's words wounded me.

My father's letter of March 8th announced that he would be discharged within a couple of days. He had procured a seat on the same plane Dag Hammarskjold, the UN Secretary General, would be flying to Cairo. Colleagues from UNESCO would meet my father at the airport. He mentioned again the pronounced burning sensation in his left calf—his polio leg. He said it felt tight, writing that rubbing it provided some relief, and adding, "Wanting to be discharged I have not brought it to the doctor's attention again." He expected to be home by 3 p.m. and looked forward to being alone with Mother. Gulnar and I would return home after 4 p.m.

The letter had an upbeat tone. I imagined our conversation in my head. "Yes," he would argue, "65% was better. Why couldn't you score 100%? As my son, you should be able to achieve that."

My reply: "Yes, I am so happy to be your son, but Daddy, I'm not you." Nevertheless, I somehow had to come up with an act to impress him, such was my hunger to restore his love for me.

A class friend, Tarek, had among his treasures a WWII German helmet and a bayonet in pristine condition, which he had found in the dry sands of El Alamein. We agreed that in exchange for the 1/72 scale Avro Lancaster Bomber I had finished building, he would lend me these two items. On March 10th I did not participate in after-school sports, coming home on the early bus to meet Daddy, hoping he would have forgotten his angry letter. I would take pleasure in his warm embrace. When I rang the front door bell, he would more than likely open it.

Hours earlier, around 8 a.m., while I was on my way to school rehearsing my act in my mind, the doctors in Beirut discharged Daddy. His pleurisy had completely cleared; he got out of bed to gather his belongings, anxious to catch his flight.

Eight hours later I rang the bell to our flat, having donned the helmet and drawn the bayonet, which glimmered in the landing's sunlight. I stood there like Caesar, poised with the dagger removed from its sheath, held in mid-air about to strike: a Roman pose of strength, in modern German regalia, a pose of manliness and defiance.

After a slight delay, Tante Mustakima opened the door, dressed from head to foot in black. Seeing my perplexed look, she drew me close to her ample bosom. "Your father died," was all she said. In my heart, I had known the instant the door was opened, for I heard the traditional wailing of women, and the simultaneous recitation of the Qur'an—both flooding through the widening door, gradually filled as if in slow motion by the expanse of Tante Mustakima's blackness.

Daddy had risen from ten days of bed rest and collapsed, dying instantly. The DC-3 carried a simple pine coffin to Cairo. It lay lengthwise across the floor of his book-filled study facing Mecca. Islam prohibits routine autopsies; the accompanying note from his physician in Beirut simply said, "Heart attack."

Was it?

Many years later, during my first year of clinical training, we learned of Homans' sign, indicative of deep vein thrombosis. An inflammation in the lining of the leg vein causes red cells to stack up one upon another like pennies, slowly growing in the deep vein of the calf and extending up the thigh into the pelvis. The clot, attached precariously to a point on the calf vein wall, waves around like seaweed as returning blood passes upwards to the heart. The clot builds during prolonged bed rest, often initiated by the presence of a systemic inflammation, like pneumonia. When the patient walks, the sausage-shaped clot is dislodged and shoots up into the heart, blocking the flow and snuffing out the oxygen of life. It is not a dramatic death, but an instant one.

Tante Souad supervised our servant making tea or cool lemonade for the guests, who sat about the wall of our entrance hall-cum-parlor paying their respects. She too was dressed in black, holding a soggy tissue to her ashen face. Auntie Jo, who spoke a lot more Arabic than Mother did, answered the constantly ringing telephone and doorbell, greeting and inviting in the guests who had come to offer condolences.

A United Nations staffer who accompanied the coffin handed Mother two envelopes. One contained £E100 (equivalent to ~$600), found in Daddy's suit jacket. The other was a signed, life-long contract with the United Nations, assuring the widow a nominal UN pension. I found my dazed Mother walking aimlessly among the mourners, wearing a light-colored spring dress. She was lost and passed me without saying a word.

A blind sheikh sat cross-legged on a cushion chanting Qur'anic verses. Three professional wailing women, all in black, sat barefoot, cross-legged next to one another on the sofa. On Tante Souad's cue they would weep or howl, individually or in unison, or between Qur'anic verses when the sheikh rested his voice. Gulnar, a lanky teenager, appeared from somewhere, speechless and dry-eyed. The headmaster, one of my father's former pupils, had given the news to Gulnar during lunch break then sent her home in his car to be with her mother.

I was bewildered, unable to comprehend the finality of the situation. Daddy's letter kept floating in front of my eyes. He would never know that in my last exam I had scored a passing grade. My effort had paid off. I had doubled my score in a matter of weeks. Now there was no way to tell him.

Unfamiliar with or disregarding Muslim customs, or expressing her anger, Mother irritated everyone by asking Daddy's sisters to dismiss the "noisy" wailing women and to pay off the sheikh, not realizing that their presence was not for her benefit, but for the numerous neighbors and friends who came calling. Many of Daddy's colleagues sat about the room in silence, their faces reflecting disbelief. I knew many of them by sight and greeted others, not remembering their names. They embraced and kissed me in keeping with tradition, saying words of comfort, telling me to be strong, and reminding me that I must now be a *man*, to protect Mother and Gulnar, according to our culture.

My mother aggravated the gathering by her persistent compulsion of shoving, with her feet, the roughly finished coffin to one side of the book-lined study, to conform to her Teutonic sense of order, allowing her to access the balcony. She should have stepped over the coffin or walked around it, as the rest of us did when we went to get some fresh air. My aunts repeatedly moved the coffin back to its original orientation with its long axis facing southeast in the direction of Mecca, without saying a word. They wanted their brother's soul to rise toward the holy city.

Around 6 p.m., the bell rang. Mother opened the door to the chauffer from the Indian Embassy. He carried platters of food—fish, chicken, salad, cooked vegetables, rice, and several desserts. The aromas immediately permeated the flat, making my mouth water. Minu, in Gulnar's class, had probably told her mother about my father's death. The Indian ambassador's family was Muslim, responding to the rituals of the moment with kindness.

Mother did not like Indian cuisine or fish. Suspecting all the dishes were curried, she refused the offerings and closed the door, telling the driver we did not eat that type of food. I was starving. Neither Gulnar, nor my relatives, nor Auntie Jo had eaten. Mortified, I hailed the driver from the balcony to return.

I did not understand Mother's actions; after all her years in Egypt, she had no comprehension of local customs or chose to ignore them. Daddy's death evoked in me a sense of *schaden-freude*—sadistic enjoyment—at Mother's pain and misfortune, giving me a feeling of retribution. I did not cry, although I tried. I was angry at receiving his hell of a letter.

Standing on our balcony overlooking the Nile, watching the day plunge into darkness, listening to the stray pack of roving dogs beginning to bark in the night, my reaction to Daddy's

Marwan on balcony of our flat

disappearance raised a series of questions in my mind. How can a son feel relieved at his father's death? How could he let himself die? Had he promised me that he would? Was he dead, or was the whole affair a cruel form of play-acting?

That night, after the guests, family, and Auntie Jo left, Mother irreverently straightened out the coffin again. She asked me if I wanted to see Daddy as she pried off the lid.

"No. I never want to see him again," I said. "The pain is too great. He falsely accused me of being lazy."

I resolved to pursue my life without the succor of a father.

25

GANAZAH

Funeral procession in Cairo Street

Oh, antic God return to me my father
—Lucille Clifton

The following morning, several of my uncles arrived on foot. The Indian Embassy's Cadillac, with Asad, took us to Tahrir Square. In the shadow of the menacingly monolithic government building—the Mogamma—a large funeral tent had been erected to one side on the grass. In keeping with tradition, we removed our shoes and entered. I joined Giddi, sitting on a cushion next to him, while he silently wept. The pillows lined the periphery of the tent, ready to receive the male family members and colleagues who came to pay their respects and then attend the funeral.

A remarkably small, shrouded body lay in the center of the carpeted floor. Daddy's numerous contemporaries, writers and friends, paid their condolences to a red-eyed Giddi and to me, and then joined us sitting cross-legged around the perimeter—a community gathering to honor my father. They murmured to themselves, glorifying God, with lips barely moving, *misbaha*—prayer beads—in hand.

Giddi, slightly sweating, grasped my arm. I could feel his fine tremor. He muttered something to me that was drowned out by the recitation of *Salat al Ganazah*—a funeral prayer—that offers a collective message of forgiveness to the dead, followed by the recitation of Qur'anic verses amplified by a loudspeaker into Tahrir Square.

Dried saliva strands webbed Giddi's cracked lips. He had not had breakfast, perhaps not even his morning tea. His weeping eyes, staring into mine, revealed the agony of his incomprehensible loss. I had *yet* to cry—perhaps I never would. Staring at the lifeless form under the shroud, I sat there trying to get in touch, to connect to Daddy, to somehow let him know that I was a good boy, that I knew he loved me, and I would miss him. The surroundings did not allow me to focus on this task. A constant stream of mourners interrupted my meditations.

Word of his death had traveled quickly. By mid-morning, a crowd of more than three hundred had gathered. Uncles and close colleagues, bearing Daddy's body on the wooden pallet covered with a red-mottled shroud, formed the head of the funeral procession. Asad and I lined up behind the body and began to walk, joined by suited dignitaries and luminaries, and followed by more uncles and Giddi in his *galabeya* making up the second row. Mourners included the Minister of Education; university professors and deans, including the head of Al Azhar University; and a number of Daddy's literary colleagues—Taha Hussein, Tawfik al-Hakim, Naguib Mahfouz. Our bank manager from the head office of The Egyptian National Bank was there, which surprised me. Less surprising was the presence of the head of the United Nations office in Cairo. Behind them, my numerous relatives mingled with Daddy's students and the young literary collaborators he had mentored. Men carrying memorial floral bouquets, sprays, and wreaths rounded off the lengthy train of mourners. Written on the banners of the bouquets were names of various university departments, faculties, teacher training colleges, and groups throughout the Arab world—places his books were in use, where he had taught and influenced a progressive national Arabic curriculum.

Family Mausoleum in the City of the Dead

The procession wound its way across Tahrir Square, against

the one-way Suleiman Pasha Street interrupting the oncoming traffic rush coming at us from the opposite direction. We walked toward Groppi restaurant. The funeral cortege edged its way through the street against oncoming automobiles, lorries, and donkey carts, parting the mid-day rush like a slow ship plowing through the oncoming waves. Cars swerved to one side and stopped, reverently allowing the procession to pass.

Was going against life's stream emblematic of Daddy's life? Fighting uphill against the odds, from an adobe hut to becoming known as a teacher and author throughout the Arab world? We walked in silence slowly along the street, Asad to my left, Giddi behind us, shaded from the mid-day sun by the tall office blocks.

If you had no father, you'd not only make an effort, you'd have to struggle, like I had to, and your life would be different, looped endlessly through my numb brain.

Overwhelmed by anger, I was convinced he had died on purpose, just to teach me a lesson. He wished to believe the worst of me based on one exam score, as Mother had tattled. Still in a state of disbelief, and draped in black, she, Auntie Jo, and most of my aunts watched the procession through Groppi Café's windows as it inched its way up Suleiman Pasha Street. Once in the Square, the mourners dispersed in groups of two and three.

Family Mausoleum. Plaques show names of those interred.

They interred Daddy in the family vault in the "City of the Dead," at the foot of the Mokattam Hills. He had bought the lot in Cairo's necropolis at the time of Sit Nazifa's premature death —ten by twenty-five meters, separated from other burial plots by high walls, entered through a locked, wrought-iron gate. Below the dirt surface of the desolate, sun-filled enclosure were sandstone crypts, reached by descending a central set of steps hewed out of the limestone. Sit Nazifa's shrouded remains lay to the left of the descending staircase, with space for family females on ledges below her. Daddy's body was placed in a freshly excavated vault to the right. After placement, earth filled in the stairs and the vaults, recreating the flat courtyard. He was out of my life, freeing me from the smarting nags.

Perhaps Sheikh Amin's tears were not only for the loss of his son, but also for the loss of the family steward. It was obvious that I would be a poor substitute.

My father's words filled me with rage against him, yet even more so toward Mother. She had set me up. It would be much more difficult to forgive her. My anger would transmute to simmering antipathy and indifference, growing gradually to approach the level of malice. Her day of reckoning would come.

Many years would pass and much personal growth would occur before I could forgive either one.

26

WHO'S THE MAN WE BURIED?

Daddy at age 20, 30 and 50

Life can only be understood backwards;
But it must be lived forwards.
—Søren Kierkegaard

T he events surrounding the arrival of the coffin brought home the fact that he was my father, one half of the two adults in my family, each with very distinct roles. Until that moment, with my father's overseas travel, the dominant figure in my daily life had been my mother. She was central in the domestic arena, refusing to bow to the culture into which she had married and I lived. He had been the breadwinner and the family's overarching guiding force. He had walked into the house and across her carpets when she implored him to remove his shoes at the door, as was her custom growing up in Hamburg. He refused. She may have thought she was the ruler of the house, but now I see that he was the pharaoh and this was Egypt, not Germany.

From 1949 to 1954, Mother had her promise of returning to Europe fulfilled. When we returned to Egypt, she suffered her husband's long absences while he worked at the university, or attended his writing group's late-night meetings, or visited his family on Fridays. He was always available to his students and colleagues and often ate out with them, giving little value to our family meals; work took precedence. She, the other half of the twosome, was the dependable stay-home wife, making sure her husband's physical needs were met in an effort to promote his career success. I cannot count the number of times after his death she said, in a self-righteous tone, that she would have preferred a new suit for him instead of spending the money on a dress for herself—a martyr to her mate.

Daddy had paid the price for his 1938 promise to return to Europe for her education; it was now his turn to proceed with his career, despite her great disappointment at being unable to work as a psychiatric social worker. In Egypt, there was no demand for her skills; family members took care of their own—well or sick.

Rents were high in upscale Zamalek when we returned in 1954. To enhance his income, Daddy once more started to consult overseas in Arab countries, perhaps seeking a better-paying job. On each visit home, he looked more tired and worn-out, with stress etched onto his face. His laughter became less frequent.

When he returned, he never seemed to be around. When he

was, he was too busy with fellow writers in his study, or irritated at his wife's refusal to accompany us to visit his family. On Saturday mornings, he took Gulnar and me to the cinema. At first, I was overjoyed, thinking he would accompany us, but he only ever bought two tickets and collected us when the program was over. Even now I recall my disappointment.

Was *this* the man who commanded a large public funeral in Cairo's city center? A shrouded body followed by dignitaries who I did not know? They were individuals who would recognize me as his son, and perhaps help me in my father's name, if only I had met them personally. I wished I had their personal or business cards, or knew the influencial positions they commanded in the government or at the university. Would they have attended his funeral had they known my side of him, the family man?

There were moments of happiness with him, when my sister and I horsed around at bedtime or on waking while we were youngsters in Cairo. At such times, he laughed a lot and seemed happy; he would hug me and sing improvised songs about my being his only son. I also recall my immense pride when he took me to visit his publisher. I saw the great variety of all his different books. What an important man he was, and how nicely people treated me when I was with him. I remember first feeling his face while I sat on his knees in the tram on our way to Sayeda Zeinab, the smell of his skin. In my first four years, I was a favored special son, cherished, rising in merit.

Thereafter my memory of him is vague, and I have more questions than answers. Why had he gotten off the train in Manchester? Was it then that he walked out of my emotional life? Where was he during the years we were adjusting to our traumatic existence in Germany? Did he approve of our absence? Did he and Mother conspire? What did they do in those two years before she started her university schooling in 1951? Did he miss us? Why had Daddy not come and taken us to live with them in Manchester? Did he think that depositing me at age four in Germany was more fortunate than his ouster at age six from Beni Harem? So many questions, and no answers.

Oma had displaced my mother, but Opa had not taken my Daddy's place. Opa engendered respect, not love. He never once held or kissed me. He taught me many practical things, other than his love for music. Among these included how to raise a new dog and ride my bicycle, but I do not recall his smell, or sleeping close to him. In Germany, I wanted my father's touch, the once familiar scent of his skin, his mere presence to hold my hand, and even scold me, knowing all the while that he loved me. Did he ever miss me?

In Wedel, I lived in the constant hope that he would come back and put an end to my misery. His only presence there was his portrait—a telling photo, one that spoke of achievement, looking off into the future, not at me. In Germany, Daddy faded gradually from my memory, like the reverse process of a developing photograph.

Apparently, he had visited once for Easter, 1950, per the date on the back of a photo taken in Oma's parlor. I search the picture for a lost memory: he sits close to Gulnar in an armchair. He looks stern, lost in thought, his gaze fixed straight ahead. Incredibly, for a Muslim, the dog sits on his lap, while Gulnar at his side wears an exuberant smile. I sit tentatively on the edge of Mother's armchair set at 90 degrees to Daddy's armchair, smiling happily. Her left arm is placed lightly about me, yet she too is stern. The picture seems staged. We are together, although the frostiness between my parents is evident. Were these, perhaps, different times when adults did not smile? Now, so many years later, I will never know.

Other photos taken during the same visit show a tense man, seemingly preoccupied. His only restful face, captured by Mother's Leica, was during his siesta with Gulnar when their heads were together on the same pillow—photos of my Daddy, but always with Gulnar. What happened to his cherished son?

There were the endless hero's tales about his life—same

story, different versions depending on the narrator: he was a self-made man; he forged his way from the mud village to success in Cairo; he studied under the streetlight to always get the highest marks. Then there were the narratives of his achievements at Al Azhar, his ability to recite the Qur'an yet speak and write English, German, French, and Hebrew. His siblings all looked up to him, admiring his determination and drive. Even Giddi contributed to these stories. The message was always clear to his grandson: be like your father—live up to his standards or surpass them.

Maybe the congregation of eminences who walked in silence behind his body knew that he had overcome many adversities. Perhaps he was the secret poster boy for his past students, but he was not mine. None of these luminaries would have accompanied him based on the picture I remember of our lives. I hated him, my Daddy. The endless stories of his successes angered me. I did not face the challenges he faced—I had my own. He failed to recognize that he had made it possible for me to have a different life than his, with other circumstances and opportunities.

I had some lingering thoughts. Was he aware he was about to die? The tone of his last letter to Mother was feeble, lacking spirits. It was the voice of a chronically tired man. When Mother read his words to us, they frightened me because they seemed to say *I am living yet dying and I want to come home to you.* Was the dramatic event of his death painful? Had he had a premonition? Did he regret sending such harsh words to his son? He could not have welcomed death, for he wrote that he looked forward to seeing his family.

On his demise, I discharged what I thought would be my final obligation to him, to appear at the head of his funeral procession. He used to say that the dead were lucky, that those who survived had all the problems, and he was right. Then he would quote Shakespeare: "He that dies pays all debts." This was also true; he had paid the debt incurred by the hasty promise prior to his marriage, almost twenty years earlier—the curse that ruled our lives.

Yet the reality of his death was painful, for in a strange way I missed his abiding influence eclipsing our home. His death began a new life for me. Now Mother, Gulnar, and I were three separate individuals orbiting in our own worlds, avoiding each other's state of distress.

I stayed away from my sister because of her heightened abrasiveness, since she feared that seventh-century Shari'ah law would empower me. *Dearest sister, I had no such ambitions to control your life.* I was only thirteen and had no desire to become the head of our household. I wanted to do what young boys do: play with my friends, clown around in school, go to school dances and to the movies, get to know the girls, read my *Aircraft Magazine,* and build model airplanes.

I shunned Mother because she tried several times to mold me into the man she had so abruptly lost. She tried to get me interested in the books that stood on his shelves. It was hard enough to keep up with school reading and homework. A few days after the funeral she took me into the bedroom and made me try on my father's suits. I had never worn a suit. I did not want to wear a suit. In my wildest dreams, I never imagined needing to wear one. As I stood there, trapped between the mirror of the open wardrobe door and Mother, I sensed she was completely out of touch with reality. She insisted I try them on, one suit after another. Their sleeves dangled beyond my hands, and I almost tripped over the long pant legs while she held up their waists to prevent them from slithering down to my ankles. All the while, she kept repeating, "They are made of such fine wool. It is a shame to waste them. Whenever we had extra money, I always wanted him to have a fine new suit." She went on, "We can't waste them. Daddy's tailor will shorten the sleeves and legs and pull the waist in . . ."

"I'll never wear suits. I like my shorts. I can't move in these things."

"But we'll take them to the tailor. He'll fix them for free because your father brought him from the village and helped him start his business. See, he'll raise the shoulders," she said as she pushed the pads over my pre-pubescent upper chest.

"No, no, no," I shouted as I wrenched off the clothes. "Leave me alone, I want to go and play! I want to go to school and be with my friends. Can't you understand that?"

In many ways, his death relieved me of a huge burden. At the time it seemed that his persona, his capability, his reputation, and his expectations stunted my self-worth—a giant oak over-shadowing a seedling. Despite my feeling of release, I had what Mother called "floating anxiety." Without my constant account-ability to my father, I was on the edge with nothing to anchor me to reality. I was freer, yet he continued to exert his phantom presence. My world was opening up, but his power over me persisted, as evidenced by daily entries to my diary in which I implored myself to work harder, using such phrases as, "I've been playing too much . . . I must work more . . . I cannot fail." Yet as time would show, his drive and determination were imprinted on me. They coursed through my blood. His body was gone, but his spirit—like a curse—remained. I had to resolve my anger at his death, the feeling that he had deserted me on the cusp of manhood when I would need him most.

This welter of unresolved feelings prevented me from going to his grave. I only visited several years later, after Giddi had also died. I went reluctantly, at my aunts' behest. After the groundskeeper had unlocked the wrought iron gate, I stepped into the stark, barren courtyard. There was no shade under the blazing morning sun. A couple of dusty cactuses grew in pots to one side. Inserted into the facing wall at the far end were marble engraved plaques recording the names and dates of Sit Nazifa, Giddi, Daddy, and his siblings who had since died.

"Say the Lord's Prayer, Marwan," urged Tante Souad repeat-edly, as she and Tante Mustakima started to mumble their recita-tions. Before I could begin, years of pent-up emotion burst forth and I broke down and wept—not for love and longing, as I did for Oma, but out of raw fury at the man whose affection, recognition, and acknowledgement I had wanted and worked so hard for, but who had only tortured me. My plea of "Why Daddy, why . . ." was drowned out as the hired sheikh standing behind me started reciting the Qur'an, while a jumbo-jet roared overhead from Cairo's nearby airport on its way to a foreign land.

27
___

EXISTENTIAL CRISIS

Giddi and Marwan

*The zebra's fur coat is black due to its black skin pigmentation.
Its white stripes are areas that lack pigmentation.*
—Scott Camazine

The feeling that I had never been good enough to meet my father's approval persisted—now much exaggerated by the lost opportunities to prove otherwise. With his death, the lack of daily opportunities to prove my worthiness weighed me down to an almost unbearable depth. Given my relative Germanic appearance and my self-conscious, inadequate Arabic, I struggled with who I was. Language and its culture confer identity.

My sense of emptiness amidst the uncertainty of our new family dynamics drove me to visit Giddi. I traveled from the cold, Teutonic environment of my Zamalek home to the once predominantly Islamic district of Sayeda Zeinab, to the flat with its comforting cooking smells and familiar noises. In Giddi's company, I felt no conflict or confusion. He was my father's father. I was of his flesh and blood, a *Sa'idi* Egyptian. I ached for his closeness. Holding me, kissing me, he transformed me within his magical embrace. I loved the unpretentious man who emanated my father's odor. Speaking softly, occasionally in *Sa'idi*, he knew I understood more than I could express.

He was clearly suffering from the unexpected death of his oldest son. He had lost his appetite, along with the will to walk to the mosque. We prayed sitting on the sofa, facing Mecca, starting by striking our thighs twice—a religious dispensation for those unable to prostrate themselves. Following a light lunch, we retired to the sitting room. He rested his arthritic hand on my arm—his physical contact signifying my acceptance and a connection to his son.

The Mosques of Sayeda Zeinab

Giddi was the only remaining male in the household. Tante Sanaa, the youngest of my aunts, remained unmarried, and wore her *thawb*—the loose, long-sleeved, ankle-length garment with black embroidery. She occasionally looked in to inquire anxiously about her widowed father's needs, or to offer us mint tea or iced water. Ten years later Sanaa, who my father had guided into teaching, would become the headmistress of a private girls' school in Saudi Arabia, amassing a little fortune, in dollars, and return to support the family in greater comfort. Tante Souad sat in the dim dining room weeping quietly, gripping a soggy Kleenex as she had done in Manchester. A hijab covered her once-coiffed hair and she wore black, replacing the flowery European dresses I remembered. She stared in front of her into the darkness, her lips moving incessantly, no doubt reciting the Qur'an. Tante Mustakima, Giddi's eldest daughter and the bastion of the female clan, was absent—now married and with a son.

We were two men—one in the spring of despair, the other in the desolation of winter—immersed in the boundless pain of our loss. We grieved. Long periods of silence cemented our love while we watched specks of dust dancing in sunbeams as the breeze coming through the open window blew the flimsy curtains. He would shed slow tears that welled up and gently cascaded down his pale cheeks, like raindrops running down a windowpane. Perhaps he was dreaming of the time his son was born, or the time when his son was six years old and he had to send him away from the village on the insistence of his second wife, Nazifa—his precious first born, off to Cairo to fend for himself—as he dreamed of greatness within his son's potential. My sadness was mixed with regrets, even though I could not have done more to get Daddy's approval. Tante Souad listening to the mid-afternoon Qur'anic recitations on the radio intruded into our reverie. These broadcasts punctuated the day, giving life its structure, providing communal familiarity, a sense of belonging, and the predictable comfort of a rhythm.

Breaking the stillness, he told me in his raspy voice, "I am certain you'll be successful like my son." He used words that conveyed the characteristics he wanted to see in me: strong, hardworking, respected, concluding with ". . . a great man. Marwan, don't forget to pray every day, thanking Allah for He is the Most Gracious, the Most Merciful." Each loaded word sent me slowly sinking into the depths of a lake made by his tears. Hypnotized by his voice I understood his urging, his expectations. I met each adjective with unquestioned agreement.

"Yes, Giddi, yes; I want that too; I won't let you down."

"Take care of your mother. Abdel Aziz always said she was a good woman," he murmured. I wondered how he would feel if he knew her from my perspective. "And Gulnar's honor . . . she is your sister, it's your duty." He was now sobbing more openly.

I put my arm about him. "Yes, Giddi," I answered tearfully. I wanted my words to carry conviction, yet doubted my ability to accomplish his wishes, despite being the nominal head of the family. Giddi repeatedly conveyed such messages in our weekly lunches—more authoritatively than the unforgivable message in Daddy's last letter, and more powerfully than his countless naggings.

Departing meant ending an afternoon of family communion at 7 Haret Omar Street, now with its neglected flat in a rundown, decaying neighborhood that had once resonated with familiar voices, joviality, my numerous uncles, and a table brimming with food and love. It might as well have been a king's villa, a pharaohs' palace.

Returning to Zamalek, I would take the late afternoon bus, riding in the second-class compartment at the rear, wedged by choice among the *baladi*—common folk—and loving their oppressive body heat crowding me. Each stop brought more fatigued riders squeezing into the overcrowded compartment, inhaling each other's fetid breaths. I wanted to blend in, to be perceived as one of my Egyptian kinfolks, for much had changed in Egypt since we had left it for Europe. What did everyone on the bus know that I was missing? How could I be an Egyptian when I was unfamiliar with the most common gossip, current cultural norms and established customs? To me, the whole *urfi marriage* business—contract marriage for a limited time to produce an heir for Tante Mustakima—revealed my lack of awareness of many aspects of Egyptian-Islamic life.

Why did President Nasser's weekly speeches start in Standard Arabic for the educated few, then quickly switch to colloquial Egyptian for the masses? Why was I going to an English school, whose mission had been to groom the next generation of Egyptian leaders with loyalties to Britain, when that strata of society were now in disfavor? How could I hope to become a pilot or a doctor without fluently speaking my native tongue in all its complex forms, as my father had done? In his absence and without his help, what was my fate? Was merely riding with the common folk sufficient to allay my anxieties?

My trepidations about my existential being and my societal acceptance continued, reinforced by my ignorance. My Egyptian stripes were pale, while my Germanic stripes betrayed my desire to be accepted as a native son. Would I ever be comfortable in my own skin?

28

THE FORLORN WIDOW

Mother

We will now discuss in a little more detail the Struggle for Existence.
—Charles Darwin

In the absence of a will, Sharia laws determined the disposition of Daddy's estate. I would get 48%, Gulnar 24%, and Mother 14%, with the remainder divided among the family. I was not interested in inheriting, nor did I expect an inheritance; I wanted a mother to continue providing a home and taking care of us. Giddi made it known that the family would forsake its share "to enable Abdel Aziz's children to continue their English School education." With the wisdom of age and that of a former teacher, he understood the effects of our five years' absence from Egypt on our Arabic language.

My European-looking mother was forty-three, fair-skinned, and no doubt attractive to Egyptian men. A string of suitors paraded through our home, each declaring that he would be our new father. Apart from Gulnar and I rating them sternly to discourage Mother from remarrying, I wondered if some were more interested in Gulnar. My mother and sister were enlightened women steeped in European values of independence, and Mother skillfully navigated social expectations.

Survival in a male-dominated Muslim society without a husband and father to financially support us became another concern. Neither Gulnar nor I had any idea of our economic circumstances. Before Daddy died, home was a second-floor flat on the northern tip of Zamalek. From our balcony, I watched the majestic *feluccas* gently sail down the mighty river

Feluccas

through the heart of Cairo, bearing goods from Upper Egypt. I wondered with envy about the seemingly carefree lives of the sailors and peasants as their cargo-laden ships glided gently for days, blown by the wind and swept by the Nile's rapid currents from its spring well in central Africa, through Sudan, Upper Egypt, past my ancestral home, Beni Harem, on for another 400 km to Cairo and past my view.

After his death, we could no longer afford the rent. Mother found a less expensive but actually nicer flat, close to the commercial center of Zamalek. The same French and Italian architects who designed elegant buildings along the boulevards in Geneva and Rome had designed most blocks of flats over-

looking the Nile in the pre-WWII era. Ours was on the top floor
of a modest high-rise at Hassan Assam Street overlooking the
Officer's Club, where President Nasser gave his numerous two-
to-three-hour Friday speeches. We managed to keep going, with
my mother teaching German at Cairo's American University and
at the English School.

Mother shared the news that the Cairo branch manager of
Egypt's National Bank had written her: "Records show that your
husband had only one wife. There was only one joint bank
account."

"Of course," she said with indignation, unaware she was
showing her naiveté; Mother was not in touch with realities of
Islamic life. I could not figure if her expression concerning the
letter was one of consternation or annoyance. She may have
rightfully trusted Daddy's fidelity; however, she lived in a
Muslim milieu. Sometimes after a man's death another family
surfaced.

Mother had to become our legal guardian until we came of
age at eighteen. She said that the bank manager was an honor-
able man endowed with Daddy's many fine personal qualities.
His name cropped up often in her conversations. She continued,
"He is very kind, most helpful in assisting me to complete the
mountain of paperwork needed by the *Maglis El Hasba*
—Welfare Council." Apparently, she had formed a gratifying
relationship with him, initially to advance her fatherless children's interests; later, through her letters, I discovered how intimate their liaison had become.

The slow process of filling out endless forms overwhelmed
her. For almost two years, she supplied a myriad of Arabic docu-
ments in support of her application in a language she did not
speak or fully understand. She had to appear before the *Maglis
El Hasba's* judges multiple times. After each ordeal, she came
home around noon exhausted, then showered and took a siesta.
When I returned from school, Mother, robot-like, made me a
tasteless German meal, for she did not like onions, garlic, olives,

or Egyptian spices. She did not like to hear Arabic songs or the hit parade coming from my room. The mood in the house would lighten when she played Mozart's Jupiter Symphony, Bruch's or Mendelssohn's Violin Concertos, or Bach's double violin concerto on the gramophone in the parlor. She did this often enough that I could whistle them.

Late afternoons she often went to see Mrs. Rosemary Johnston. While the women visited, I eagerly played outside with the twins. On the Saturday closest to my April birthday, Mrs. Johnston arranged an afternoon American-style barbeque. Almost thirteen, I rode the elevator to their penthouse to find Mother in earnest discussion with Mrs. Johnston. They quickly stopped speaking when they saw me.

I joined the boys at a separate children's picnic table. Their *sufragi*—butler—cooked hot dogs on a grill and served them to us on sweet rolls, garnished with ketchup, mustard, and relish. These American flavors were new to me, and very different from the savor of Egyptian cooking. Homemade vanilla ice cream topped with Hershey's Chocolate Syrup followed. The twins wanted marshmallow fluff topping.

"Marshmallow? What is that?"

The boys explained its sweet taste and gooey consistency in detail. The dishes returned with white "stuff" plunked on top of the chocolate. I took one bite expecting heavenly delight. I spat out the lot. "It's revolting! It tastes like mayonnaise." Sure enough, the *sufragi* had mixed up the Hellman's Mayonnaise jar with the marshmallow fluff. They looked alike to someone who could not read English.

Mother sat near the penthouse railing. She looked down at me sitting at my lower perch on the children's picnic table.

"You know that the Johnstons are returning to the States in about a month. They want to adopt you. You would grow up in California with Jamie and Jeffery. You will love living there."

I could not believe what I was hearing. There was a searing pain in my stomach. I nearly vomited. Once more she was going to abandon me, to dump me with strangers. She was taking me from my Egyptian homeland again. I was stunned speechless that she was going to give me away. Her very words sliced open my wounds of rejection. I got up, burning with hatred for the woman who did not value me, as the others faded away. Mother and I stood facing each other, and as I approached her, God help me, I wanted to shove her backwards over the seventh-floor railing. Instead, I ran to the exit and down the stairs.

Nothing came of this adoption scheme. I was fatherless, not an orphan. Adoption of non-family members was not encouraged in Islam. Did Mother not know that? How could she? She was not familiar with the tenets of Islam and its cultural teachings. Neither Sheikh Amin nor I would have consented. The subject did not arise again, but emotional pain had been inflicted once more, weakening any tenuous bond that remained between us.

A few weeks later Mother suggested I join the Egyptian Boy Scouts. "Since you speak German, you can join them at the summer Jamboree in Germany. Once there, you should not return to Egypt. Go to Oma." Again, I was shocked. Did she not get it? Egypt was my home.

Even so, I gradually began to understand how difficult life in Egypt would be without my father to open doors, place me in privileged positions, and advance my career. Who would protect me? My uncles held allegiance to their own families. Mother was far too independent to consider becoming a second wife or a dependent to one of the brothers.

By the time I was thirteen, one year after the end of the last Israeli-Egyptian war, military rhetoric in the press and on the radio was rising once more. I became aware of the approaching age of conscription—sixteen. My friends and I realized that to the government we'd be cannon fodder. Little by little, I began to see Mother's efforts to get me out of Egypt in a changing light, given the escalating verbal and propaganda conflict with Israel. My understanding was slow in coming, given the permanent emotional gap that existed between Mother and me. Gulnar, though not worried about conscription, feared being married off. We listened to Mother's suggestions with suspicion as to her motives, because we did not trust her.

My need for a Plan B, to avoid conscription, was spurred by a letter from Mrs. Johnston typed to "Margarite, Marwan, and Gulnar." It arrived from Sonoma, California, in 1957:

```
We think of you often and fondly,
always, and many times speculate on
whether we couldn't talk you into
leaving Egypt, with all the happy and
sad memories it must hold for you all,
and starting a new, freer, happier life
with us back in our wonderful little
California town of Sonoma. Did I ever
tell you, Margarite, that we live about
a mile from the California State
Hospital for mentally retarded "chil-
dren"? How happy they would be to snap
you up and put you on their staff! You
must really give us a chance to try; at
least, to talk you into coming home with
us. You really owe it to Marwan and Guni
to think it over. It would mean such
happy prospects for their young lives.
```

The last sentence stopped me short. I had no thoughts of going to America; Egypt's educational orientation was British. Mrs. Johnston's words stayed with me, planting the idea that I would have to devise a plan to get a passport with an exit visa, independent of my mother's impractical exit schemes that would likely be transparent to military authorities. They hung on to any young man who was a potential soldier.

29

INFATUATIONS

1957-1960

Body and mind, like man and wife, do not always agree to die
together
—Charles C. Colton

W hen I was four years old, Baba took me onto our
Giza balcony to show me the blazing Mokattam
ammunitions dump. This was in 1948 during the
first Arab-Israeli War. The conflict ended indecisively; the
Armistice Agreement signed in 1949 meant Egypt remained
technically at war with Israel.

We were in Manchester in July 1952 when we learned from
the BBC that the Free Officer Movement had deposed King
Farouk. Colonel Nasser, with his junta, was in charge of Egypt.
This included two junior officers, Sadat and Mubarak; together
they had served during that Arab-Israel war. Baba, considering it
progress towards a modern Egypt, had been upbeat about the
news. Mother was indifferent. I overheard no debate concerning
the abolishment of the monarchy, or the establishment of an
Egyptian Republic, two topics much discussed on BBC's Radio
3. Prior to our return to Egypt, I recall no discussion following
Baba's return from the London embassy with our new passports

about the implications of a pro-Palestinian national agenda, or the ending of Britain's eighty-five-year occupation.

In the decade of the Fifties, nationalism was constantly whipped up in the government media—movies, songs and press. The political atmosphere remained tense, with the propaganda stream against the Zionists hyped by the daily news of Egyptian commando raids launched into Israel. The pro-Palestinian agenda was to liberate occupied Arab lands.

Egyptians were proud of Nasser's leadership role in the Non-Aligned Movement, joined by Prime Minister Nehru of India, President Tito of Yugoslavia, and two-thirds of the countries in the United Nations. The Movement was against the great powers (Britain and France), imperialism, colonialism, foreign aggression, and domination. Their political stance was for the middle course between the Western and Eastern Blocs in the Cold War.

Some of my friends were ardent proponents of the military government, leading to heated playground debates. Despite Nasser's non-aligned stance, we felt assured that the World Bank would approve Egypt's 1954 request to finance the $400 million needed for the construction of the new Aswan High Dam in Upper Egypt, the cornerstone of the country's future development plan. It would control the annual Nile floods, triple the generation of hydroelectric power for industry, and increase the agricultural acreage to feed the growing population. We fervently supported these goals, which promised the modernization of a prosperous Egypt that our generation would inherit.

John Foster Dulles changed my life around my twelfth birthday. He recommended that the U.S. Congress and the World Bank refuse funding the dam. In response, Nasser addressed the people of Egypt. I lay on a chaise lounge on the balcony one hot July Cairo night, watching the stars, cooled by the Mediterranean breeze that came down to Cairo from the north, listening intently to the President's lengthy speech. He declared in colloquial Arabic that he had nationalized the Suez Canal to finance the Dam. Jubilation followed. Crowds of proud Egyptians poured into the street celebrating. At last, we could say "our Suez Canal." We could collect the revenue generated by the Suez Canal, about $400 million per year, allowing the High Dam Project to continue.

The English language *Egyptian Gazette* reported anger and consternation in London and Paris at the loss of the $400 million revenue from the British and French corporation, *Universal Company of the Maritime Canal of Suez*. The corporation had constructed and operated the canal between the Mediterranean and the Red Sea through Egypt from 1869 until the 1956 Suez Crisis.

The previous year Nasser had closed Britain's military bases that had protected the canal during WWII, and evicted British soldiers. Now Nasser had grabbed the Anglo-French canal itself. In an effort to cripple it, British and French ship pilots who steered the oil tankers transiting the narrow canal were promptly withdrawn. These ships guaranteed the continuous supply from the oilfields of the Middle East to European industry. Egyptian and Eastern-Bloc pilots replaced them and the canal continued to function smoothly. Revenues poured into Egyptian coffers. Egyptian nationalism soared.

During this time, France supplied Israel with Mystère jets— modern fighter planes. We followed daily reports of the progress made by a French naval convoy sailing to Haifa with uranium for Israel's first atomic bomb. We worried. War tensions sharply increased when the West refused to supply Egypt with modern weapons. Czechoslovakia did, pushing Nasser into alignment with the Soviet Bloc.

My cousins and I watched the annual parades of Egypt's modern military might, standing in the street among the crowds, seeing rows upon rows of commando and infantry units march by. We cheered, unaware that the poorly paid conscripts had no incentive to fight. Endless columns of Soviet T-32 and T-34 tanks and armored vehicles followed the marching men past Nasser's reviewing stand. Russian Mig-15 and Mig-17 fighter jets, accompanied by Ilyushin-18 jet bombers, flew overhead in gleaming silver formations. Our pride was palpable.

To reclaim the canal and destroy the new Egyptian military there followed the disastrous Suez War in late October 1956. Prime Minister Anthony Eden of Great Britain hatched the plan. Israel would attack Egypt by invading the Sinai, threatening normal shipping in the canal, which would limit oil supplies to the European market. The newly equipped Egyptian Army advanced into Sinai to stop Israeli progress onto the canal.

We listened to the BBC World Service on our little short-wave radio. A few days later, British and French forces attacked Port Said and Ismailia, on the pretense of separating the fighting armies, to repossess the canal. From dawn until dusk, the terrifying air raid sirens wailed as British, French, or Israeli planes attacked vital communication centers around Cairo.

The military built brick walls across apartment entrance halls, converting them to air raid shelters. I snuck onto our balcony during one air raid. Across the Nile, black puffs from anti-aircraft guns filled the bright sky. I was excited—a real war! Suddenly a high-flying silver speck exploded. A parachute emerged from the falling debris and floated downwards toward the opposite riverbank. I cheered, until I saw an angry mob, like a pack of wild dogs, arms extended skywards and wielding sticks, move like a tsunami toward the descending pilot. The police reached him first, snatched the pilot in mid-air and placed him in a protective cage. The frenzied mob surrounded it, shouting, and beating it. This was the reality of war—nothing like what I had seen in movies.

The Israelis, with British and French help, trapped and annihilated the Egyptian Army in the Sinai, seizing the canal and humiliating President Nasser. Radio Cairo proclaimed vastly exaggerated Egyptian victories. Public knowledge of the disaster's extent led to anti-government demonstrations, which failed to displace Nasser. On December 24, 1956, President Eisenhower forced the foreign troops to withdraw after Mr. Khrushchev threatened nuclear war. The lack of accountability and veracity by the Egyptian government undermined my confidence in wanting to live in a future Egypt.

During the summer of 1957, smarting from the loss of my father, I rose with the *fajr* prayers at four in the morning. In the quiet hours of dawn, my recitations engendered a sense of determination. I tried to communicate with Daddy, promising him I would do my very best at school. A few days before the anniversary of his death I always felt downhearted, the effect of my anger for his unjust punishment. I wanted him to be proud of me. My summer followed a routine that would have pleased Opa. Following prayers, I walked to the nearby Gezira Sporting and Jockey Club and swam laps in the Olympic pool, which I usually had to myself. Exhausted yet revived, I returned home around eight for breakfast. I settled at my desk to study, including Arabic—reviewing my past lessons, preparing for the next term. Our servant made me a light lunch, and then I would nap, visit with Hassan or Asad, or go to the club seeking friends.

Then came Kinga.

Kinga

I met her by the pool. In the blaze of afternoon light, she was a tall, slim, blonde-haired girl in a red bikini with her hair casually pinned up. About my age, she appeared unexpectedly in front of me. There was a soft radiant vibrancy about her. She smiled at me brightly, exposing her most unique feature, the gap between her upper front teeth. We introduced ourselves. Her little sister tried to pull her into the water, though she continued looking at me with interest. She was Hungarian. I was smitten.

She spread a large red towel in the shadow of a tree, inviting me to join her. She propped herself up on her left elbow, innocently exaggerating her slim figure like no Egyptian girl would, comfortable in her body. We told each other our stories without haste the whole afternoon. She lived on the east bank of the Danube in Pest, the more affluent part of Budapest. I had nearly forgotten the annoying little sister she was babysitting. I savored the tone of her voice and every word uttered from her delectable lips. She attended the American school; we did not have mutual friends. We parted, and I hoped to see her again. Fortunately, I encountered her at the club with daily anticipatory joy. We spent the summer afternoons getting to know each other and became fast friends. She taught me *saratlak*—Hungarian for *I love you.* I taught her the same phrase in Arabic—*bahibak.* How easy it was to fall in love. I learned she was not a morning person. On the afternoons she did not appear at the club, I frantically searched the grounds, wanting her. Not finding her, I would worry she had forsaken me.

I adoringly called her Pussy, a term of endearment, for she seemed exquisitely soft, gentle like a kitty, and as I had first read in Lear's poem *The Owl and the Pussycat*, not knowing it had a sexual connotation. One day when I visited their home to present her with a model plane, her mother asked me why I called her daughter that. She could see from my gooey-ness that I was a very romantic thirteen. Her father, the commercial attaché at the Hungarian Embassy, asked if I would like to come with them to Agamy, an exclusive beach community west of Alexandria, where they had rented a house. I could sleep in the guesthouse. Without hesitation, I agreed. Mother was surprised. "I didn't know you had a girlfriend." There was a lot I kept from Mother.

I spent four days on the soft yellow beach under a bright blue umbrella with her parents and her annoying eight-year-old sister. I chatted with her father, who seemed to miss having a son. We kidded around. His wife rebuked him when, laughingly, he taught me some naughty Hungarian words. Kinga rarely joined us until eleven in the morning, when we would go for a walk along the firm sand, the rolling waves rushing in to cool our feet. I was love-struck by her smile, the gap in her teeth, and her blonde hair, but too proper to hold her hand—let alone to try doing more than that.

Her father was recalled to Hungary and Kinga threw a huge party. We danced to songs by the Everly Brothers, Neil Sedaka, and Paul Anka. She was a party girl. She danced with all the young men and I felt pangs of jealousy. The musical messages of the hope, the pain of love, and of love lost and found touched my adolescent heart. When I left the party to meet my 11 p.m. curfew, she hung onto my jacket, imploring me to stay longer. I can feel the lingering farewell kiss she planted on my lips, her arms embracing me closely. I floated home with the Everly Brothers refrain, *Never knew what I missed until I kissed her/How did I exist until I kissed her* ringing through my head. We remained occasional pen pals for the next three years. I attempted to visit her, but the Hungarian Communist authorities would not grant me a visa.

That autumn term one-third of the class were girls, and they were smart, multilingual, and came from affluent families. Among them was She'ham Shaffei, very bright, smart, good-looking Egyptian, the daughter of my parents' friends, both of whom were physicians at the university.

Prior to my dad's death, he, Mother, and I had gone to their house for dinner. The conversation revolved around She'ham and me. Both families agreed that we would make an excellent couple for eventual marriage. We became friendlier during class, but I never felt the same sensations of passion and longing I had for Kinga, or the same thrill when I saw her on a daily basis in class.

Perhaps it would have turned out very well had an arranged marriage taken place in the absence of passion. My future in Egypt would have been secure under such a union, and my anxiety would have evaporated. Perhaps. But that wasn't what I had imagined my future would hold.

30

BROTHERLY BONDS

1957-1960

Hyim, Armenag, two friends, and Hossam—Brotherly Bonds

*Don't walk behind me; I may not lead. Don't walk in front of me; I
may not follow. Just walk beside me and be my friend.*
—Albert Camus.

I was thirteen and in the coming years I forged bonds that
remain to this day. Without a father I turned to friends,
and at the English School Cairo, we set about expanding
and testing our developing male confidence. The school's philos-
ophy was to deliver a first-class education that required of the

students the surety and ability to perform under pressure. I loved it.

President Nasser's weekly two-to-three-hour Friday speeches echoed across the cool evening breeze to our balcony in the late spring. I listened with passion, wanting to believe him since he spoke with a clear, authoritative voice similar to my father's. Addressing the Egyptian people—addressing me—his voice poured over the rooftops of Zamalek as he talked about building the massive High Dam. Nasser wanted a modern Egypt.

He spoke of the dangers of the Muslim Brotherhood, emphasizing his opposition to their antiquated Sharia laws. His voice boomed, "The Brotherhood's chief policy theorist, Sayyid Qutb, came to see me today telling me to pass a law dictating women wear the hijab. I told him, 'How can I make millions of women cover their heads when you can't make your daughter, a physician, cover hers?'" The audience roared with laughter. With time, he jailed most of the group's leaders and executed Sayyid Qutb. To the Egyptian people he was a soft, beloved, yet forceful leader. I would read in the paper that in the elections held the day before, he had won by 99.9%. I believed it, because he made me feel relevant and important as a young Egyptian—we were the future.

To the larger Arab world, he whipped up anti-colonial fervor, berating the Western military for their bases in Libya and Cyprus. He used poetic Arabic phrases, threatening to push Israel into the sea, liberating occupied Arab lands. Not that the Arabs were planning to do this exactly, but to reflect the injustices we felt committed against us. We wanted them recognized and corrected. What young man could be against such sentiments?

He embellished the theme of national Pan-Arabism, proposing a union that brought together the 360 million Arabs under his political umbrella. The union would have extended from Morocco in the west to Syria in the north, the Gulf States including Saudi Arabia to the east, to Sudan and Yemen in the south—the United Arab Republic. I liked the idea, and never for once imagined it would be difficult to do. After all, there was the United States of America.

Nasser promoted the sentiment of Egyptian nationalism, underpinning it with the idea of military might, elevating the armed forces into the ruling class. My heart swelled with pride, wanting to believe and support what I heard, yet the prospect of achieving these goals with my looming army conscription unsettled me.

From the same stage, the internationally famous singer and national icon, Umm Kulthum, sang in her low contralto, chanting intimate love songs. The emotionally roused audience encouraged her with encores.

I lay on the balcony listening to both of their voices in turn wafting over the rooftops. One engendered pride in the Egyptian nation, the other captivated the population, including myself, singing the sentimental refrains of my favorite song, *Enta Umri* —You Are My Life—yearning more just to love than addressing anyone in particular.

Hossam, Mohammed, Henry, Barete, Amr, Armenag, and Ibrahim

With the 1957 spring term, Hassan and I, like brothers, jumped into the second class of Senior School based on our

performance. Asad, a year younger, entered the first. I was apprehensive about skipping a class once more, for it meant huge
knowledge deficits, especially in math. It was comforting being
with Hassan, although I was sorry that our band of friends had
dispersed. Carol went to Geneva and Cynthia to the American
School in Cairo. We made a new set of friends, among them
Armenag, his cousin Atkin, as well as Ibrahim, Samir, and
Mohammed—all of whom, along with Hassan, would meet
again at school reunions in London, where most of the class
eventually settled.

Our band of friends attended each other's birthday parties,
where we mixed freely with our classmates—boys and girls. The
focus was on the generous buffets. Hassan and I hung around
the entrance to the dining room, where the servants were placing
the dishes on the table. Our motto was first in last out. However,
since Mother always fed me a sandwich laden generously with
German cold cuts before she drove me to a party, I tended to
gravitate towards the dessert end of the buffet, and load my plate
at that end. Despite loud background music by contemporary
American artists, which I loved, our socials seldom became
dance parties. It was more of standing around with friends chatting up the flame of that night. Frequently, adolescents from the
American School were also invited such that I met new girls. My
diary is scribbled with their names; Evelyn, Rita and Mary-Lou
followed by paragraphs of overflowing lush fantasies about our
togetherness.

Hassan's and my obsession with aircraft continued to grow.
We formed an Aeronautics Club, inviting all the students to
join. We promised quizzes on aircraft recognition with prizes,
which we did not specify; regular fact sheets on interesting WW
II airplanes; seminars on model building; talks on the principles
of flight; and group meetings to review aircraft identifications.
Several of our friends joined. Armenag suggested we adopt code
names similar to those used by NATO to identify Soviet planes:
Armenag became Tupolev, I was Mig, and Hassan was Yak,

while Ibrahim insisted on remaining Peewee, which had always been his nickname. These names made us feel that we were members of a close band of brothers and provided a sense of security.

Ibrahim, Marwan, Hassan and Derek at Almaza

On the event of "Open Day" at Almaza Military Air Force Air Base in Heliopolis near our school, a parent dropped four of us off to spend the day moseying about the aircraft line-up along the tarmac. We were very familiar with the Russian aircraft on display; of greater interest were the old British airplanes along the base's perimeter. We snuck away from the conducted tour and fanned out toward the abandoned aircraft set beyond the runways. The "running amok" of four boys seen to be climbing over a derelict World War II Lancaster bomber, a Vampire, and a Meteor jet caused alarm in the control tower. An MP jeep soon found us, and the occupants wanted to know what we were doing. We thought this was obvious. We were having fun. They demanded our personal ID cards, reviewed them, and wrote down our names. Throughout we joked with them and finally reassured the cops that we would not harm ourselves. They drove off while we continued to discover older cast-off planes, among them a Miles trainer and a Mig-15 UTI-trainer, which was a tandem-seated jet trainer. I loved climbing through the Lancaster and over the other aircraft and prying lose souvenirs to take home. Sitting in the front seat of a discarded Mig 15, I discovered that, unlike a car, there was no key to start the engine —only a push button.

Our confidence in recognizing aircraft, especially those flown by the Israelis, gave Hassan and me the idea of cycling one afternoon to the southern tip of Zamalek, where we understood the military intelligence headquarters was located. Laying our bicycles on the grass, we walked in unchallenged. Two officers sitting behind a desk were curious about how we had gotten in and what we wanted. We offered our services in silhouette recognition of Israeli, British, and French airplanes, and lectured them about the benefits of such knowledge, which every Egyptian soldier ought to possess. Amused, they listened politely to these two 13-year-old boys. We left in a buoyant mood after they assured us they would seriously consider our offer.

In the meantime, I had an appointment with the editor of Cairo's English daily, *The Egyptian Gazette*. We met in his office, where I showed him a sample manuscript on the evolution of the Mig-15—the first in a series of columns I proposed to write. He reviewed it, suggesting changes and additions to the text. I left with the promise that the column would be published. I was ecstatic at my achievement, yet did not follow through with further installments. In fact, I had no plan or outline, and was too busy with my real homework anyway.

At school, the character of the staff and the level of discipline had changed. My new class teacher was a middle-aged, uninspiring Egyptian who seemed to be treading career water. The school had recruited a couple of young Irish teachers on their first assignments, one of whom taught history, where we continued with the old curriculum of learning about the British monarchy. It was a boring subject, memorizing lineage, battles, and dates. Prior to each weekly test, we wrote the relevant information in Arabic on the blackboard's left-hand side with a note in English, "Do not erase." The teacher thought the Arabic had been written by the last teacher and was our homework assignment, so she didn't erase the information. She always beamed with pride at our grades, not knowing that we were copying the answers to her questions from the Arabic notes on the board. She seemed mystified at finding puddles of water in the open handbag sitting on her desk. When she turned to write questions on the blackboard, Hassan would squirt his water pistol with great accuracy into the open target.

We played cross-cultural tricks. The biology teacher, an elderly Egyptian, taught us botany. When we learned about flowers, Derek Farawagy raised his hand repeatedly to ask how to spell "bud." The teacher would face the class, spelling b-u-d, eliciting a general giggle; in Arabic, it meant "my balls." Whenever the teacher said "plant tissue," Derek responded, "Bless you." The poor teacher didn't catch on to our mischief.

Our English teacher assigned us to learn Wordsworth's "The Daffodils." Hassan and I fooled about with the first line, once again laughing at our own silliness. The next day, during English, the teacher called on me to recite the poem. I stood in front of the class petrified; my fear of public speaking prevented me from starting until she prompted me. Staring at the back wall, I said, "The Daffodils, by William Wordsworth." I took a deep breath and continued, "I wondered lonely as a clown." The class erupted in laughter. The teacher angrily called me *Homar*, a donkey and sent me packing to my seat. During another lesson, she spoke about the British in Egypt having lived in "bun-Gal-oos." We were perplexed. Addressing the class, our Egyptian teacher said in a condescending voice, "You, the children of rich parents, educated by the British all these years, and you don't know bun-Gal-oos?" No one knew. She went to the blackboard and wrote the word.

"Oh! Bungalows," we cried in unison.

School was fun that year, distracting me from my grief and worries about the absence of a male guiding father, looming conscription, unknown financial circumstances, all adding up to an uncertain future.

An opera troupe from La Scala, Milan, visited the Cairo Opera House. For three years, Mother allowed me to choose only four tickets for each season to attend the Sunday matinee. The standing "seat" was at the back of the balcony.

I took the overcrowded bus to The Royal Opera House in Al-Azbakeya—a historic garden district in the northwest of the city known for its flocks of ibis, their indiscreet white droppings, and the myriad of secondhand bookstalls lining the pavements toward the cultural building. I rushed through the gauntlet of aggressive booksellers and hawkers, evoking more an atmosphere of a bazaar than of the silent reverence of a library, aiming to claim a good perch beside the balcony's central aisle.

The Royal Opera House stood at the periphery of Al-Azbakeya public gardens. Despite the building's neglect, the imposing architecture of the Opera House set it apart from the surrounding dilapidated dwellings, offices, neon lights, and the bustling tram station. The architectural opulence was a reminder of the grandeur of the former Ottoman Empire. Khedive Ismail ordered its construction to celebrate the inauguration of the Suez Canal in 1869 as a lasting and outstanding symbol of the performing arts. The era ended with Nasser's 1952 revolution and the installment of a military technocratic, authoritarian government bent on reclaiming Palestine rather than lifting the standard of living of the average citizen.

Dashing from the sunbaked square into the cool interior, its lofty majesty transported me into a sumptuous world of marble and red velvet. I climbed the grand stairway with remnants of Egypt's once prominent Levantine business class in formal dress, embarrassed that I was conspicuous in my everyday clothes. The majority, in their Sunday finest, entered the Orchestra section while I slinked up a side stairway to the top floor, making my way up to the gods to stand behind those seated below in the balcony. I claimed my vantage place to get a clear shot of the

distant stage. Over the years I saw, but mainly heard, performances of Puccini, Verdi, and my favorite opera, *Rigoletto*; how I
related to the sad tales of human despair and felt joyful ecstasy at
the soaring melodies.

When *Nabucco* was on the program, the poignant and
powerful "Chorus of the Hebrew Slaves" conjured up the story
of exiles singing about their homeland, and wanting to escape.
The song's first words, "*Va, pensiero, sull'ali dorate*" ("Fly on the
golden wings") tapped into the audience's sentiments. Roused by
the music, they joined with the chorus to express their
anguished solidarity over the changing political environment
that had sidelined them. The overtures, melodies, and
atmosphere conveyed them to a sentimental world beyond
Cairo. They were born in Egypt, yet were considered foreigners,
about to be banished, their property confiscated by the new
order. The predominantly Italian, French, and Greek expatriates,
and members of the Armenian and European communities who
the Nasser regiment had not yet expelled at the tail end of the
Suez conflict rose in their seats at the end of each aria and
cheered with elation. It was here that I first heard "bravo," "bra-
va," and "encore," exalting the singers as roses were thrown at
their feet. I easily sublimated my need for close love into
passionate music.

During intermission, I sometimes met Armenag, Atkin, and
our friend Henry, who also enjoyed musical experiences.
Although born in Egypt, they had foreign passports and related
to their distant homelands. Like them, I longed for a brighter
future outside Egypt, where the arts could feed my soul.

As the military rose in prominence, the once-cosmopolitan
student body at the English School lost favor. On the last day of
class, we gathered once more for a photograph. My classmates,
now approaching military age, were terrified of conscription and
searched for opportunities for schooling and success out of
Egypt.

31

GULNAR ABSCONDS

1958-1960

Resentment is anger directed at others—at what they did or did not do.
—Peter McWilliams

With rising military tensions, the policies regarding leaving Egypt had become progressively more restrictive. Departing citizens could not legally take more than $12 out of the country. Neither Gulnar nor I had passports. Egypt allowed a joint passport for children in the family under age five and ours had expired long ago. With Daddy's death we had to forfeit our UN documents. Getting new ones under the current political climate was nearly impossible. While Mother carried an Egyptian passport, she would never leave her children once more, not to mention her money. Even if she had wanted to exit, she would need a male's written permission—in this case, mine, as I was the head of household. Leaving Egypt as a family was not an option.

To help us get by, Frau Reiner, a teacher at the German High School, moved into our guest bedroom. She was a strange, middle-aged woman who spoke little, kept to herself, and had a persistently worried look on her face that tended to age her. She took most meals with us. Sitting at the table, I tried to engage her in general conversation about the last war. She stated, between sips of tomato soup, that the winter of 1946 had been particularly cold. Having lost everything, she stole a blanket from the British occupying forces. The four of us sat in silence following that disclosure. To provoke her into further revelations I asked, "Isn't that a sin?" She looked up, spoon halfway to her mouth, and gaped at me across the table without a reply. She completed her meal without another word, rose, and left, closing the door to her room.

Mother, Frau Reiner, and Marwan in our dining room

Mother and Gulnar were fighting over almost everything. Gulnar seemed unhappy most of the time. The root cause was her grievance at not receiving her 24% inheritance. I did not understand her discontent. Minors were not entitled to such funds. Besides, Mother was feeding us, clothing us, and paying our private school tuition. If we knew what funds might be due us, what exactly would Gulnar have done with the money? Even so, Mother was unwise to dismiss her complaints as trivial.

As a family, we had no fun. We had no social togetherness, no trans-generational parties involving mother's friends and their adolescent children—only parties I arranged with my school friends. As a teenager I was emotionally alone and awkward around girls. Apart from the girls I knew from class and the club, I did not know how to develop intimate friendships, nor the progression of friendship to the development of love.

In May of 1958, Gulnar graduated from the Senior School with her English O-levels. She celebrated by attending a dance party at school and falling in love with a fellow student, Mansur. After that, she consistently broke her curfew, generating ongoing tension and endless arguments with Mother, who kept insisting her daughter not compromise her reputation by violating the 10 p.m. curfew. As head of the household, I agreed with Mother in principle but sided with Gulnar to spite Mother.

Minu, Asad's sister, invited Gulnar to a graduation party at the Indian Embassy. Gulnar returned with the gift of a sari. Its silk sheen made the reds, greens, black, and gold glimmer magnificently when Gulnar paraded in it, whirling around and catching the sunlight. Mother showed only passing interest in the present and pondered aloud, "What on earth are you going to do with it?" Disappointed, Gulnar stopped her sari modeling. Gulnar was growing into a young woman and Mother couldn't handle it.

Around that time, I overheard Mother and Frau Reiner discuss transferring Gulnar to the German School. She was almost seventeen. From that point onwards, our lives diverged even further. Entrenched in two different cultures, we progressively became strangers. Gulnar spoke German to Mother—but I spoke in English to both of them. I focused on learning Arabic and tried to maintain contact with Giddi; she showed no such inclination. Her new friends were German; she dropped her English School links.

Our daily family existence was bizarre. Mother was gone all day teaching, while Gulnar was involved with German School activities. I hovered between the dual orbits of my Egyptian family, with prevailing Muslim mores, and British school with its European culture. In our schools and at home we lived according to the Gregorian calendar instead of the Islamic

calendar that was in use throughout Egypt. Each culture celebrated holy days at different times, leading to social discon-
nection.

My mother recognized Christmas. Prior to Christmas Eve,
she would string up seasonal decorations, make special meals,
and sing along with carols on our
shortwave radio. Relative to
Christmas events in Wedel it was a
stripped-down affair. These activities seemed to fit her memories of
Christmas, but there were no
presents, no fun, no cheerful
togetherness, and no Stollen.

It was not clear if Mother was
indifferent or unaware, but she did
not observe Muslim holidays. She
did not anticipate the dates that
changed each year due to the
Islamic lunar calendar, nor did she
understand their societal signifi-

Gulnar—forever moody

cance, their meaning of gratitude, or their importance to me.
The timings of Eid Al-Fitr, celebrated at the end of the one
month fast of Ramadan, and four-day Eid Al-Adha feast, the
Feast of the Sacrifice, took me by unpleasant surprise always too
late to find my way to family members and participate. I wanted
to live as an Egyptian, and yet gradually saw less of them, even
my beloved Giddi. Limited contact with my Egyptian family
meant I lived in a German bubble.

Mother did not celebrate our birthdays—no cards, no
cake, no presents. Since the national holiday *Sham El Nessim*
—rites of spring—fell like Easter around my April birthday, I
was conscious of becoming a year older. When I reminded her
that it was the day of my birth, she generally replied, "I was
there." At such moments, I yearned for the geniality and
belonging of Wedel, with Oma's cakes and celebratory gather-

ings. I couldn't understand why Oma's warmth had not passed on to Mother.

A week after the date of my birth, to which I could hardly refer as my birthday, Mother received a letter and proclaimed with pride, "Freimut has written from Hamburg. He is on a trip around the Middle East. He wants to visit Tante Gretchen in two weeks." She emphasized *Tante*. "He's the twenty-four-year-old son of Hildegard Duve, who was with me in England in the 1930s." Mother continued, "A handsome young man." Gulnar's eyes lit up.

Freimut's arrival was imminent, and Mother wondered how we should entertain him. As she considered this, Gulnar appeared in a cocktail dress secretively tailored from the sari. It was strapless, barebacked, and narrow at the waist, with a full skirt ending above her knees. She looked stunning, twirling around in her high heels. I told her so. She smiled and twirled again.

Mother was shocked. "Oh, my goodness! You look naked. You are much too young. You cannot wear it in Egypt. Your father would never allow it." Gulnar was defiant, belittling, and dismissive of Mother's jealousy packaged as conservative sentiments. Arguments between them ended with Mother in tears, and Gulnar slamming her bedroom door. The conflict revolved only partially around the dress; in actuality, I could see it was more about Mother's realization that "her baby" was growing into a desirable, beautiful woman and that her own influence was waning.

Freimut arrived with flowers in hand for Tante Gretchen, talking nonstop in a jovial mixture of German, English, and rudimentary Arabic. Mother had baked a cake—imagine, a cake for him but not for my birthday! We sat enjoying afternoon tea. The pull between Gulnar and Freimut was magnetic. She spent most of her time with him during his weeklong visit. Mother at first seemed delighted by the friendship that developed between the two young people, but became increasingly concerned as

Gulnar repeatedly defied her nightly curfew. Tension simmered between the two women throughout Freimut's visit.

During her two years at the German School preparing for her Abitur, Gulnar had obsessively propagated rumors among her teachers, particularly her advisor Frau Dr. Förster, that as her legal guardian I would marry her off to an Egyptian to forge a strong family alliance, thus securing my and Mother's future in Egypt.

Mother and Freimut

Approaching marriageable age, Gulnar embroidered her fear of my power over her. Her teachers were appalled by the tenets of seventh-century family law—men's dominance over women's fate—that remained indifferent to any appreciation of their social context. Frau Dr. Förster took me aside and lectured me against forced marriage whenever I attended Gulnar's school functions. Unaware of Gulnar's covert crusade of instilling alarm, this puzzled me since I had no such aspirations. I was preoccupied with my interest in airplanes and gliding, as well as studying for my final exams in mid-1960, and the prospects of my own survival, given my potential for conscription.

Her teacher, Mother, and Gulnar maintained a conspiratorial silence to get Gulnar out of Egypt. On passing her Abitur in the late spring of 1960, she became eligible to enter a German university. With the intent of removing her from the perceived danger of my marrying her off, Gulnar's teachers sponsored her for a scholarship to study pedagogy at Heidelberg University.

The Egyptian Overseas Office of the Ministry of Education enabled Gulnar to obtain a passport, assuring her an exit ticket from Egypt. The scholarship covered the cost of tuition and living expenses. My mother's banking friend suggested she use this opportunity to legally transfer funds out of the country on a monthly basis, ostensibly to support her daughter. In actuality, the money would be banked and saved for Mother to live outside of Egypt someday when she could leave the country.

One day Gulnar simply disappeared. She left in the early hours of the morning while I was asleep. I, as nominal head of the household, had been sidelined, ignored, deceived, and kept entirely in the dark. It was only upon returning from my last O-levels and *Tawjihi* examination, exhausted, that I learned of my sister's departure that morning. At the same time I discovered that Mother and Gulnar had conspired for at least two years behind my back. The perception of my being a villain, and my exclusion from family discussions, hurt me deeply. Gulnar didn't even say goodbye or leave a note. I felt betrayed, distrusted, and inconsequential. I was sixteen, the age of conscription, and the one at risk of becoming a common soldier. Yet they had not included me in an exit plan from Egypt. Once Gulnar left, she did not correspond with us.

An overseas bank account was desirable. Mother had trusted Gulnar to open a joint account in Germany in both their names. Mother eagerly transferred money on a monthly basis to a bank in Heidelberg, failing to recognize that it was only in Gulnar's name. Gulnar kept the money, claiming when she was eighteen that it was rightfully hers, part of her 24% inheritance. Gulnar's deceit caused the beginning of an irreparable fissure between the two women. In hindsight, had Mother missed a crucial indicator of the depth of her daughter's deep-seated insecurity or was it revenge or spite? It was not about the money; it was my sister's chronic fear of the loss of her independence and want for love. To Gulnar, money meant control, a mindset that started with the stealing of Oma's money when she was seven.

Mother never told me of Gulnar's embezzlement—she was too embarrassed. I only learned of this and subsequent costly thefts when I acquired an extensive, acrimonious correspondence between them years later, finally explaining their treacherous, life-long battle over finances.

32

PLAN B
1956-1960

Gomhouria *trainer*

The gull sees farthest who flies highest
—Richard Bach

In the years following Daddy's death, the entries in my diary showed I was very conscious of the looming date: May 1960. I would be finished at the English School, sixteen years old, and eligible for conscription. This ominous date caused me constant anxiety given the unending warmongering between Egypt and Israel. Passing the obligatory Egyptian *Tawjihi* examination and the equivalent Oxford O-Level (ordinary level) was crucial; both would allow me to proceed with further education, perhaps deferring the draft for a few years. Of course, the better educated one became, the more desirable one was to the military in an era where electronic warfare was being introduced.

Gulnar had gone. Mother and I never discussed my fate, and I was not sure what lay ahead. The murmured buzz among my male school friends hinted at their plans for leaving, although specifics were never mentioned for fear of the all-pervasive *Mukhabarat*—the State Security Secret Service. I became obsessed with the idea of leaving Egypt.

Some friends seemed to have a plan crafted by their parents, while others seemed ready to take action themselves. Hyim Sakal, a friend and classmate, along with most of the Jewish community, immigrated to Israel—a permitted exit. Ibrahim and his brother took the train to Upper Egypt where they crossed into Sudan. They bought tickets for a British Airways flight from Khartoum to London. He told me later that they breathed a sigh of relief when their Comet-4 took off from Khartoum—they had escaped—only to discover that the flight had a stopover in Cairo. They locked themselves in the bathroom, convinced the Egyptian authorities would haul them off. Such was the degree of fear and helplessness.

Despondency and paranoia fed my determination to develop my own viable exit plan. I was interested in becoming a pilot or a surgeon, with no clear idea how to achieve these goals. Furthermore, I did not know how to get a passport, which was rumored to be impossible. President Nasser's socialistic policies banned overseas travel unless one had an offer for an educational opportunity abroad.

When the Suez Crisis had interrupted our schooling in October 1956, Hassan, Asad and I, along with other classmates, attended private tutoring arranged by the Thai Embassy. Egyptian teachers taught English, geography, and maths during the morning.

During our free afternoons, Hassan and I cycled out to the edge of the western delta, where green alfalfa fields met yellow desert sand on the fringes of Embaba, one of Cairo's poorest suburbs, to visit an air cadet field.

It was a huge expanse of compressed black alluvial dirt dotted with tufts of grass. At its southern end was a white military barrack with a small control tower. Parked on the tarmac were several single-engine, side-by-side pilot and instructor *Gomhouria* trainers and a couple of Tiger Moths. Air cadets of 16 and 17 years of age were learning to fly, subsequent to graduating from the glider program. After their maiden flight they got their license, which was their entrance ticket to the Egyptian Air Force as pilot officers and a secure career.

Marwan with TigerMoth trainer

The afternoon sun beat down on us as we lay our bicycles down beside the field. There was no breeze, and heat shimmered as it rose off the compacted mud. We gravitated toward a group of people gathered around a long-winged yellow Slingsby T.21, a side-by-side training glider resting on the grass.

Chatting young men surrounded a military figure in fatigues. After greeting us, Sergeant Mohammed surprised me by asking if we wanted a joyride. We were thrilled at the offer, not realizing at the time he was recruiting for the Air Force. I volunteered to go first.

The glider lay on its left wingtip. Its massive wingspan of 54 feet was fixed to its flimsy wooden body above and behind the open cockpit. I climbed into the right-hand side and sat on the plank seat, resting my feet on the two pedals before me, a joystick between my knees. A young English instructor cheerfully got into the pilot's side on my left and harnessed me in—shoulders and lap straps—cautioning me not to move the joystick or use the rudder pedals. "Hold the stick lightly with your right hand and place your feet on the pedals to get the feel of the movements while I fly this bird."

Before we started, he familiarized me with the instruments. "I'll lean on the stick in the direction I want the glider to go—forward puts the nose down. If I move it to the left, she'll bank left."

"What about the pedals?"

He stepped back and forth on them. "The rudder makes the glider's nose *swing* to the right or left." He pointed to three dials on the dashboard installed between us. "This 'turn and slip' indicator shows the angle of your wings relative to the horizon." Next, he pointed to the airspeed indicator and an altimeter. "Once we're aloft, I'll show you the most important lesson you must learn to stay alive." My heart pounded. Was this joyride dangerous?

Picture of Slingsby T.21 glider

Sergeant Mohammed hooked the glider up to a tow cable lying in the dirt in front of its nose. The cable connected to a gigantic winch at the furthest point of the field's western edge, more than 1,000 feet ahead of us. The pilot gave the thumbs-up; the assembled group raised the glider's wing to the horizontal position, another thumbs-up. Sergeant Mohammed waved and I felt the jerking tug as the winch took up the cable's slack. When it became taut, we rolled forward into the oncoming dry desert wind. The others ran with us, supporting the glider's wing until the speed became sufficient to lift us off the dirt.

Gaining height, we climbed smoothly, sharply, and swiftly, pulled almost vertically by the cable, rising like a kite, climbing through progressively cooler air. The white yaw string in front of us, which had hung limply, became straight in the slipstream. My excitement grew and my apprehension vanished.

I was no longer earthbound but suspended aloft, seemingly weightless; the desert's fresher air rushed into my face and past my ears, pressing me into my seat. We climbed sunward as the green delta dropped below my right wing, and we sped toward the majestic Pyramids shimmering on the horizon due west. The glider had rapidly gained 900+ feet and seemed to level out, reaching the crest of a hyperbolic curve. The pilot pointed to the yellow cable release knob and mimicked a pulling motion. I pulled and the cable fell away, unshackling us, freeing me of my dreary anguish and worries.

The oncoming wind kicked us higher into the blue sky, for a moment leaving my belly behind. He thrust the joystick forward; the nose pointed down below the horizon, the flickering desert replacing the blue sky as we gained speed and amazingly climbed farther, the earth below speeding under us. Rising currents of cooler and more breathable air coming off the desert buffeted the plane as it lifted us aloft, up, up, until we were riding the thermals with the birds at about 2,000 feet. The feeling was like none I had ever experienced. I whooped into the onrushing wind, delirious with the joy of freedom.

An invisible draft of dry air carried us higher, straight toward the Pyramids, to a height where the sun felt more intense. I was riding the wind. The instructor looked over and must have recognized my state of total ecstasy. He lightly banked to the left, swung a gentle downward swoop through a section of cloudless blue sky around the airfield below, with its miniature planes and ant-like humans. I saw a *Gomhouria* taking off and thought, *that will be me one day.*

Gusts lifted the sailplane in harmony with the wind yet higher to 3,500 feet, driven first by the desert thermals and then by the heat of the alfalfa fields that sped under my wings as we banked over into the delta, with Cairo a flickering haze in the distance. We reached a tranquil altitude of 4,000 feet, where we glided with the current like a boat sweeping along a fast-moving river. I became one with the craft, mesmerized by the wonder, sensing the joystick and the glider's movements. The occasional turbulence bounced and danced me in airborne suspension; new movements and sensations, yet I could have stayed aloft forever.

The instructor woke me from my reverie to teach me how to get out of a stall that would lead to a free-fall plummeting to certain death. "Always keep the nose down to maintain speed and height," he yelled. "Watch the yaw string, and listen to the wind when I pull the joystick back." The nose rose above the horizon. I was pressed into my seat, and the rush of wind softened until it almost disappeared. The altimeter spun counterclockwise as we lost altitude and our airspeed decreased. The yaw string flapped wildly about, and we began to slide uncontrollably sideways. He shoved the stick forward, pointing the nose down, heading straight toward the earth—a frighteningly dangerous moment. The glider regained speed, the wind resumed flowing past my ears, the yaw line straightened out, the altimeter needle twirled in the clockwise direction again, and we rose up past the birds on a river of hot current. Reassured to be back in control, I had learned my first lesson—how to get out of a stall in order to survive.

We soared for a while longer, circling the field. Then the pilot lined up into the wind to land. As we descended, the crowd on the field grew steadily larger, and as we approached, they scattered from our flight path and likely landing site. Our approach was too high—we would overshoot the field. He motioned for me to yank the lever to my left. Dive brakes popped up from both wings. The glider forcefully shuddered—the vibrations seemed so abrupt and dangerous. Would the wooden plane disintegrate? We dropped like a stone as our airspeed and height precipitously decreased. When he indicated one, then two and finally three fingers as my signal, I released the brakes and abruptly smooth airflow replaced the turbulence over the massive wings. We came in gently, first hopping over a railway embankment, then a convoy of lorries belching black smoke at the airfield's perimeter road, touching down close to where we had taken off. We rolled a few feet before the long wing tipped into the ground, halting us, and the group of youths ran up to help retrieve the glider. Hassan beamed. Though it was probably only a ten-minute ride, it felt like forever—I was hooked!

Hassan's turn was next. As part of the team, I stepped forward to stabilize the glider, still on my high. I held the body between the wing and the horizontal stabilizer instead of at the wing tip. The glider began to roll and I ran with it until it started to rise. When I let go, pleased with myself at having helped, the satisfying feeling of being part of a team, I turned to see the stabilizer coming straight at me, about to transect my spine. I dropped. A whoosh of air passed millimeters above my body. The sergeant ran over, an expression of horror on his face, which turned to relief as I dusted myself off. It was *maktoob*—fate—I survived.

Mother did not like the idea of me flying. When I first started to get free lessons in 1957, she refused to sign the permission form, claiming she had lost a husband and she did not want to lose a son. Whenever Sergeant Mohammed asked me for the "signed form," I would lie that I had forgotten it. Finally, either he forgot to ask for the permission slip or he gave up. As a pupil, I had the potential for a pilot's permit. Eventually, he gave me a glider pilot's logbook into which I carefully recorded each flight and its duration. The sensation of gliding, of floating in the air, entered my very bone marrow, so that at night while I dreamed I would experience the feeling of hovering above the earth.

As a group of enthusiastic and carefree young men, the regulars varied in age from barely teenagers to a twenty-two-year-old engineer. They called themselves *Shabab Nadi Gliding El Masri*—Youth of The Egyptian Gliding Club. We joked at the presumptuous name, since there was an official Egyptian Gliding Club. They did not belong, nor were they affiliated. As I got to know the group, I formally joined their Egyptian Gliding Club. "We," this band of ragtag Egyptian youngsters, were "the club" and for the next few months we hung out together and competed against one another, avoiding any discussion of our motives for learning to glide. Sergeant Mohammed was the honorary president. We were aware that the frequency of our training flights depended on him to achieve our goal to obtain a glider's permit, which would allow us to advance to training on the *Gomhouria*. None of us discussed this intent, because we did not know who was an informer for the *Mukhabarat*. We claimed we went up because it was fun. There were days when Sergeant Mohammed was absent and his subordinate, Ezmat, would try to supervise us. At such times, we instigated games well beyond the scope of regular flight training.

The most popular was to draw a large cross in the alluvial mud some distance from the perimeter fence. The winner was the pilot who could land on top of the "X." This meant coming in to land at a shallow angle and crash landing on top of it—never popular with our instructors or Ezmat, for it potentially damaged the glider. The first two pilots to go up had the best chance of success, because after that, the flight instructors would catch us at our game and forbid it. I dropped close to the "X" a couple of times by suddenly yanking the air brakes, jarring the plane, the instructor, and myself. He threatened not to take me up again if I repeated the treacherous maneuver.

In subsequent flights, I took progressively more control of the joystick, gliding from one thermal to another, following the circling birds, staying in the air for longer and longer periods. Flying required judgment and alertness. I liked touching down near the take-off area rather than farther down the field to avoid having to drag the glider back to the starting point for the other students. Yet, landing my huge bird smoothly where I wanted was a challenge. The compressed air between my wings and the dirt resisted my touchdown and led me to float a few feet over the grass for some distance before I had to push the joystick forward and force the nose down for a less than smooth landing.

One day, well into my second gliding year, Mother picked up my shirt to wash it. The Student Pilot License bearing my photo fell out of my pocket. Dumbfounded, she said, "I told you, no. It is dangerous. I refused to give you permission to go gliding." I explained my elation and joy at soaring, its safety, and my sense of independence and accomplishment. She did not agree but did not prevent me from continuing my training, learning the capricious ways of the desert winds. I did not share with her my audacious plan that gliding was a means to a propeller plane, whose maiden voyage was my exit strategy —Plan B.

During my summer holidays, we were in Cairo, since we no longer went to Balteem. Hassan had dropped out of the gliding program so I cycled to the field alone almost every morning, after *fajr* prayers, my swim, and my studies, or in the afternoon. I would go up with different instructors under varying weather conditions.

Now and then, a looming sandstorm would prevent me from going to Embaba. The atmosphere over Cairo would become dark beige from the diminished sunlight, heralding the storm's advance from the Western Sahara. An eerie silence preceded the approaching solid wall of sand and dust, pushed by gale force winds, reducing visibility to almost zero. With the storm, the streets emptied. The blizzard engulfed every neighborhood, and often brought traffic to a stop. Caught outside once, the particles stung my skin like a thousand needles, invading my mouth and ears, making visibility and breathing difficult. The howling wind swirled the sand, beating against the windows more forceful than the rains in Manchester. Fine granules filtered around window frames and through nooks and crannies; every surface in a room was yellowish brown. After the storm, entire sand dunes had settled in streets and against buildings, while yellowish-red dust coated cars and leaves. On these days, flying was out of the question.

There were other days I could not sneak away to "visit my friends," my usual alibi. Mother prevented me from going, claiming I needed new shirts and insisting on taking me shopping in Cairo. There were two variations of this distasteful enterprise, and both were mental torture. In the first, after parking near the Royal Opera House, we walked some distance through the bustling streets, reaching the Hennawy Department Store by ten. On the fourth floor were three bins of jumbled shirts that stood aside from the regular racks and displays of men's clothing. The first bin contained an assortment of sports shirts priced around 30 pence (then the equivalent to $6). The cost and quality of the shirts decreased with each bin, as did the variety.

"You can have three new shirts from these," she said, sweeping her arm over the bins as she saw my eyes wander to the racks of shining new merchandise, each shirt wrapped in cellophane. "These are good enough."

They were terrible in color and pattern, and looked like cast-offs or secondhand stock. When I refused to select one, she would pull out one or two from among the heap and hold them up. "What's wrong with these?"

"I don't like them."

"They look nice on you. Try them on."

"No. I like the ones I already have."

"You're a growing boy. You need some new shirts. I can't get the sweat stains out of the old ones."

So, the tug of wills continued. Finally, I would take the one she liked best merely to end the torture, believing we could head home.

Following her unenthusiastically at some distance, we landed in the women's dresses department trailing a young shop clerk with arms full of clothes, skirts and blouses, to the changing room. I sat outside waiting with my one new shirt in a bag, wondering what I was missing with my friends at the Gliding Club.

She eventually appeared in a new dress, and after climbing a platform, gazed into the panorama of mirrors. "Do you like this?" she would say while the shop girl nipped and tucked at the sleeves, hem, and shoulders, sticking pins in here and there.

"Yes, it looks fine."

"No, do you really like it?"

"Yes, Mother."

She would disappear into the changing room with the assistant in chase, only to reappear to begin another performance —this time with a skirt and a blouse. In the end, we left the shop with only my shirt. It took me a while to realize she had no intention to purchase anything. When she wanted to go to Ades, Carol's family's upscale shop, I stopped dead in my tracks on the pavement with people rushing by.

"No," I yelled over the hawkers' calls, car horns blaring, and from some distance the ring of tram bells. "It's hot and I'm tired. You go shopping. I'll take the bus home."

She relented. The sun beat down and the inside of the car was blazing, the plastic seats scorching and steering wheel burning hot. The mid-day crawl home in a boiling car surrounded by dense slow traffic, donkey carts, and jaywalkers made me long for the liberation I found in gliding.

At the field, the usual group of boys and Sergeant Mohammed was there. We took turns going up with one of the

Egyptian, English, or Swiss instructors. I tried to squeeze in three to four flights in an afternoon, each lasting seven to fifteen minutes. With each flight, I progressively mastered the intricacies of the wind and weather. In between flights, I helped launch the glider for the others. Standing around waiting for them to return, I glanced at the other end of the field and observed the ground crew preparing the *Gomhouria* for the cadet pilots' solo flights, while another trainer came in for a landing.

I finally reached the amount of flying time where the instructors felt I was safe enough to be in command of the glider. From then on, I could choose to glide and be the pilot; the instructor was the passenger there to bail me out in the event I placed myself in a dangerous situation. I loved making the decisions, knowing there was a guardian angel.

Early logbook entrances with flights, credited by director's signature.

A few weeks later, I met a middle-aged German engineer from the Bücker company near Berlin at the southern side of the field. He befriended me when he discovered I spoke his language. He offered to take me up in a trainer. I thought he only meant the Tiger Moth; instead, he pointed to his red monoplane glistening in the sun. He had flown from Germany on his way to Cape Town, and Cairo was a stopover. How could I resist? We sat side by side in the enclosed cockpit. It was like a hothouse under the canopy until he started the engine and the air conditioner cooled us off. Following an "all clear" from the control tower, the engine roared as we bounced over the dirt, taking off parallel to the glider on my right in the distance. The engine hummed, pulling us into the blue desert sky. We gained height rapidly, flying higher than I had ever been in my glider. He throttled back, noise abating, as we cruised, still rising.

He asked in Hochdeutsch, "Do you want to see the Sphinx and Pyramids?" I nodded enthusiastically, wanting to prolong the flight. We steadily approached them flying northwest. The altitude gave me my first aerial view of the Pyramids-Sphinx complex sitting on the Giza Plateau, a perspective I could not have appreciated from the ground. The view was grand. The monuments loomed progressively larger as we approached.

Above the Cheops Pyramid, he yelled over the engine, "Do you want to feel the force of one G?" On my thumbs-up, he dipped his left wing, pointing at the Pyramid's apex, pirouetting above it. The great pyramid spun round. My vision grayed out as blood pooled in my legs; the engine seemed to howl louder. I felt sick to my stomach and hung onto my seat. He straightened out to level flight beyond the plateau, and looked over at me. He grinned as my vision gradually returned. I registered my joy with a big smile and two thumbs up.

Flying on, I got a critical view of the desert to the northwest. The desert floor dropped considerably beyond the Giza Plateau, continuing flat and empty to the horizon: no buildings, no trees. I pointed in the direction of our flight. "Sidi Barrani?" I yelled.

He nodded over the roar of the engine, making a sweeping right-hand bank to give me a better view. He flew a few minutes in level flight. Yes, the desert was flat leading toward Sidi Barrani, which was more than three-quarters of the way to the Libyan border, only 240 km from Tobruk in Libya, and my exit. In that momentary view, I saw the beckoning promise of what lay over the horizon: the distant American airbase. Yes, I was going to learn to fly the *Gomhouria*. It was my Plan B exit strategy out of Egypt—a daunting prospect, yet I was determined to succeed.

He glanced at me. Was he reading my thoughts? I'd be stealing one of his company's trainers, even though it belonged to Egypt and he might be involved in the scandal. I tried to look interested at his dashboard dials to distract him.

He banked to the right, heading toward the airfield, silence descended in the cockpit. My mind raced. I had two stripes—Egyptian and European. Which was the more dominant? Did I have to choose again? The price of flying out would be to forfeit my cultural heritage.

The *Gomhouria* was an Egyptian built version of the German Bücker Bü 181 and had a range of about 800 km. If I flew it low and used the uplift of the blazing heat reflected from the sand, I felt I could coax it to Tobruk. The Egyptian radars faced north, tracking British flights from Cyprus, and east, fearing an Israeli strike. After taking off on my maiden flight, with a full tank in my *Gomhouria*, I would head west past the Pyramids. I would then drop low, throttle back and fly just above the desert floor, gaining extra lift from the rising heat—saving precious fuel—while crossing the vast empty desert toward Sidi Barrani. Past the oasis, I would correct to a northwesterly direction and cross the border into Libya and freedom. One full tank, I calculated, might barely make it. I hoped that I would be picked up—an intruder worth checking out—by the U.S. Wheelus Air Force base radar.

Meanwhile, life was permeated by the constant threats of war. There was no let-up in the daily flow of bombastic nationalistic rhetoric from Cairo radio, keeping anxieties high. In school, we entered the Officer Training Corps. It was uncertain how official the "officer" part was under the checkered instruction of Sergeant Shawky. Some weeks he appeared, others not. His emphasis was on the spit and polish of our ill-fitting uniforms, lecturing us to shine our buttons and belt buckles and to keep the spats white. He taught us to crawl single file, dig zigzag trenches, and then camouflage them. We drilled endlessly and competed with other OTCs at a shooting range. We were issued old British Lee-Enfield bolt-action, magazine-fed rifles or captured Italian FAW guns from WWII. In the confusion, not knowing which was my target, I managed to fire one shot that rang loudly in my right ear, giving me instant vertigo and life-long tinnitus with deafness. I recognized that I would never be a warrior. The very notion of conscription was anathema.

An unwelcome letter arrived.

———

The Recruitment Center was near the English School in Heliopolis. My uncle Fareed drove me and waited outside. Hundreds of young men stood in their underpants in a line that snaked from one room to another. I was the conspicuous odd man out—European features, pale skin, glasses, white Marks and Spencer Jockeys. The others were men of peasant stock, with pale chocolate complexions. None were myopic. They wore long-legged underpants with a web of cloth that dangled from the crotch, facilitating their squatting or sitting cross-legged. Two or three physicians in each room briefly eyeballed us from a distance to evaluate various systems—a cursory military exam-ination.

Eventually, I left the center with a certificate of "Final Exemption Status." I'd failed because I wore glasses. I now had the most crucial document needed for getting a passport.

I joined Uncle Fareed. Fareed, as I called him from time to time, was the younger brother of Uncle Mustafa who had married Tante Amal, one of Daddy's sisters. He'd joined the military academy in Cairo and on his days off we frequently met. Had I had been recruited, Fareed, wearing his officer's uniform, would have intervened.

Since he was congenial, fluent in English, carefree, and unmarried, and I had no male relative similar to my age, we bonded easily. He invited me during my school breaks to join him for lunch at one of the downtown restaurants.

"Marwan, have you ever eaten Nile *gambari*—shrimp?"

"No."

We feasted on an endless supply of *gambari*, which was a novel taste and one I enjoyed. Our ease of conversation, flip-flopping between English and Arabic, and our lighthearted banter and joking cemented a brotherly love, for I admired his modesty, politeness, and tactfulness when discussing a range of family matters. After such a meal, we rode the bus to *Khan al-Khalili*—the bazaar—and quenched our thirst on sweet black tea at Cafe el-Fishawy. Ambling through the bazaar we held hands, and in the narrower and more crowded alleys arm in arm, expressing the traditional affection between men—a sign of solidarity and kinship. In the absence of my father, I developed a welcomed and strong friendship with Fareed, which did not parallel the closeness to other male relatives.

Coming out of the recruitment office, breathing a sigh of relief, I waved the exemption certificate. We headed for one of downtown Cairo's restaurants.

33

THE MUKHABARAT

A fox in the Western Desert escaped to Libya.
He was asked, "Why do you come here?"
The fox replied, "Because in Egypt they arrest camels."
The Libyans said, "But you are not a camel."
The fox said, "Of course not, but try telling that to the
Mukhabarat!"
Egyptian Joke

Born out of desperation, Plan B, although reckless, was my secret salvation. I furtively nurtured it and did not share it with anyone, least of all Mother, whom I mistrusted.

The Mogamma represented everything I detested and feared about Egyptian bureaucracy. A monstrous fourteen-story administrative building in Tahrir Square, it was a gift to the Egyptian people from the Soviets. All paperwork for Egyptian government agencies was handled centrally in that *one* building. It also housed the *Mukhabarat*—State Security's Secret Service—whose rumored motto was, "Whosoever is afraid remains unharmed."

During 1959 and into the early months of 1960—without knowing any of my father's influential friends who could have helped me—I went to the Mogamma several times a month in the vain attempt to acquire a passport.

I would take the early bus to Tahrir Square to enter this intimidating, drab edifice. Inside was a rabbit warren of endless corridors, crowded offices, filthy marble floors, worn-down marble steps, overcrowded elevators that frequently broke down, and stinking, overflowing toilets. The building lacked air conditioning, so the summer sweat of the thousands of teeming, hassled citizens mingled claustrophobically with the atmosphere of uncertainty, paranoia, and fear. Egyptians from all around the country rushed from office to office, trying to navigate the bureaucratic red tape. Tea boys pirouetted through the milling crowds, balancing trays of boiling, sweet mint tea-filled glasses high above their heads, darting in and out of offices, avoiding cross-legged scribes seated against the walls of the passageways. For a negotiated fee, the scribes handwrote yet another petition. Their illiterate clients squatted next to them on the floor, trying to explain their perceived injustices. Sandwich sellers hawked their goods, laid out on newspapers in temporary stalls on each of the fourteen landings, raising the pitch of the noise to above-shouting level.

Business was conducted by 18,000 poorly paid, languid public servants—mostly men. They seemed less interested in doing their jobs than socializing, always seeking late-afternoon independent income opportunities. I bounced futilely from one office to another, submitting completed forms. Each time I went, I related my request to a different government official sitting in the same office, hoping to garner his support. Their questions had mostly to do with my background and family history, as if to determine how they might benefit from helping me. Some discreetly opened their desk drawers, hoping for me to drop in *baksheesh*—bribes—to grease the wheels and move the process along. These government employees were paid a puny salary, and saw me as an opportunity to enhance their take before they disappeared to their second unofficial job after mid-morning prayers. The forms would get lost, or a different official would tell me I had not completed them or he did not have them. I had not made any headway in months and my frustration mounted.

Progress depended on who one knew or could befriend, not to mention a healthy underground economy of *baksheesh*. At one point, I tried to contact a distant cousin who worked in the *Mukhabarat*. After more aggravation and never getting a direct answer, I came to understand that he was a member of the banned Brotherhood and that he had gone to work one morning and never came home.

Allah intervened in the form of a man named Mr. Mukhtar. His wife was studying German, taught by my mother at the American University. Mother asked her student if her husband could help me. I was invited to his home. He was a connection —someone who knew someone.

My July, 1960 visit was in the late afternoon—an informal, friendly call following the traditional siesta time when government officials went home for lunch and to rest from the oppressive summer heat. Mr. Mukhtar was asleep when the servant led me into their parlor filled with gilded furniture, cool and dim by virtue of the closed shutters. She knocked on her master's bedroom door. I could hear him as he rose, splashed water onto his face, and cleared his throat before closing the bathroom door.

Mr. Mukhtar appeared shortly thereafter. The servant turned on the lights, bringing a tray with two cups of traditional Turkish coffee. Mr. Mukhtar was very informally dressed in a brown open-neck shirt and brown pants, wearing slippers without socks. I handed him a colorfully wrapped box of chocolates, which elicited a quick smile. He slouched casually in a straight-backed, upholstered chair.

Despite the brief smiles and social niceties, the mood in the room changed the minute he began to run down his list of anxiety-producing questions about why I wanted a passport, each response sandwiched between prolonged silences when he fixed his inquisitive eyes on me. I averted my eyes from the constant nervous jerking of his leg to avoid distracting myself. He challenged my loyalty. He scrutinized my past behavior. He questioned the motive of my visit to the intelligence headquarters in Zamalek, the reason I had drifted to the periphery of Almaza Airport on its open day, my peripheral involvement with the Officer Training Corps at school, and my learning to glide during the summer. I sat in fear, wondering if he somehow suspected my secret Plan B. It seems that all the military personnel I encountered somehow saw me as a suspicious individual. Suspicious of what, I wondered. Or did they routinely report all contacts to the *Mukhabarat*?

Was Mr. Mukhtar's interrogation leading to confirmation of Plan B? Many of his questions were direct, concerned not only with my background but my future intentions and my current military status. He noted some replies on a piece of paper. Most frightening were the long silences between questions, when he looked directly at me, propping his head on his hand. He jiggled his right foot ceaselessly. I wondered if he was completely awake.

When I asked him a question about how I was to proceed in getting a passport, he told me it depended on what was in my dossier. He would first have to see the file that State Security had on me. I was stunned, taken aback, wondering why the *Mukhabarat* would have a file on a sixteen-year-old boy. Apart from my interest in learning to fly, and being less than a model of obedience by challenging Sergeant Shawky's irrational commands at Officer Training Corps, I could not think of any issues warranting a personal dossier.

My meeting with Mr. Mukhtar lasted about forty minutes. On leaving, I asked myself if I had made any progress. At least I had a scheduled meeting with him at the Mogamma in two days. I rode the overcrowded bus home, speculating whether he could be a police officer in State Security rather than the helpful father figure I needed. Mother did not question me when I got home. I assumed Mr. Mukhtar's wife received very special attention, becoming a stellar German student, with excellent grades to show for it.

I met Mr. Mukhtar two days later around eight in the morning in a small, whitewashed office on the fourth floor of the Mogamma. He produced a dark brown dossier from among a stack of files. He wore civilian clothes, an open-necked crisp white shirt, and sat behind a government issue grey steel desk on which sat two small flags: one Egyptian, the other of the Police Academy. He looked awake and smiled benignly.

Tall, locked, stainless steel filing cabinets lined the walls. On the cabinets sat whirling electric fans. A huge portrait, one of many official versions of Nasser, hung on otherwise bare walls. There was a narrow, open window to combat the early morning summer heat. A naked, buzzing neon strip provided some light, while traffic noise from Tahrir Square invaded the office. A policeman in a white summer uniform and a black, ill-fitting beret guarded the door and kept out the crowds, including people my newfound friend had asked to wait outside. We were left alone. I was served a glass of sweet mint tea, and he had Turkish coffee. The trappings were consistent with the rank of a colonel.

Once more, we went through the series of questions. After flicking through the pages in my dossier, he finally filled out a form, signed it, stamped it, and called the policeman into the office, instructing him to go get somebody's signature—a name I did not catch. The man departed after saluting. When we were alone again, Mr. Mukhtar directed the conversation to my knowledge of German and his wife's desire to learn it and do well in her studies. The message was not lost on me. I merely smiled in acknowledgement.

Through Mr. Mukhtar's invaluable assistance, I must have received security clearance. There followed numerous additional trips to the dreaded Mogamma. Matters appeared to move smoothly and rapidly in the different offices in which I completed my business. Regrettably, I did not encounter Mr. Mukhtar again. I liked him. He was an efficient man of few words.

I finally received a passport allowing me to travel to England by train or car via Italy, Austria, Switzerland, Germany, Holland, and France. It was early September 1960. Unbeknownst to me, Mother had been secretively making other plans to help me, working her influences in Manchester, where she had worked for the City Council. Suddenly Mother declared she had arranged for me to finish my secondary schooling—grammar school in England. Pandora's Box opened. I received an exit visa via the Overseas Office of the Ministry of Education, and she got permission to send money abroad to support me.

Partial Clan Gathering. Top row: Aunts Souad, Amal, Mustakima, Sanaa, & Mother, Bottom row: Uncles Mustafa husband to Amal, Abdel Shaffei with Ali son of Sanaa, Ali son of Mustakima, and Mr. Zahran husband to Sanaa.

Before leaving, I insisted to Mother that I see the Egyptian branches of my family once more. They were now scattered in different districts all over Cairo. She arranged a family gathering at the Mena House, the once royal lodge for Khedive Ismail near the Pyramids and now a hotel with luscious gardens. As with all extended families, misunderstandings and rivalries between siblings limited the number that attended the get-together on a warm and sunny Friday afternoon. I reveled in their company, enjoying their hugs and kisses and comforting banter. Giddi was too frail to attend.

Mother and I packed our bags. To my surprise, she placed one-half of our family's red and blue kilim carpet in my trunk. It was a present to her from my father and hung adorning our living room wall throughout my childhood. Apparently, Gulnar had taken the other half out of the country, and Mother hoped one day to reunite the two halves.

Mother and I crossed the Mediterranean again on the *Esperia*, this time heading for Venice. There our VW would be unloaded and Mother would drive on to Hamburg before our arrival in Manchester, where I was to be enrolled into Burnage Grammar School (Burnage Senior High School).

Esperia

When we had returned to Cairo in 1955, I imagined I'd go to an English School and we would resume the visits to Sheikh Amin and my warm Egyptian family in Sayeda Zeinab. I envisaged the dining room table laden with delicious dishes, the air saturated with their aromas, the love of my aunts and uncles and that Arabic would become my language.

It didn't happen that way.

Daddy and I, Gulnar and Mother had returned to a different

Cairo. Sit Nazifa had died. My uncles and aunts had married and moved out of the family nest. No.7 Haret Omar became a cold abode, more dilapidated then before, where an infirm Sheikh Amin resided with a rejected, aging aunt Souad. Only the feral cats inhabiting the stairwell seemed to have given meaning to constancy.

Standing at the rail as the Esperia moved out of the harbor I remembered the comfort of my father's arms about me when I was four on our first sea crossing. How I wished he was next to me now.

Near me stood the only other male of my age leaving Egypt at the same time, a young Egyptian-Frenchman named Georges watching Alexandria fade away even more intently than I.

Speaking aloud he said he was never going to return, singing, *"Non, je ne regrette rien."* Georges Moustaki was restless, endlessly scribbling on a piece of paper, humming.

"What are you doing?"

"Composing a song for the most famous French singer."

Months later, Edith Piaf sang the hit song "Milord."

> *Sometimes it's just enough*
> *For there to be a boat*
> *To make everything fall apart*
> *When the boat leaves.*

ACKNOWLEDGMENTS

I am deeply grateful to the many people who helped this book come into the light of day. First and foremost, my profound thanks to Jennifer Brice who has gently encouraged me from the start of the writing process through the full circle. Ellen Lesser's and Leslie Rubinkowski's thorough editing during the developmental writing stage kept me from repeating or making a fool of myself in print. I am thankful to Lori Handelman for her psychological insights encouraging me to go deeper into matters I would rather have avoided.

I am indebted to Joan Gerberding and Vera Thieme for their valuable help in transcribing and translating the voluminous letters in my library. Other thanks go to my longtime supporter Dawn Jensen Nobile who helped me through a rough writing spot. My appreciations go to the good souls of a local book club on Marco Island, Florida, whose feedback was invaluable. My thanks to Dr. Hilary Wise and Allison Ouverson for their part in giving life to this book.

At English School Reunions I have had the privilege of clarifying memories & moments of truth with Samir, Armenag, Mohamad, Hossam and Hassan, and to Carolyn Ring who took a manuscript and made it into a book. And lastly, grateful appreciation to my dear Jo-Ann Sanborn who has been a constant encouraging force. Her devotion and reassurance as we talked through the ideas and stories cheered me to the final pages. Lucy, my faithful Chihuahua sat by my side throughout the years of writing.

ABOUT THE AUTHOR

Born in Egypt, Michael M. Meguid spent his childhood in Egypt, Germany and England, and attended University College Hospital Medical School in London followed by a surgical residency at Harvard Medical School. A surgeon and a Fellow of the American College of Surgery, he studied human nutrition at MIT to benefit cancer patients and was  awarded a PhD. He is the recipient of numerous national and international honors. In addition to his demanding operative schedule, he ran a research laboratory which was funded by the National Institutes of Health for twenty-five years, and his research has won awards and continues to be cited.

Michael M. Meguid is a Professor Emeritus of Surgery, Nutrition, and Neuroscience in Syracuse, New York, and an Editor Emeritus of *Nutrition: The International Journal of Applied and Basic Nutritional Sciences*. On his retirement he earned an MFA from Bennington Writing Seminars in Vermont, and attended workshops at Queens University of Charlotte, North Carolina, and Non-fiction Seminars at Goucher College, Maryland.

Meguid's short stories have been published in *Bennington Review*, *Stone Canoe*, *Columbia Medical Review*, and *Hektoen International*. He has given readings in Florida and London and has a thirty-episode podcast entitled "Making the Cut" currently subscribed in thirty-eight countries.

Roots & Branches: A Family Saga Like No Other is the first in a series of biographical stories. The sequels, *Mastering the Knife: Seeking Identity and Finding Belonging* and *A Surgeon's Tale*, will be released in 2021.

MASTERING THE KNIFE
SEEKING IDENTITY AND FINDING BELONGING

Please enjoy an excerpt from Michael M. Meguid's sequel, *Mastering the Knife: Seeking Identity and Finding Belonging,* which will be released in 2021.

Mastering the Knife is dedicated with gratitude to:

Ray Forbes MD, who started me on this the road of seeking identity.

Rich O'Neill PhD, who provided insight into my belonging.

Robin S. Pilcher FRCS FRCP, who encouraged my interest in surgery.

WG Austen MD FACS, who enabled my surgical training in the U.S., thus changing my life.

1

THE TERROR OF FAILURE

JANUARY 1970

The greatest barrier to success Is the fear of failure.
—Sven Eriksson

I faced the written primary surgical fellowship exam with trepidation. Passing it would indicate to the surgical world that my specialty was surgery, and after passing it, I would be eligible for surgical registrar jobs. Seventeen months previously, I had sat for the Licentiate of the Society of Apothecaries examination where, in a matter of several hours, I had poured out five years of accumulated medical knowledge gained in medical school at University College Hospital into blue-covered answering books. I passed this examination. Passing earned me a license to practice medicine in the UK. A few weeks later, my quest to attain the academically acclaimed and more important degree of M.B. B.S. was less satisfying; the tension to pass the definitive General Medical Council's qualifying examinations was less urgent, and my desire to purge myself of my accrued learning was less pressing and more tedious. Yet, passing the Medical Council's qualifying exam, I was rewarded with the title "doctor." In both exams, I had a sense of confidence that I knew the information—the medical school curriculum—from which the examination questions would be asked.

The primary examination drew from no such set curriculum. The morning of the examination I woke up early to the smell of bacon. Victoria, my wife, made me a smack-up breakfast along with my favorite tea. She too had passed the essential requisite medical degree exam and was making plans to pursue a career in pediatrics.

"This is to fortify you." She must have sensed my tension and reassuringly urged, "Read the questions carefully. Sketch an outline of your answer and then proceed to write." I nodded as I ate my eggs and bacon. "You've been studying for months. I'm sure you'll do fine." She paused before adding, "You always do."

I wish she had not said that. If she only knew how I had been attending to other parts of my brain and body. I had short-changed my studies—the painful deception of a parallel life. I felt awful. Looking up, I saw her beauty and all the virtues I had admired and overlooked for the past months. All the virtues which made me fall in love with her. I didn't deserve her, nor did I deserve to be rewarded with passing the exam.

In the grand scheme of things, I could say that I had studied. Yet I didn't feel prepared, not enough to assuage my sense of apprehension—the terror of failure was ingrained into my DNA. Had I covered the fields of anatomy, physiology, and surgical pathology appropriately? My fear of failure, along with the distraction of covering Dr. B's GP, general practice for six weeks, a stint working as an internist for ESSO, plus my inability to find and review past primary surgical fellowship exam papers, added up to a profound lack of confidence. But the major factor in this brew was my habitual attention to Hanna instead of my studies.

Loaded with this baggage, I walked briskly through a cool morning to the front entrance of the examination hall—Queen Square in Old Gloucester Street—as if heading to an abattoir. A beadle barked at me, "Candidates enter the examination hall via a basement door," and he redirected me around the building to a narrow back street.

There, Mr. Palmer, a formidable army type in a smart mauve frock coat directed me to a murmur-filled hall with examination desks. I recognized no one as I took my seat. Face down in front of me lay a white sheet of paper and a blue examination booklet.

The anatomy questions were obscure, nuanced, and I could barely understand them. By asking *this* question about *that* anatomical structure, I wondered *what* answer they were seeking. My answers became convoluted and meandering in the hope of befuddling the examiner. Matters didn't improve with the physiology questions or even the surgical pathology paper. I was a driver careening down the road with no control of my car, heading for a crash.

———

Two days later, I faced the dreaded *viva voce*—the orals, with four different examiners who could quiz me about any aspect of surgical anatomy, histology, physiology, and pathology. From the very beginning, my composure, demeanor, even my posture, reflected my lack of self-confidence. Sitting in front of my two surgical anatomy inquisitors, I waffled my way through the examinations, my answers lacking conviction. It was painful to hear myself. My strategy was to prevent the examiner from asking another question by talking endlessly because I knew, for sure, I wouldn't know how to answer their next question. I felt a real fraud for bluffing my way into a profession whose standard I knew I had not earned and did not deserve. When it came to their interrogation of physiology, I wanted to melt away in my chair.

I could barely look the last two surgeons in the eyes. The first asked, "What is a sphincter? And give me some examples."

I heard myself say, "What do you mean by sphincter, sir? I don't understand the question." What was there not to understand? Where was my mind? The first surgeon impaled me on his examiner's sword of questions, while the second finished any prospect of my passing by skewering me with my ignorance. Both watched me metaphorically crumble and bleed to death.

By mid-day, cross-examinations in all topics relevant to passing the first hurdle of starting a surgical career had concluded. We were advised by Mr. Palmer, in his booming voice, that the examiners would release the numbers, and thus the names of the successful candidates after *their* customary sherry, which preceded a traditional three-course lunch that was served by elderly helpers, finally concluding with a selection of delectable cheeses and crackers with a glass of Port. Following lunch, Mr. Palmer would announce the numbers that indicated the names of those who had earned the honor of an elevated status—"the three 'P's that deservedly placed a candidate onto the first rung of the ladder to 'power, prestige and pocket-book'"—as he phrased it, to "righteous membership in the profession of barber surgeon."

I retreated to The Swan, which was a few minutes from the examination hall and open for lunch. Several other candidates had congregated there, and together, we commiserated, drawn by the certainty of having done poorly but longing for some glimmer of hope in our gloom. I sat among the other candidates, nursing half a pint of lemonade shandy and licking my self-inflicted wounds—more attention to Hanna than to my books. The mood among my fellow candidates swung from foul to fouler to desperate, like a dark and hopeless plot in a Kafka novel. I heaped all sorts of punishing and self-deprecating names on myself, castigated myself for ill-preparedness, squandered energy, obsession with another woman, and my deceitful behavior. I hated myself. Sitting in this stew of self-made shit, I waited in agony for the four o'clock congregation at examination hall with Mr. Palmer. It was like waiting for the hangman, I imagined.

He boomed out successful candidates by number. Unperturbed by the howls from failed candidates, Mr. Palmer continued down the list to pronounce with gusto the number of successful candidates, all of whom exited via the front door, eyes averted, leaving behind their failed friends. When he called a number after mine, I knew I had failed, as I had feared, as I suspected. I was among the contemptible 80% who did not satisfy the examiners—the dross, the unworthy, the undesirable, the disreputable, the despicable of surgically aspiring degenerates.

The failed candidates departed via the basement door through which they had entered. I joined a group of disappointed wretches who wanted to express their misdirected frustration and anger at failing. As we ambled together along the outside of the back of Queen's Hall, talk of disappointment at failing and the need for revenge toward the examiners grew. In an act of retaliation, the failed candidates pissed in unison into the ventilation system of the examination hall—ten powerful streams of urine aimed right into the vents.

I limped home to a cold, dark, empty flat and crawled into bed without eating dinner. At least I was alone; Victoria was on duty in the hospital. As I drifted asleep, I had two thoughts. First, I had to pass this exam if I wanted to become a surgeon and possibly go to America. I resolved to sign up for the courses at the Royal College to better prepare myself for the repeat exam some seven months away. And second, I was determined to cease my distractions by ending all contact with Hanna and rebuilding my love for Victoria.

2

PRESENCE OF HER ABSENCE

OCTOBER 1960

I want to leave behind me the name of a fellow who never bullied a little boy, or turned his back on a big one.
—Thomas Hughes

Mother and I arrived in Manchester from Cairo some six weeks into the autumn term at Burnage Grammar School. I was sixteen at the time. The headmaster's Oxford gown complemented his portly good looks. He asked a few bookish questions in pretentious, cultivated Queen's English, distinct from the charming Lancashire dialect I heard all around me. Since my declared career choice was aeronautical engineering, my A-level majors for the next two years before university were math, physics, and chemistry. He offered Mother a cup of tea and then marched me to my new Lower Sixth Form science classroom, telling me that apart from a Jewish boy in a form below me, I was the school's only other foreigner.

Mother had found me a bedsitter in a semi-detached duplex near the school. The next day, she took me to a cooperative for a school uniform—gray shirt, school tie, flannel trousers, a blazer embossed with the school crest—woolen underwear, and long johns for winter. The sturdy black shoes, unlike my brown Egyptian lace-ups, would not melt in the persistent Mancunian rain.

She opened a joint bank account in our names to deposit funds into from Egypt. To ensure my healthy relaxation, she bought me season tickets to the Hallé Orchestra, Britain's oldest symphony orchestra. Mother's idea was that attending the Saturday night symphony would prevent me from mixing with the wrong crowd while inculcating me with a classical repertoire and further developing my love for music. For the first time, my school life would not include girls—which was totally unnatural for any adolescent but was exceptionally hard on me because I had always enjoyed the female companionship to a co-ed school.

Having ensconced me in the bedsitter, Mother returned to sunny Cairo. She had fulfilled her maternal duties in every way except one: giving me her love and emotional support, the thing I needed the most.

I could hardly bear to see her go. Her abandonment inflicted the unbearable pain of rejection of forsaking me, as she had done in 1948 when I was four years old after deserting me in post-war Hamburg, depositing me with despotic war weary German grandparents I had never met before. As I learned only when a teenager, she joined my father at Manchester University to pursue the promise my father had made to her on their marriage in 1939—a promise to follow her academic career at the university. In Hamburg, she departed without a word of explanation—age four was too young to understand. Still, she left me. Just gone. I felt worthless and helpless. And now, at sixteen, the festering wound reopened and with it reappeared the feeling of vulnerability and impotence. I detested her for deserting me yet again. She was a widow, so what drew her to favor Cairo over providing a home for her son?

I failed to grasp how she could leave me when family-based loyalty and friendships were so much a part of the Egyptian side of my cultural heritage. Her father, my Opa, was an autocrat and disciplinarian—difficult to live with to say the least. To avoid, him she spent many hours at school, happily involved with extracurricular activities. But I wanted to come home to a warm nest, not to a lonely bedsitter. My pleading did not persuade her to stay in England.

After she left, I sat sobbing on the edge of my bed, unable to control my hurt as rain streaked down the windowpanes in sunless, cold, smoggy Manchester. I convinced myself that her repeated abandonment reflected her inability to love me, or some form of punishment for a sin I had committed, or an error I knew nothing about and that I deserved to be punished for.

The landlady of my bedsitter, Mrs. Bagley, was a widow who kept to herself. For four guineas a week, she provided me with a room and a cooked English breakfast. On my return from school at 4 p.m., she served high tea, which in the north of England was the equivalent of a light, hot meal like baked beans on toast. I could only have one or two baths per week.

I ate my meals alone in the front parlor, listening to BBC radio. At the same time, I could hear Mrs. Bagley's TV in the back room. After tea, I retired to my bedroom upstairs and tried to do my homework, but my mind drifted to my school friends in Cairo and our comforting camaraderie.

At nine, Mrs. Bagley left me watered cocoa with a dry biscuit in the downstairs parlor. I was forsaken by friends and family—adrift and alone, with no salvation—and stranded in miserable Manchester. I ached for the warmth of the life my family had in Manchester when I was between the ages of eight and ten and attended Burnage Primary. I had a pretty blonde girlfriend and was a member of Roy's tough gang of boys, chasing girls during recess and smoking Woodbines behind the garden shed. I sensed having lost something warm and good.

I liked a British breakfast, particularly when my landlady substituted back bacon for the bread-filled sausage. Meals were not provided on weekends, so on Saturday mornings, accompanied by loneliness, I sat in front of my books in the Central

Library in the heart of Manchester. I read. Nothing seemed to be absorbed, even understandable. I lunched alone at Lyons Corner House and then sat in front of my books in the afternoon, and once again, nothing seemed to stick in my mind. Saturday evenings, I'd forsake dinner to attend every recital, orchestral, operatic, and ballet performance at the Hallé—a welcomed distraction from my gray life. Sir John Barbirolli, the conductor, delighted the audience during performances, as rumor had it, with gin-enhanced athletics, which became wilder as the evening progressed. I sat with people whose faces had become familiar, season ticket holders, strangers yet human company nevertheless. Even though we didn't exchange words or acknowledgments, there was comfort in those strangers.

Music had always been a balm to my soul. Now, it carried me back to happier times when we lived in Cairo, when Mother played Mozart, Bruch, Mendelsohn, Bach—records handed down from departing German ex-pats. They were the background music of stability in our ménage. At school and birthday parties, we danced to lively music from the American and British hit parades, along with the occasional French or Italian songs—romantic songs that stoked my teenage hormonal urges. But my soul was captured by the torturing laments of Egyptian love songs that whined and pined for the love of a woman not yet met, kissed, or even envisioned—the elusive *sehnsucht* of love, the *mirage* of deserts.